MEETINGHOUSE HILL
1630–1783

MEETINGHOUSE HILL IN ROXBURY, MASSACHUSETTS, ABOUT 1790.

From a copy by Samuel Curtis of a painting by John Ritts Penniman of Roxbury. By courtesy of the Roxbury Historical Society.

Meetinghouse Hill

1630-1783

BY

OLA ELIZABETH WINSLOW

WITH A NEW PREFACE

The Norton Library

W · W · NORTON & COMPANY · INC ·

NEW YORK

FOR

B. R. B.

First published in the Norton Library 1972
by arrangement with the Macmillan Company

Library of Congress Cataloging in Publication Data

Winslow, Ola Elizabeth.
  Meetinghouse Hill, 1630-1783.

  (The Norton library)
  Reprint of the 1952 ed., with a new pref.
  1. New England—Church history. I. Title.
BR530.W5   1972   277.4   79-39172
ISBN 0-393-00632-8

SBN   393   00 632   8

PRINTED IN THE UNITED STATES OF AMERICA
1 2 3 4 5 6 7 8 9 0

Preface to the Norton Library Edition

EARLY New England had many meetinghouse hills, some of them still bearing the name after more than three hundred years. In the beginning the Committee appointed to "fix the center" had another name. Hills sometimes being too far between, they were content with finding mere "rising ground." On the spot chosen they placed a heap of stones and then drew a line to each of the four corners of the newly assigned acres. One more line was then drawn to the center of the nearest village or town and the distance carefully measured. The new town now had a place on the map and also a neighboring settlement, perhaps also a name.

Around this central heap of field stone the small wooden houses of the first pioneers would be "orderly placed." The first building would be the "common house," designed primarily as a place of meeting. On Sundays when weather made the "shade of the mighty oak" no longer adequate, the "common house" would be the place of preaching. On Monday, very soon, it would be the place of Town Meeting, and at all other times, at the beat of the drum, it would be the place of immediate assembly without asking why.

To follow through more than a century the sermons preached, the decisions made, and the action taken here is to see a small company of men and women without a country beginning to build a new nation. They were strangers one to another except that they had shared a two-month uncomfortable and somewhat perilous sea-journey. They were now huddled together on the fringe of a vast wilderness. They were beginners and would learn by doing, for there were no blueprints.

Preface to the Norton Library Edition

How does a new nation begin? Read the meetinghouse story in any New England village of the seventeenth century. Step by step in uncounted meetings from appleblossom time to the first snowfall, year after year, these pioneers forged a group unity and made it durable. How? By testing it over and over not by procedures but by the principles and loyalties with which their lives were guided. Finally the day came when every man's uplifted right hand and his signature to the covenant they had themselves written made them one in the faith they all professed. As many early covenants expressed it, they were now "bound up together in a little bundle of eternal life" and the bond was strong.

To transfer this group unity into the concerns of everyday life no doubt looks easier than it was, but that too was accomplished. Mistakes were made, of course, many of them; meetings were by no means always peaceful. Sometimes there were blows; yes, blows of the fist from neighbor to neighbor, and sometimes benches were broken, but presently the unity of a self-governing citizenry came to pass. Henceforth every man must have a voice in the decisions, and every man in his turn must perform a share in the humbler services of the community such as chimney-viewing, fence-viewing, and night-walking, as well as cast his vote in weightier matters.

It would all happen in the sturdy little building on the "rising ground," where as generation followed generation, the lookout tower would be replaced by a white spire against the sky. Worshippers would sit more comfortably as the hourglass on the pulpit turned, once, twice, or once in a while three times, and there might even be a Paul Revere bell to call them to meeting. The word *wilderness* had been forgotten. Instead, the wide spaces in all directions had become "Our Country."

Ola Elizabeth Winslow

November 24, 1971.

"There is one thing stronger than all the
armies of the world, and that is an idea
whose time has come."

Preface

THE story of religion in colonial America has been told many times and with many different accents. This book dares tell it once again, this time with the colonial meetinghouse of early New England in sharp focus. The object is not to repeat the familiar outline of early religious history, nor to exhibit the meetinghouse as a period piece, but so far as is possible to put it back on Meetinghouse Hill, where it stood in the day of its authority, and, by recalling typical procedures in relation to various aspects of community life, to suggest attitudes which it helped to establish and patterns of group action which it helped to make habitual.

Obviously the New England story in any line of inquiry is only one chapter in the colonial record. Obviously also, in any inquiry concerning religion, the procedures of the "standing order" are only one portion of that New England chapter. To tell the story fully would be to include also the rôle of the Church of England, and of the smaller religious groups for which in the earlier days New England was inhospitable territory. If there is justification for emphasis on a more limited area, it is that thereby the familiar picture of the whole may be somewhat enriched.

Town and church records, sermons, diaries, letters, and various other memorials surviving from seventeenth and eighteenth century America supply most of the first-hand data for this late version of what (with Thomas Fuller's permission) may still be called "a velvet study and recreation work". To thank once more the custodians of these materials, now so freely and conveniently accessible in research libraries, is to call the roll of names familiar to all scholars in the field. I wish to acknowledge with particular gratitude the hospitality shown me at the Boston Athenaeum, the American Antiquarian Society, the

Massachusetts Historical Society, the Essex Institute, the New England Historic Genealogical Society (by courtesy of Miss Martha Hale Shackford), the Congregational Library in Boston, the Boston Public Library, and the libraries of Bowdoin College, Dartmouth College and Wellesley College.

It has not seemed necessary to list once more the standard general works or the many specialized treatments of American colonial history, indispensable to the student of any corner of the subject. Specific acknowledgment is given wherever possible.

The word *meetinghouse* is used throughout as in the early town and church records, meaning a place of assembly, not in the better known sense of a house of worship for Quakers.

O. E. W.

Wellesley, Massachusetts.
March 31, 1951.

Contents

Illustrations

Prologue

THE white beauty and grace of the village meetinghouse have long been, in Emerson's familiar phrase, "part of the New England sky", but not long enough to take us back to the beginning of the story. Until late in our national day of small things, no white spire lifted itself out of the elms on any village green. Instead, a sturdy little structure, fully exposed, and possessing neither beauty nor grace to invite the eye, fronted the gradually receding wilderness from the highest point in the settlement—any settlement. The spot might be the merest hillock, but at least it could be called "Rising ground", and as such had been carefully selected by the committee appointed "to fix the Center". From this spot they had taken measurements to the four corners of what would presently be a town; on the summit they had "subdued the underbrush" and to it they had cleared a path.

As soon as this committee had made report, the settlers, met in formal session, would first dignify the "said Rising ground" by the name Watch Hill, Fort Hill, Town Hill, or more commonly Meetinghouse Hill, and then vote at this "Center of ye wholl circumference" "to build our Meetinghouse and to underpin the same with Good, Handsome stones". Very probably this vote would be the first corporate act of the new settlement.

So runs the record year by year and town by town. In main essentials the story of one is the story of all. Sometimes the rising ground "nigh unto some convenient Trees" was hard to find. Never the "Good, Handsome stones". Not on a New England hillside. The meetinghouse was accordingly framed, raised, set; and, wherever it stood, there was the center not only of another pioneer town, but of life itself and that according to a deliberate purpose and pattern. In due time the houses of the settlers would be "orderly placed about ye midst", as the early rules for laying out a town required, and henceforth around this homemade little building on the hill the main currents of American life would flow for more than a hundred and fifty very important years.

In the village mind this unpretentious little building was all but inseparable from the ideas for which it stood. In fact, it was itself an idea and had been one long before it was a building, but an idea too deeply taken for granted for anyone to have stated. In some way not easy to explain, the meetinghouse stood for a way of life both civil and religious and, in the thought of those who acknowledged it, a way of life shaped to the divine intent. When deacons and elders and laymen, working together, set the corner posts, laid the sills, and erected the frame, they were also consciously building a world, and their unshakable conviction that they built according to the Book was by all odds their best piece of equipment. It may also be the best reason some of the ideas they thus translated into hand-hewn beams and hillside stone were written indelibly on more than the town records.

Theirs is a village story in a day of small things, but small things that determined the shape of larger things to come. Taken out of their frame and setting, the ideas and behaviors which made up the first generation design for living lose much—too much. To a day that has gone after other gods their rigidity seems fantastic; their fine-spun distinctions academic and dull. The throb of life is not in them. In these latter days we can no longer listen as the sheep-pen pews listened, or build the meetinghouse as the sons and daughters of the "elect" built it in the day of their faith. It is many generations too late in the story of things American for that. But put these ideas back under the pulpit sounding board on a village Sunday morning, deacons and elders and tithingmen in their places, and the sheep-pen pews crowded and tense. Watch the behavior of a congregation "stayed" by the pastor for the easing of an erring brother's conscience, or the excommunication of an offender past reclaim, and many of these same ideas and behaviors take on something of the accent and gesture of reality.

In its own time and setting the meetinghouse story made sense. Even today, when a little of the village soil is pulled up with the record these men and women left behind them, theirs is the story of a way of life still recognizably American. Here and there through the years one also catches hints that some things in contemporary life and what we are pleased to call the "American character" may still be measured, as colonial records tell us distances from town to town were once measured; namely, "in a straight line from the meetinghouse door". But let the story speak.

BOOK ONE

~~~~~~~~~~~~~~~~~~~~~~~~~~~~~~~~~~~~

"BOUND UP TOGETHER IN A
LITTLE BUNDLE OF LIFE"

CHAPTER ONE

"God Makes Roome for Us"

WHEN John Cotton came down from Old Boston to Southampton in 1630 to bid godspeed to the vanguard of the Massachusetts Bay Colony, he took as his text, II *Samuel* 7, 10,

> "Moreover I will appoint a place for my people Israel, and will plant them, that they may dwell in a place of their own, and move no more".

He could hardly have opened his Bible to better purpose on that particular morning. The men and women before him were for the moment men and women without a country. They had just uprooted themselves from all that was familiar and precious in their lives, both immediate and ancestral. They had no return tickets. In this state of suspension between worlds, the long and hazardous sea journey may well have seemed the only reality. Beyond that the future was a blank. Suppose that after all, the "new heaven and the new earth in New-England" should prove merely another Utopian dream. What then? Favoring winds had not yet come. There was still time to listen to prudence and withdraw.

No one would have confessed such thoughts openly, but John Cotton was too wise a realist not to guess that they might be lurking. Accordingly, from the moment he began to "open his text", he set himself to give a hopeful preview of the New World and all that it promised. His Scripture context provided him with an almost perfect rôle for the purpose, that of Nathan the prophet, sent to David in a dark hour, "to shut up his speech with words of en-

couragement", and so to remove his discouragement "two wayes".
John Cotton straightway donned prophetic robes and proceeded to do
likewise.

He called his sermon, *God's Promise to His Plantation*,[1] and made
it a promise of room, plenty of room, room that is ours for the taking.
Such was inspired *Doctrine* for this particular occasion. Whether by
tact or genius, or something less than either, he had hit upon the perfect theme-song for pioneers in all ages. In his own best phrase, "No
binding here, and an open way there", he was sounding a refrain
which would be a poet's choice more than three centuries hence when
the American west was being opened up to other bold ones.

"Room! room to turn round in, to breathe and be free"[2] was
Joaquin Miller's way of singing it, and it was a verse to stir men's
imagination and awaken courage in his far safer day. So in all days. In
1630 and the intellectual climate of Dissenting opinion it was a theme
to dilate the imagination and challenge the zeal of potential pioneers,
in spite of being kept within the white lines of pulpit idiom and
biblical analogy.

Sermon orthodoxy did not permit John Cotton to present either
England or America directly, and he stepped over the line only twice,
once when he mentioned the persecutions of Queen Mary, and once
in his sixth and last counsel, "Offend not the poore Natives". Otherwise he kept strictly to biblical history and geography. His hearers,
to whom the analogies of Scripture were a familiar language, translated his words easily into their own sternest convictions and dearest
hopes.

Everyone who listened knew that God's "Plantation" was the
Massachusetts Bay Colony and that II *Samuel* 7, 10 was His promise
to each of them personally. Stripped of its biblical footnotes, the
core of the sermon argument is a series of affirmations.

Yes, God has designed a place for His people.
It is a spacious land. There will be room enough for all.
Here God's people will dwell "like Freeholders in a place of their
owne".

Here they will have "firme and durable possession, they shall move no more".

They will have "peaceable and quiet resting". "The sonnes of wickednesse shall afflict them no more."

Yes, it is God Himself who has made room for them in this spacious land. He has done it in three ways.

He has cast out enemies.

He has given foreign people favor in the eyes of native people.

He has made the country "void of Inhabitants" in those places where His people will reside.

Yes, it is true God's people need neither buy this land nor ask any man's permission to settle there. God Himself is landlord and where-ever He has made "so convenient a vacancy"—"there is liberty for the sonnes of *Adam* or *Noah* to come and inhabite, though they neither buy it, nor aske their leaves". This right is theirs by virtue of the "grand Charter" given to Adam and his posterity in Paradise.

> "In a vacant soyle, hee that taketh possession of it, and bestoweth culture and husbandry upon it, his Right it is."[3]

Not that we would "rush into any place, and never say to God, 'By your leave' ". We must find out why He has appointed us this place, else we are but intruders on God. But have no fear. You are appointed of God.

At this point in the sermon John Cotton was probably aware that he was stepping into what had doubtless been a zone of uncertainty for many of those before him during the preceding weeks. For some, perhaps for most of them, religious motives had tipped the scale. It therefore mattered and mattered deeply that they have assurance of divine warrant for the step they were taking. How could they be sure that they went to the New World by special "Commission" from God Himself? With John Winthrop this was a firm conviction, as he was to announce some days hence, when on board the *Arbella*, admiral ship of the fleet, he preached his famous sermon, *A Modell of Christian Charity*.

"Thus stands the cause betweene God and us",
he said;

"Wee are entered into Covenant with him for this worke, Wee have taken out a Commission, the Lord hath given us leave to drawe our owne Articles".[4]

It was a comfortable assumption for those who could posit it, but the preacher in John Cotton would not let him take it for granted. He must needs present the A B C's of such assurance. As he proceeded to do so, he was probably conscious that at no time in the sermon thus far had he been listened to so intently. Bluntly he stated the question.

"But how shall I know whether God hath appointed me such a place, if I be well where I am, what may warrant my removeal?"[5]

"There be foure or five good things", he replied, "for procurement of any of which I may remove". There be also evils we may wish to avoid, such as sins which threaten the land, debts and miseries, persecutions, for any one of which we may lawfully transplant ourselves. And lest these two categories might not take in everyone, he found a third which he called "speciall providences or particular cases". Altogether John Cotton gave his hearers eleven chances to leave England behind and to set sail with a clear mind. Only one of these eleven was strictly the reason of a Dissenting clergyman. The other ten were merely good and sensible reasons why any spiritual legatee of Drake, Gosnold, Raleigh, and all other pioneering Elizabethans might naturally be responding to the pull of an unknown continent.

In bare statement, all eleven sound flat enough, but put them beside the anxieties, the restlessness, the fresh hopes of the 1630's, and they might easily have seemed far otherwise, particularly to men and women with a license to sail in their pockets.

First, we may remove for the getting of knowledge.
Secondly, "for merchandize and gaine-sake".
Thirdly, "to plant a Colony, that is, a Company that agree together to remove out of their owne Country, and settle a Citty or commonwealth elsewhere".
Fourthly, to employ one's talents better elsewhere. Witness Joseph,

who "in wisedom and spirit was not fit for a shepheard, but for a Counsellour of State, and therefore God sent him into *Egypt*".[6]

Fifthly, men may remove "for the Liberty of the Ordinances", and here only John Cotton spoke as a Dissenter to Dissenters. For the militant minority within the reforming ranks (and some of them were before him) this was the very taproot of their purpose and design. To "purify the Ordinances" of all "Mixtures and man-made Corruptions"—the incense, the babbling prayers, the "tossing to and fro of Psalms and sentences like Tenisse plaie", and greatest "Abomination" of all, "the enormous crime of kneeling at the Sacrament"—this was the obligation God Himself had laid on those who would carry His banners into the wilderness. Otherwise indeed, "What needed they to have removed from England", an Election preacher would say a generation hence, when John Cotton's four other reasons had become realities.

At the 1630 stage of the English Reformation these alleged corruptions of a ritualistic worship were still main-line issues throughout the Dissenting ranks. Danger lurked not so threateningly in the dark corners of men's hearts as in the rail around the communion table, in the sign of the cross at baptism, and in that "emblem of heathenism, the wedding ring". The phrases "Liberty of the Ordinances", "Reformation in the positive Part", were watch-words in the crusade against all such "hellbred Superstitions", "Abominations and Patcheries, stitcht into the service of the Lord". The list was as familiar as a catechism answer, and recited almost as unvaryingly. Had the members of this or any other migrating company in the 1630's been polled at the dock on sailing day as to their reasons for removal, and had they dared to speak their minds openly (as is of course unthinkable) many among them would have given back this familiar catalogue, as their first and perhaps their sole reason. To enjoy freedom from all such "Pollutions" was to "cast off the yoke of anti-Christian bondage" and be free men indeed.

If it seems a bloodless formula for the Four Freedoms in any age, one need only remember that *freedom* is a word of many meanings, each for its own day and for no other. It is also a magic word in any generation and it was a magic word in this limited sense at the time of this sermon. Protest against a "toying worship" gave concreteness to large, though as yet only half-formed, hopes for a better way of life, and concreteness was imperative. No crusader has ever gone forth to battle for freedom in the abstract, nor have such battles ever concerned merely the side issues of life. "Liberty of the Ordinances" was a vital concern in 1630 among intellectuals as well as tradesmen and indented servants, and the very phrase a powerful enough slogan to evoke an emotional response in any company representing such a cross-section of English social classes as was about to embark in Winthrop's fleet.

One might expect for this reason that the future author of *The Way of the Churches* and *The Keys of the Kingdom of Heaven* would have made more, on this occasion, of an issue so vital to many in the move they were making, but John Cotton knew better. This was not the moment for protest or controversy. He was painting on a large canvas this morning, and only ultimates concerned him. He was also reading the minds of his hearers, giving assurance at their most sensitive points of doubt, and lifting their thoughts above the immediate distresses of parting. Everything else could wait. Besides, in his own thought, he had already jumped this hurdle as to ceremonials. Six years earlier he had written Bishop Williams that he had "come of late to see the weakness of some of the grounds against kneeling, which before I esteemed too strong for me to dissolve".[7] This farewell sermon, however, was neither the time nor the place to declare his own personal change of position on this vexed issue.

Instead, he contented himself with giving the "Ordinances" strategic place among the reasons which might justify a man's removal, and with making their "planting" and "maintaining" not only a major obligation, but also the safest guarantee that this new land would remain theirs "forever". Once again he stated his thought "two wayes". First,

"Have speciall care that you ever have the Ordinances planted amongst you, or else never look for security. As soone as God's Ordinances cease, your security ceaseth likewise".

And second, let history be witness that I speak truth;

> "Looke into all the stories whether divine or humane and you shall
> never finde that God ever rooted out a people that had the Ordi-
> nances planted amongst them, and themselves planted into the
> Ordinances; never did God suffer such plants to be plucked up".[8]

He made it all sound easy, and also sure. The case between God and
man in this new relation of landlord and tenant was as definite and
certain as two sides of an equation. On the one side, defraud not God
of His rent, serve Him, teach your children to serve Him, and in return claim security, permanence, and prosperity *forever*. Comfortable
words these, and buttressed at every turn by assorted texts, conferring
by chapter and verse an authority that was not to be gainsaid, "as
though God Himself were speaking to us". Difficulties? Certainly,
but God

> "hath given us hearts to overlooke them all, as if we were carried
> up on Eagle's wings".[9]

It was a safe Scripture promise, and if it did not always work, erring
Christians would know where to lay the blame.

Don't forget us, the preacher paused to say, with admirable tact
and a doubtful pun, just as he was about to turn his last page.

> "Even ducklings hatched under an henne, though they take the
> water, yet will still have recourse to the wing that hatched them:
> how much more should chickens of the same feather, and yolke?"[10]

His barnyard figure spoke present truth, but not prophecy. "Chickens
of the same feather, and yolke" at that moment they were indeed, Dissenters who took the water and Dissenters who stayed at home; but
very soon it would not be so. For those who went to the New World,
new and very insistent realities would quickly shape their thought and
the action which would stem from it, and shape it in determining
ways. The derivative would quickly bend to the yet unknown; far
sooner, in fact, than anyone would imagine. Although for a long
time the ways of parish life would remain essentially English at the
core, they would be quickly overlaid with much that John Cotton

himself would presently claim as New England's own. But he did not know that on this particular 1630 Sunday morning.

With or without its biblical scaffolding, John Cotton's subject would have held an audience anywhere in England at this date. Reports of the vast and empty space that was America had set notions spinning in the minds of men on all levels of English society. Both inside the church and out of it forces were at work which gave men courage to think once more that they might build the world over to their own desire. Each built it in his own way. Colonization projects had been launched at precisely the right moment to seem a practical answer to the new urge toward a freer and better way of life.

Dissent along with other restless groups was responding to currents of change which ran far deeper than they knew. For this reason it is nothing to the point that when these religious adventurers talked of the "wide doore of libertie", which was opening up to them in America, they had in mind a door which to later generations looks very narrow indeed. Their strictures, like those of other restless groups, were only the fringe of the great argument. They were in reality caught by the perennial dream of the protesting few in all generations—the dream of beginning over.

Read without reference to its occasion, this is not a great sermon. One looks in vain for originality of thought, or even new and arresting ways of saying familiar things. Perhaps it is unfair to expect them. Sermons are made to be spoken and heard in a given hour, not read when they are cold in print after many generations. If they deserve to be called in any measure great, it is because they combine in some indissoluble proportion the man, the idea, the moment. Whether there is much or little of John Cotton, the man, in this sermon, it is hard to say, for we know too little of his personal quality; but as a leaf out of English thinking in the uncertain 1630's it catches a mood when, to certain bold ones, New England seemed the way out.

Addressed to a company of those who had dared to take the risk, and listened to by them at the port of embarkation in the tense atmosphere of farewell and departure, this neat justifying of the great migration, now at last to begin, may well have been electric in its effect. It would be easy to believe that those who heard never forgot, and that long afterward they took strength and courage from their memory of these hopeful and reassuring words. For Puritans of the Dissenting wing the particular power of such a sermon would have consisted in precisely what makes it seem unimportant today; namely, the insistent literalness with which biblical texts were made to fit the case of those about to embark. Assurances made to Noah and Abraham and David were neatly fitted to 1630 doubts and questionings. Such matching of human need and divine resource over the centuries seemed incongruous to no one. That the Bible was the ultimate and unequivocal authority in the affairs of men, past and present, was a major premise on both sides of the desk. In learned hands it could also be an oracle, and on this occasion it spoke favorably.

Unfortunately, what the congregation thought of the sermon is not recorded. John Winthrop, who as leader of the company would almost certainly have been present unless the great "busyness" of which he speaks prevented, does not mention it, but the fact that it was almost immediately printed in London suggests that someone (possibly one of John Cotton's friends who had come with him from Lincolnshire) thought it worthy of preservation. Fortunately so, as it is one of the very few farewell sermons in print, and as such, like John Robinson's last counsels to the Plymouth company at Delfthaven, it takes on a certain historic importance. Read in later times, it is a revealing document. As point by point John Cotton built his argument, bringing forth Scripture proof upon Scripture proof that the homeland no longer bound these men and women about to sail, and that the New World was neither a mirage nor unlawful territory for God's English children, he not only quieted immediate fears but also made vocal the unspoken and still largely inarticulate dream of certain middle class Englishmen for a better way of life temporally as well as religiously.

At the time he preached this hopeful sermon, thoughts of the "open way there", the roomy place, the new chance, were already spinning in John Cotton's own mind, although he had not yet decided to come to America. Less than three years later his own loyalties had crossed the ocean and begun to root themselves in a Boston parish. Had he in time returned to "the wing that hatched him", he would have been intractable and also lonesome. The New World would win and he would be one to boast of the victory.

After he had been in Boston a year, he wrote down his reasons for coming. They were the reasons of a practical man and he made no effort to ennoble them. In sermon fashion, he listed and annotated them.

First, God having shut one door and opened another, "who are we that we should strive against God, and refuse to follow?" If we may and ought to follow God's calling three hundred miles, why not three thousand?

Secondly, there be times when one should suffer imprisonment, "but not in case men have ability of body and opportunity to remove, and no necessary engagement for to stay".

Thirdly, why "sit down somewhere else, under the shadow of some ordinances, when by two month's travel we might come to enjoy the liberty of all?"[11]

These are not the answers of a saint or martyr. They are the answers of a practical man, facing a practical dilemma, and making a sensible, matter-of-fact decision as he saw how the columns added up. Other men, who were not of so practical a temper, did likewise. The "gratious, sweete, Heavenly-minded, and soule-ravishing Minister, Master Thomas Shepard", one of the most spiritually minded of all early New England leaders, looked himself straight in the face and admitted that his reasons were many, his "ends mixt", and that he looked much to his own quiet. Therefore he came. The "mixt ends" were chiefly personal. He "saw no call elsewhere to any other place in Old England and no way of subsistence in peace and comfort" to himself and his family. Some of his friends had gone and others were going.

"I did think I should feele many miseries if I stayd behind", he wrote. Besides, "my deare wife did much long to see me setled there in peace & so put me on to it".[12] Therefore he came, although after his first "sea-storme" he wished with all his heart he had stayed and felt miseries. No wonder his Cambridge people loved Thomas Shepard. He was an honest man and put on no saintly airs.

A later generation would not have it so. Patriotism (likewise a word of many meanings) changed these earlier "mixt" motives into something more single and also more spacious than they could possibly have been. The sons and grandsons of these first men relieved them of any desire to "live in the large place" John Cotton's sermon had promised, to "gaine knowledge", profit by merchandise, have a chance, like Joseph, to become counsellors of state instead of shepherds. These later generations made them into single-minded champions of a freedom they could not yet have comprehended. Even William Bradford's pleasant phrase, "the Lord's free people", was more prophetic than actual; it had to be so. First generation blueprints for freedom suited the first generation only. *Liberty* and *freedom* were words they all used, but they used them in straitened senses which would presently not be agreeable to their own children. To Richard Mather, as he listed his reasons for removal, the liberty of New England included the chance to exercise church discipline more rigorously and "to censure those that ought to be censured"; to others in matters civil as well as religious it meant something more or less straitened, but it was not a spacious concept with any of them.

Nor was spaciousness greatly important. Tenacity was what mattered and these men and women had it. If they envisioned a limited kind of freedom, at least they knew the kind they wanted, and they were ready to pay the asking price in full. Some fourteen years before the Winthrop fleet sailed, the doughty Captain John Smith had written of Massachusetts, "the Paradise of these parts",

> "For, I am not so simple, to thinke, that ever any other motive then wealth, will ever erect there a Commonweale; or drawe companie from their ease and humours at home, to stay in *New England*, to effect my purposes".[13]

He was wrong, or at least half wrong. So were the later historians who brought them here by religion alone.

"Nothing sorts better with piety than competency", realistic John White declared in his forthright *Planter's Plea* of this same year, 1630, recognizing at the same time that

> "Intentions are secret; who can discover them?"[14]

He spoke wisely. His own recommendation, as to sound guiding purposes for these English gentlemen who were turning their faces from east to west in 1630, was to make "reason and religion" equal as the grounds for their decision. It was the answer of a sensible man.

John Cotton would have agreed. His sermon closes on a note hospitable to these twin safeguards. Trust in God for peace and safety, he said, but at the same time

"Neglect not walls, and bulwarkes, and fortifications for your own defence".[15]

In other words, keep your sights high and watch your step. Shrewd counsel which would presently be labelled true Yankee. No one who reads the record as these first immigrants left it in their own luminous story, printed or unprinted, can doubt their ability to do both simultaneously. Practicality did not deny vision but gave it substance. As for freedom, a word which sometimes appears on their every page, had these men and women, who were known to the world to love the smoke of their own chimneys so well, but who were now daring "to go farre beyond their owne townes end", found only freedom of the sort they came to seek, their story would be far less worth the telling. The "wide doore of libertie" would grow wider as they walked through it. It could grow wider in no other way.

CHAPTER TWO

"Gathered"

THERE were seventeen ships in Winthrop's Fleet, and in every one of them were men and women minded to join themselves into a church society or to unite speedily with one already formed. Likewise in every other westbound ship during the migrating decades. Those so minded were usually a small company. Just a "little Knot of Christians", as they said, men and women intensely eager to end the dubious state of being "out of a church order". Until they were a regularly organized society with a minister to shepherd them, they were deprived of all church benefits except preaching, when they were able to "hire" it. The Sacrament of the Lord's Supper, in their eyes the most precious privilege of Christians on earth, could not be celebrated. Their children could not be baptized. When John Cotton sailed on the *Griffin* in 1633, he had been an ordained minister for more than twenty years, and yet he could not baptize his own son, born during the voyage. The child must needs wait two weeks longer than the usual time before being presented for baptism in the properly constituted church at Charlestown. Here he received the absurdly literal name of *Seaborn*, thereby memorializing his infant discomfiture throughout a long and useful life.

Had he been born of parents sailing in the *Mary and John* in 1630, there would have been no such delay, for the ship would have served as a church. The nucleus of the Dorchester congregation was on board, and they had duly organized themselves before leaving Plymouth, England. They also had with them John Warham and

Samuel Maverick, properly chosen as pastor and teacher respectively, so that they "sailed as a church", bearing all their privileges and prerogatives with them. Ten years before, the Plymouth company had done likewise, but this was a rare distinction. Formal organization was usually postponed until the New World was reached.

Meanwhile eagerness increased on board while prospective "saints" put themselves in a proper state of mind by a plenitude of sermons and "other agreeable devotions", as the weeks passed. The *Griffin* in 1633 boasted three Sunday sermons, one by John Cotton in the morning, one by Thomas Hooker in the afternoon, and still another by Samuel Stone after supper. The Dorchester group did even better, "having Preaching or Expounding of the Word of God every Day for Ten Weeks together, by our Ministers". Such rich fare filled the "longsome voyage" with so much of religion that every day was something like Sunday.

> "Even the ship master and his company used every night to sett their 8 and 12 a clocke watches with singing a psalme and prayer that was not read out of a booke",[1]

Francis Higginson rejoiced to report of his own "pious and christian-like passage". During an eight- or ten-week voyage in kind, something like a year's normal allotment of such neo-Sabbaths was possible for those who wished to claim them. In such an atmosphere it is not surprising that the importance of setting up "a spiritual house" grew apace; so much so that once on the American side the earliest companies made it their first business, sometimes even before they had houses to live in.

Perhaps this sense of urgency helped them to cut corners. Perhaps they conceived of their task of organization more simply. At any rate the earliest groups accomplished it more simply and with considerable more dispatch than those who came later, even in the same decade. They also succeeded in keeping main issues main and making procedure of secondary importance. Having as yet no precise model, they were freer than later immigrants would be, after a pattern had taken shape and precedents had been established. Inevitably the pattern came, but for a long time it was uncomplicated by minor specifications.

Salem had led off in 1629, a year before Winthrop's first ships arrived. For reasons that go well beyond church history as such, this first Salem chapter deserves to be on the record in all its details, but unfortunately it is not, because by a strange irony the first record book of the church society was lost in the very effort to preserve it. After being carefully "reviewed" by the pastor, two deacons, and three other laymen in 1660 and certain passages "struck out" (one wonders what and why) it was put on view for a month and then either destroyed or so carefully "bestowed" that it has not since come to light. Almost any other New England church record might be spared more willingly. As a result of this mischance we have only the barest outline of what happened between June 29th, when the two ministers, Francis Higginson and John Skelton, landed, and August 6th, when a covenant was pledged. Had Francis Higginson lived, he would have seemed the natural annalist of this beginning in which he had played a leader's part, but he was gone within the year.

All that survives in contemporary record from which to construct this first chapter of the Salem society is mention of two occasions, neither of them indubitably certain as to date, but both of them probably belonging within little more than the space of a fortnight. Each of these occasions represented various steps in the gathering of the Salem church. Each step broke a precedent centuries old. Each of them also set the pattern for a long future.

On the first of these occasions, probably July 20, 1629, the thirty prospective members of the new church society, previously chosen by mutual agreement, cast their ballot for their pastor and teacher. In the forenoon of the day which had been set apart by Governor Endecott as a "solemn day of humiliation", the whole settlement made preparation for this important choice by prayer, praise and "teaching"; in the afternoon they proceeded to the election. There were two candidates and two offices to fill. Each candidate was fully qualified for either office. Each also acknowledged himself twice called, once by God Himself and once by the people of Salem. Both men had come to New England by invitation of the Massachusetts

Bay Company, and both were under contract with this Company to preach to the people of Salem. The area of choice therefore left open to the thirty members would seem to have been small indeed, but the privilege of casting each his own vote for his own pastor and teacher was immense thirty times over.

According to the word of an eye-witness, Charles Gott, who wrote an account of this day's business to Governor Bradford, the two candidates were first examined by the members, and having cleared all by their answers, they awaited the verdict while

"Every fit member [probably meaning the thirty self-gathered men who were eligible to take covenant together] wrote, in a note, his name whom the Lord moved him to think was fit for a pastor, and so likewise whom they would have for a teacher".[2]

This is the first recorded use of a written ballot in America. When the votes were counted, it appeared that John Skelton had won as pastor and Francis Higginson as teacher. Although the duties differed somewhat, only a thin line divided the two offices as to prerogatives and honor, and if either man was disappointed in the lot he had drawn, he gave no sign.

This election accomplished, the thirty men next proceeded to the "full choice of elders and deacons", but according to Charles Gott, who was one of those proposed for deacon, these officers were only named on this occasion, and the "laying on of hands deferred", until the members saw "if it pleased God to send us more able men over". Those named had no choice except to acquiesce in this qualified sanction. Other early church groups took similar action. If they saw none accounted worthy, they waited. Why not? They had all the time there was. In a sense these early elections were the beginning of political life, but it was political life on a high level; not only may the best man win, but if he is not already present, maybe he will be on the next boat. We shall wait for him. So ended the first day.

The second precedent-breaking occasion came presumably on August 6th, when the thirty eligible members pledged themselves publicly in a covenant framed by one of themselves, presumably by John Higginson. Thirty copies of this covenant had been prepared in advance, we are told, and distributed among the prospective members, who by this instrument of union would be bound together in a church society. The covenant itself, as preserved, is notable for its simplicity, and in what might very well have been its original version, notable also for its brevity. It is shorter than a night letter.

> "We Covenant with the Lord, and one with another and doe bynd ourselves in the presence of God to walke together in all his waies, according as he is pleased to reveale himself unto us in his Blessed word of truth."[3]

The significance of this brief pledge lies not only in its simple expression of a high purpose, but also in the fact that Church of England communicants had written it themselves and that in so doing they were laying the foundation stone of a new church order.

If it were in line with later practice on similar occasions, this simple ceremony probably consisted in no more than the public reading of the covenant, perhaps in concert, perhaps individually, and then the pledging and signing of it by each man in turn. It probably took place in the open air, in the presence of the whole settlement, and at the conclusion of a sermon appropriate to the occasion. Salem at this time numbered some two hundred persons, and since this day also had been set apart by Governor Endecott as a "solemn day of humiliation", attendance by all two hundred would have amounted to an obligation. The thirty men who took the covenant were presumably heads of families and would have represented the sympathetic majority. The minority group, led by the Browne brothers, John and Samuel, loyal Church of England adherents, was probably also present, partly because of Endecott's proclamation, and more because of their deep concern over the gigantic impropriety of a self-gathered church society. Their views were probably well known to the community, so that as they listened to the sermon and witnessed the strange procedure which followed, their unsympathetic attitude may well have brought a note of tension into this solemn assembly.

On the afternoon of this same day, the now covenanted laymen proceeded to the ordination of the pastor and teacher whom they had previously elected. Almost all that we know of this ceremony comes once more in the letter of Charles Gott to Governor Bradford,

> "Mr. Higginson, with three or four more of the gravest members of the church, laid their hands on Mr. Skelton, using prayers therewith".[4]

The ritual was then reversed, and Mr. Skelton with the same three or four "gravest members" laid hands on Mr. Higginson. The self-gathered church now had a self-elected and self-ordained pastor and teacher. The participation of the two ministers, both of whom had previously been ordained in England, of course kept this ceremony from being an entirely lay ordination, but to John and Samuel Browne and their adherents such procedure was presumptous and unwarrantable in the extreme; in fact, monstrously so. Their subsequent protest and urgent entreaty to be allowed to read the Church of England service among themselves, instead of worshipping in the new congregation, was presently rewarded by what amounted to exile and the loss of all they had hitherto ventured in the Salem project. It is a black page in the non-toleration record and may possibly account for some of the deletions in the first Church Book.

In these various steps on these two occasions, the Salem group, just as Plymouth before them, had assumed "Complete liberty to stand alone". No notion was more deeply rooted in the minds of these early protesting Christians than the notion that a church, being a body of "covenanted saints", possessed within itself all power requisite to manage its own affairs, or as John Cotton was presently to say, "to walk upon her own legs". In daring to do so, both Plymouth and Salem had written significant early chapters in the long story of independence in more than church affairs.

Almost precisely one year later John Winthrop and his like-minded fellow passengers in the *Arbella* added still another chapter in accordance with the same pattern. Some six weeks after they had first sighted the Maine coastline, been refreshed by the "sweete aire" and caught for the first time the "smell off the shore like the smell of a garden", four men, John Winthrop, Governor; Thomas Dudley, Deputy Governor; Isaac Johnson, largest financial contributor to the venture; and John Wilson, presently to be elected teacher of the church, stood under a "brave old Oake" in Charlestown and covenanted together to form what became the First Church of Boston. This was on July 30, 1630. They took this pledge not as officials or as an elected committee, but merely as four Christian gentlemen to whom the founding of a church society in the new colony was a matter of first and major importance. Ten days later the church was "gathered", probably under the same "brave old Oake", and still two weeks later, on August 27th, Master John Wilson was elected teacher by written ballot, or "paper votes", as the saying was. He had no rival. Covenant members were merely claiming their individual privilege of choice and also confirming a pre-ordained selection by what seemed to them "decent and orderly" procedure.

The Boston covenant, which soon counted some sixty signatures, is also a memorable statement of singleness of purpose. It contains only one hundred and thirteen words.

"Wee whose names are hereunder written, being by His most wise, & good Providence brought together into this part of America in the Bay of Masachuesetts, & desirous to unite our selves into one Congregation, or Church, under the Lord Jesus Christ our Head, in such sort as becometh all those whom He hath Redeemed, & Sanctified to Himselfe, doe hereby solemnly, & religiously (as in His most holy Praesence) Promise, & bind orselves, to walke in all our wayes according to the Rule of the Gospell, & in all sincere Conformity to his holy Ordinances, & in mutuall love, & respect each to other, so neere as God shall give us grace."[5]

The first four names are of course the names of the four men who first took the covenant together.

On the same day of the first ceremony under the Charlestown oak, forty members of the Watertown group covenanted together in similar fashion. A Dorchester group, already organized before sailing, had also arrived. Other gatherings followed, as Winthrop's other ships came in. Before the end of the year more than a thousand new settlers had landed in Massachusetts alone. In 1633 another wave of migration brought several thousand more, so that by the end of the decade the Massachusetts population numbered more than ten thousand. This meant a succession of gatherings, although by comparison with population totals these covenanting groups were small indeed. Most of them came under the leadership of a former pastor, who having helped them over the first hurdles of organization usually became their first pastor in the new settlement. Thomas Hooker, arriving in 1633, en route to Cambridge, had been preceded in 1632 by a group from his former St. Mary's congregation in Essex; John Lothrop in 1634 brought a small group to Scituate; Thomas Parker to Newbury in 1635; Peter Hobart to Hingham; other ministers likewise. A non-conforming minister seldom came alone, and wherever he settled, a few of his former congregation were likely to be the nucleus of the new society. The similarities in early group organization owe much to this ministerial direction at the outset.

Two sentences in the *Diary* of John Lothrop suggest how simple these gatherings could be. Under date of Jan. 8, 1634/5, he wrote,

> "Wee had a day of humiliation and then att night joyned in covenaunt togeather, so many of us as had beene in Covenaunt before".

And on January 9th,

> "Another day of humilation att my house, upon wch day I was chosen Pastour & invested into office".[6]

It is all there, the solemn preparation, the fraternal agreement, the individual vote and the investiture. The imagined picture of thirteen men standing quietly in the minister's "parlour" while he spoke the words,

> "I take this people to be my people",

and their corresponding pledge in reply matches in impressiveness the scene in the "Umbrage of a Giant Oake" or around "the great flat Rock", which figure often in other records, public and private.

As soon as the first movers in any church venture had drafted a covenant and subscribed to it publicly, the way was open for others who could qualify as "saints" to take the covenant likewise. Sometimes they did so immediately; sometimes on the day following, or shortly thereafter. It all depended on whether or not individual "Professions" had been duly prepared beforehand, so that they could be heard publicly and judged acceptable or not by those already inside. This was a fraternity, and the acceptance or rejection of candidates rested entirely in the vote of the membership, acting as a group. In the beginning complete unanimity was required; majority decision came later as a reluctant compromise.

It would be difficult to overstate the almost desperate eagerness with which the privilege of "laying hold of ye covenant" was regarded by those who hoped that they were eligible. When the first Cambridge congregation was gathered at Newtowne in 1636, the wife of Thomas Shepard, minister, was too ill to attend the ceremony, but so keen was her distress that her fellow-Christians, fearing "her end was not far off", went *en masse* to her bedside immediately after the ceremony, and making certain concessions because of her weakness received her in covenant with them before it was too late. As her husband reported it,

> "She said to us that she had now enough; and we were afraid her feeble body would have at that time fallen under the weight of her joy".[7]

Instead, the end came two weeks later, and though by her husband's eulogy, "she was fit to dy long before she did dy", she was far safer inside the fellowship than out of it.

That one's name signed in the book put one in such a marginal zone of safety is attested by numerous early church entries, recording the deaths of those who died outside the charmed circle. Two which might be called typical occur in the Roxbury Church Book for 1643; one of them concerning Goodman Stone, "an old Kentish man" who had died, and of whom it was written,

> "He was not of the Church,
> *yet* on his sick bed some had some hopes of him",

and another (more hopeful) concerning "Mary—the maid serva't of Mr. Prichard",

"She was a godly maide & was to have joyned to the Church, but the Lord p'vented her & tooke her to Heaven".[8]

In determining who were "visible saints" and who were not, social status was completely ignored, equality before God being assumed with complete literalness. Later on, seating committees would sort out a congregation, at least for their Sunday appearance, according to external criteria. Men would sit high or low, in the front or in the rear, in the draught or out of it, under a window or on the gallery stairs, in accordance with their age, their official position, their social status and what would correspond to their bank accounts, but not in the beginning, and not at any time would an application for membership be honored on any such basis. To be "wounded in their hearts for their original sinne" was all that mattered.

As the story of these gatherings multiplies from town to town, it leaves one wondering a little as to the strength of the bond these earnest men and women thought they were forging. The covenant, as a basis for their union, was of course entirely scriptural in the literal sense which seemed authoritative in their eyes. Any layman could have produced texts and biblical analogies to match any skeptic's demand. *Psalms* 50, 5, was a favorite in kind:

"Gather my saints together unto me; those that have made a covenant with me by sacrifice".

The covenant relation was also in line with the strongly marked social emphasis which the Reformation had taken in Britain. During the memory of the first emigrants to New England popular English preachers were emphasizing religion less as an intensely private experience, more as a basis for mutual privilege and obligation. One might almost say they were making it a group enterprise. Professing Christians were conscious members of a special kind of society, and their relation to each other was deeply fraternal. John Winthrop's phrase in his *Arbella* sermon,

"Wee must be knitt together in this worke as one man, wee must entertaine each other in brotherly Affeccion",[9]

meant something very real to the church-minded minority; in fact, real enough to be fought for.

They could hardly have expressed this meaning better than in another phrase which closes many of their early covenants—"as befits those whom God has bound up together in a little bundle of eternal life". It was precisely so in their own thought. They took their group unity literally and wished it to embrace the whole of their lives. Briefly, it almost did. Private interests were almost in second place. Town and parish were still one, as they had been in the Old World, and yet, in their own thought of their relationship to one another, those inside the church fellowship had something very special; those outside were very far away indeed. The covenant pledge bound them together finally and irrevocably; it also embraced future generations. In typical covenant phrasing,

"Our posterity is bound up with us in this gospel covenant, perpetually and without any alteration for ever".

So they wrote it, and so they meant it to be. Presently they would learn that *forever* is a long word. But not yet, although these were realists who wrote it thus—men who went out from the "upper room" atmosphere of these early "gatherings" and covenant pledges to clear their fields of stones, to hew, to plant, and to build. They met the daily and very insistent realities of their grim chapter in pioneering with a keen awareness of fact; they made a blueprint for the religion of future generations without it.

The naturalness of the covenant idea for Englishmen is clear enough. Its roots were deep in Anglo Saxon tradition and practice. For men and women of another cultural heritage some other basis for organized life, both civil and religious, might have been chosen; but for Englishmen government by compact was almost foreordained. The idea of a holy community, or church within a church, was also not new. It was basic in Calvinism, and in some form had survived in most Puritan groups. For English Dissent it had received strong, fresh emphasis, and in a somewhat different direction, from Robert Browne and the gathering of the Norwich congregation in 1581.

"The Kingdom off God Was not to be begun by whole parishes, but rather off the worthiest, Were they never so fewe",[10]

Browne had declared. Therefore let these come out from the parish and form a society of their own. Under Robert Browne's leadership the Norwich congregation had administered just such a purge, leaving only those who by their own group judgment were "pure saints". Their boldness had been widely published, and to some extent had been imitated by other restless groups.

Although the Norwich affair was well out of the personal memory of the earliest New England settlers, it was on the record. It was also in line with the militant urge of these first comers toward self-determination in matters of church polity. Transferred to the New World, both the root idea and the *modus operandi* of this self-administered sifting process had a new chance and a hospitable one. Such a basis for church membership seemed inescapably logical to those who thought of a church as

"a city, compact within itself, without subordination under or dependence upon any other but Jesus Christ".[11]

It flattered the courage of those who dared to be so bold. It was clearcut, easy to understand and could be translated into action. Best of all, in terms of success the purpose was single. Dissent wanted a pure church. Here was a practical way to get it and to get it quickly. Most early groups were small enough to put mutual consent within possible reach, at least to the excluding of the ungodly. For these and other reasons it is not surprising that the idea of a gathered society took firm hold in a restless time.

As more New England churches were gathered and as precedents multiplied, procedure became more deliberate. Preliminaries took longer. There were more decisions to make, more requirements to observe, more permissions to obtain, more courtesies to extend to neighboring churches. The gathering soon became an event which, even without a governor's proclamation, concerned the whole community, as well as those who hoped to be included within the small circle of the fellowship. For purely secular reasons there had been no more important day in any settlement since town lots were first assigned; for by charter provision the organization of a church brought the town one step nearer to recognition as a corporate body in full charge of its own affairs.

The average freeman had also a personal stake in the founding of a church, although he might not have been articulate as to the need he felt. To the seventeenth century Englishman—church member or not, religious or not—life on this earth had eternal consequences, and he lived out his span in that unquestioned conviction. Sermons by "sound, learned, godly ministers" offered the best means at hand to help him unriddle the enigma of life and death to his own satisfaction, to measure his chances in what he had been taught to believe came after, and to learn the code of righteousness in this life. A town needed a minister as it needed a blacksmith, for the reason that community life was not complete without him. The charter gave no help as to a blacksmith; hence, if he were not already present, the town appointed a committee to institute search and offer inducements, even if it amounted to giving him a lot and building him a house. The charter required a minister, but even without this requirement the need would have demanded him, because he represented a part of life not yet open to question in the mind of the average man. Consequently, when any new settlement came to the point where a church society was imminent, everyone, saint and sinner alike, would sleep better at night. As for the ceremony itself, no one able to walk would have missed it.

To be one of the men who had helped to bring about this new era in town life increased a man's sense of community importance, forgivably enough.

" 'Tis a great Thing to be a Foundation-stone in such a Spiritual Building as is now to be erected at Newbury",[12]

Samuel Sewall wrote to Cousin Henry Sewall, who was to be so honored in 1724, more than a century after the first church was organized in Massachusetts. It continued to be a "great Thing" for several generations afterward.

Every new town had seven men so honored, for very early in the story someone discovered *Proverbs* 9, 1,

"Wisdom hath builded her house, she hath hewn out her seven pillars".

It seemed a direction made to order. What could it mean except that the seven pillars were seven men who would sponsor the church society? The idea pleased; it also spread. And after several sermons had made this interpretation authoritative, seven pillars became standard, as though by official decree. No newly arrived group, eager to organize themselves, would have risked a structure supported by less than seven. There was even some transient anxiety felt as to the stability of those earlier churches symmetrically held up by only four pillars.

As soon as these seven men were chosen, everything moved along fairly smoothly, or might do so. One step led to another, but getting started was difficult. To find in each small company seven men of blameless life, good conversation, and burning zeal was not so easy as might have been anticipated. Besides, since there was no prior organization to provide means for their orderly nomination, and since the best men were sometimes loathe to nominate themselves, things often got off to a slow start. One solution was for the whole group interested in being a church to make informal suggestions of a larger number than seven, leaving the final choice to the mutual agreement of those chosen. New Haven did it somewhat more democratically, when after much prayer, long discussion and some fasting they met in formal session and voted for twelve men from whom the seven were to be selected. More often, one man offered himself and invited others to join him.

With a nucleus chosen in some such fashion the real struggle was only beginning. Back of many a public gathering (if not most) lay weeks, even months of parley and often bitter argument behind closed doors, as the eligible candidates achieved a mutual approval of seven of their own number. Seven must survive. Seven must also approve of seven. To this end the candidates subjected themselves to a heart-searching exposure truly amazing among men. Their deliberations were of course private, but hardly secret; not in a one-street village. Much leaked out; how much not one of the seven quite knew.

They had won, but they had been victors in a hotly contested race, and when it was all over, each knew in his own private thoughts that he had probably come to his high rôle with barely an inch to spare. He might yet lose, for gathering day would pose one more test.

As time moved on and many churches were gathered, the setting shifted for most weathers from the "great flat Rock" or the "giant Oake" to a barn, "a mighty Barn", to quote the Town Book precisely. Why not? Cotton Mather asked, by way of apology for Robert Newman's barn at New Haven, the scene of two gatherings on successive days in 1639.

> "Our glorious Lord Jesus Christ himself having been *born* in a *stable* . . ., it was the more allowable that a *church* . . . should thus be born in a *barn*."[13]

That (or something else) had settled it for Milford, and as barns became more numerous, for many other prospective congregations as well. Only an occasional minister, holding out for strict scriptural literalness, insisted on writing down this humble setting as a "threshing floor" instead. The town clerk, however, had no such scruples. To him a barn was a barn.

The scene deserves a mural, although, viewed as spectacle, what happened was less than nothing. To an observer from another century the crowd would be far more impressive than the ceremony. They came on foot, on horseback, in all seasons, in fair weather or foul, and always in full numbers. Whatever town it was had never before seen so many strangers within its precincts. The Governor of the colony was always expected. He would of course sit high, as befitted his rank and station, magistrates and other dignitaries grouped around him. Visiting clergymen, distinguishable by their white bands, deacons and elders from neighboring parishes, would likewise have seats of honor. The atmosphere was always tense. Something deeply important was about to happen, and all had eyes and ears for the main drama.

The chief actors were of course the Seven Pillars. To a modern reporter, sent to cover the occasion, they would hardly have looked like chief actors in a significant drama, as one after another they spoke their pieces on the barn platform. Except for an occasional minister among them they were not accustomed to speechmaking, but the tenseness with which they were heard conferred dignity upon what they were saying. They spoke carefully, as though every word counted or any word might entrap them, as well it might. In these seven, usually long speeches, they were detailing the proofs of their eligibility as pillars in the house of God and it behooved them to speak carefully. Any barn audience on any gathering day was well sprinkled with detectives, to whom the soundness or unsoundness of a "Profession" was clear as sunlight. Eloquence in reciting it was no more a recommendation than fumbling one's notes was a disgrace. All that mattered was clear evidence for one's present state of grace and accordingly one's eligibility for pillarhood.

After each speech objections were invited, and fortunate was the would-be pillar who did not at this point find himself suddenly under a cloud. This was the moment when some hitherto unconfessed or probably forgotten sin, which someone had pocketed for last minute deadly use, might be brought forth. Fortunate also, if such "Impediments" were raised by impartial strangers among the visiting elders and deacons. One's next door neighbor could be less easily silenced in this critical moment. If there were no such "Impediments", however, or if they could be safely removed so that the seven men stood unchallenged before the assembly, the high moment was now at hand. The covenant, which was to bind the many into one, could now be taken. The ceremony remained as simple as it had been under the first great oak; so simple, in fact, that an uninitiate on the front row might have missed it altogether, or failed to understand how the raising of seven right hands and the signing of seven names could be central to all this intensity of interest, this weight of solemnity. It was a solemnity almost palpable, we may believe, so deeply felt that even the ungodly went away awed.

For Milford, Connecticut, in 1639, as for various other towns, the gathering of the church marked the actual beginning of the town's existence, and in a rather special way. Immediately after the seven pillars had put their signatures to the covenant, and the forty-four "free planters" had signified approval of the principles by which they

were to be governed, "no man dissenting", the newly gathered congregation filed out of Robert Newman's barn in New Haven, their
place of sojourn for the preceding year and a half, and struck off
through the woods to Milford, their new home. Their pastor, Peter
Prudden, was their leader and Sergeant Thomas Tibbals their guide,
"he having been there a number of times before". They took with
them their sheep, their cattle, their household gear and all their personal belongings, materials for the common house having already
gone around by water. Had the pillar of fire suddenly appeared to
these 1639 wanderers in the wilderness, as the first night-darkness
came down, not even the ten "Inhabitants" among them, who could
not qualify as church members, would have been greatly surprised.
Milford was their destination, but Heaven was their "dearest cuntrie",
and now with their names in the church book and a covenant to bind
them together they were on their way in a new and very important
sense. Likewise every other church group, as one gathering date after
another was written into the record. Only for a brief moment could
each "little bundle of eternal life" be tied up with such complete confidence that the covenant as pledged would be a bond indissoluble, but
for that moment the "mutual walk" had about it something of
apostolic earnestness and elevation of spirit rare in human association.

Looked back upon after many generations, the break with traditional procedures which these gatherings represent is nothing short of
startling. When a group of self-chosen, self-approved laymen laid the
foundations of a church society by subscribing in public to a covenant of their own making, they were challenging the old ecclesiastical order at its very foundations. They were also breaking the organic
unity of the church militant, as it had been cherished from apostolic
days down. No longer would a man assume the lifelong privilege of
church membership by virtue of having been born into the church
of his fathers before him. He would be admitted by vote of his fellow-
members. Instead of being parted from the company of saints on earth
by death only, he would now remain a member by the continuing
approval of his fellow-members. His "Carriage" among them would
be under ceaseless scrutiny, and in their hands alone would lie the
power of excommunication, should his conduct be not acceptable.

Viewed in the long perspective of known church history this was indeed a new order, newer than any seven farmer-tradesmen-men of affairs-ministerial leaders realized when they stood under many great trees or on many barn platforms and laid the foundations of many "spiritual houses".

They had done more than organize churches. By the time gathering day came in any town, a group of early leaders in that town had already taken certain first steps in setting up what amounted to a miniature republic and a republic in which they had a supremely important stake. In so doing they had usually shown an ability to distinguish between main objectives and mere machinery, surprising among men to whom bending the knee or not bending it made the difference between purity and corruption. They had also gone a short but very important way toward balancing respect for individual rights and group unity. It was a prophetic combination.

CHAPTER THREE

"*Foundation Work*"

Detailed first steps in this long process of setting up a form of government which would permit a church "to stand on her own legs", as though she were the only church in the world, are hard to come by, as these preliminaries were not part of the church record. They survive in private memorials only, and very few of these represent the lay view. We have many words from early leaders in church and state—men of affairs trained, to some extent experienced, in government, and for that reason measurably sure of their ground in such matters. Some of them had given much thought to government in abstract theory as well as in practice. In so far as these leaders published their findings, many, in fact, most of them, were on the side of the more aristocratic forms of government, and openly distrustful of the people.

Said John Winthrop,

"Now if we should change from a mixt Aristocratie to a meere Democratie, first we should have no warrant in scripture for it; there was no such Government in Israell. We should hereby voluntaryly abase our selves, and deprive our selves of that dignity, which the providence of God hath putt upon us: . . . A Democratie is among most Civill nations, accounted the meanest and worst of all formes of Government . . . and Historyes doe recorde, that it hath been allwayes of least continuance and fullest of troubles."[1]

Said John Cotton (probably consciously or unconsciously quoting Henry Ainsworth),

"Democracy, I do not conceyve that ever God did ordeyne as a fitt government eyther for church or commonwealth. If the people be governors, who shall be governed? As for monarchy, and aristocracy, they are both of them clearly approved, and directed in Scripture. . . . Theocracy is the best form of Government in the Commonwealth as well as in the Church."[2]

There is much more of this from clergy and civil rulers alike.

Laymen would have been unable to argue their case successfully against such pronouncements. Governmental theory was a maze in which they would have quickly lost their way, but they were uncannily shrewd when it came to seeing the practical implications of a structure of government, particularly in so far as their own individual rights were concerned. They foresaw the places at which dangers to these rights would be likely to occur, and they could devise practical means of avoiding them. Fortunately, they also saw their own main objectives very clearly. They wanted a pure church and they wanted to run it themselves. Accordingly, they shaped their entire structure of government to these two ends. As to the how of it, that also was very clear in their own minds. The Bible was their chief guide, as it was also for their leaders. Outside the strict limits of the Old and New Testaments all was "*Terra incognita*" indeed, as many a preacher put it. Hence with a zeal which knew no tiring, Bibles in hand, they went to work to find line and verse and chapter which would show them the next step to be taken, the more literal the correspondence the better.

Thereby hangs many a tale, unfortunately lost beyond recovery. Such tales would doubtless supply illuminating and manifold answers to the question as to how inexperienced Englishmen, representing various levels of middle class society went about it to set up a form of self-government. If the process were long and fumbling, so much deeper the imprint for similar tasks in days yet to come.

One fairly complete log of procedures in one small group, prior to the gathering of their church, survives from Dedham, Massachusetts. This was the fourteenth church to be founded in the colony. Every detail of this record can be matched elsewhere many times over and for a century still to come, but so full an account belonging to any one group so early in the story has not yet come to light. As a continuous record, which may be regarded as fairly typical, it deserves a hearing. It was set down by John Allin, a Dissenting minister, who, before the deliberations were over, was elected first pastor of the group he had helped to organize. In his own words, he kept this record "for future ages to make use of", and in order that "light may be fetched from examples of things past".[3] He knew what he said. Much light may be fetched from it, and light thrown backward and forward, as well as on the immediate foreground he thought to illuminate. As the "little Knot" of Dedham Christians labored with great zeal and painful honesty to get ready to unite themselves in a church society, they not only laid bare the values by which they lived, but also wrote a pioneer chapter in self-determination which is a strange blend of inexperience and rather surprising wisdom; of literal-minded adherence to precedent (both biblical and English) and bold originality. At times they showed a naïve caution, and then again they took leaps in the dark. There are certain moments in this paradoxical procedure which are arrestingly prophetic as early moments in the history of a republic.

At the time this record begins in 1637, Dedham was a settlement of some thirty families, or about a hundred and twenty persons. They were newly arrived in this part of Massachusetts and mostly strangers to one another. Almost immediately they began to gather in a neighborly group, first at one house and then at another, on the "5th day of ye weeke" (Thor's day being too heathen a name to utter),

> "lovingly to discourse & consult together such questions as might further tend to stablish a peaceable & co'fortable civill society, & pr'pare for spirituall co'munion in a church society".[4]

No troublesome questions arose in connection with the establishment of the civil society, but when they came to the "chiefe scope" of the meetings, namely, "the spiritual house", they struck snags and were confronted by questions which necessitated prolonged discussion.

Fortunately, having expected disagreement, they had prepared for it. The purpose of the meetings was inquiry and all inquirers met on the same level. They met devoutly; each meeting began and ended with prayer. Each member came prepared to speak his mind openly on a topic announced a week in advance. When they assembled, the host led off, others following in turn, "as they saw cause to ad, inlarge or approve" what was spoken, until presently a sense of the meeting agreement had been reached. No new topic was proposed until all had taken complete satisfaction in the discussion of the former one. Throughout the discussion objections were welcomed, in so far as they came from teachable hearts, and were offered in humility and without thought of "cavilling or contradicting".

Apparently the program justified itself, for according to the record such was the spirit of this free questioning and debate that the "reasonings were very peaceable, loving, & tender, much to edification". True Dissenters that they were, however, they took nothing for granted and, ignoring the experience of the thirteen societies already organized in their immediate Massachusetts neighborhood, they went at their own organization as though they were the first Christians since apostolic times even to think of joining together in church fellowship. To do otherwise would not be "to stand on their own legs".

To begin with, did they have a right even to meet, being as they were "out of a church order" and strangers to one another? Yes, they decided, after prayer and long discussion. Had not St. Paul urged Christians, merely as Christians, to exhort, admonish, and comfort one another? They were doing a little of all three. Next question: then why be a church at all? Why wasn't such informal exhortation, admonition, and comfort sufficient? Why not "rest in such a condicion and looke no further?" Whoever asked the question knew the answer before he asked it. Because they had no choice. God had commanded it. The Bible was full of texts and examples to the purpose. From the days of Abraham down, God's people had been joined together by covenant. Besides, until they were a church, they could not enjoy the ordinances, and as ordinances were necessary for "ye repaire of ye s[ain]ts", the question answered itself. All agreed. It remained to discuss through many meetings the nature of the covenant relationship, its obligations, its privileges, its scriptural foundations and examples, until before anyone quite realized it, spring had come in Dedham, and as yet they had not taken even the first step toward formal organization; namely, choosing the Seven Pillars. They must get on to this important business at once.

Not being sure of procedure, they first asked several members of the Watertown church who lived in Dedham to join with them and help in the laying of foundations, but the Watertown church refused to grant this permission. Until a settled church existed in Dedham, how could members from another settled church be dismissed to join with them? What would be the status of these members? They would meanwhile themselves be "out of a church order". It could not be. At this point, John Allin, being urged, took over.

He first chose Ralph Wheelocke, a neighbor of whom he approved and who fortunately approved of him. With great solemnity, and after due preparation, the two men "opened" to each other their "spiritual conditions" and found that they still approved. They then chose a third man who in turn "opened his spiritual condition" to them both. These three chose a fourth and so on, until by mutual agreement they had ten men who looked reasonably hopeful. With only Seven Pillars required, they thought to allow generously for shrinkage; wisely so. It was slow work, for each time the approval must face both ways and also there was one more man to be satisfied. Even so, with ten candidates, seven survivors looked possible, and the ten men proceeded hopefully to the screening process, or in John Allin's phrase the "scanning". Not until the Last Judgment would these ten men face a more devastating scrutiny, particularly since long before this point in the program they had ceased to be strangers. Each man knew far more about the other nine than the "soul mercies" each had experienced, and some of this knowledge might well prove fateful. However, they dared to begin.

To get themselves into a proper state of humility they first observed another day of fasting and prayer and then set to work. The first item on the agenda was the setting up of suitable qualifications for pillarhood. Long preliminary discussion and the pooling of their individual religious experiences produced three main categories of eligibility; namely, soundness in grace, wisdom and discrimination in judging others, meekness, amiability of spirit and innocency of life.

Each of the ten men agreed to be tested by this standard and to abide by the decision of the other nine. Each also agreed to lay aside "all ambitious desyres of being taken into ye worke" and, if chosen, to lay aside also

"o'vr much bashfullnes in refusing the same and to regard the choice as ye call & voice of God".[5]

So saying, they were off again; John Allin being the first to submit to the test. He recounted his personal religious story from its beginning to the hour at hand, and was then excused, leaving his state of grace, his judicial abilities and his character to the mercy of the other nine. Apparently predestined for approval, he survived, and thus became Pillar Number One. In turn each of the others followed suit, hazarding his all likewise, with the result that after many meetings by day and by night through many weeks, and after various exhibitions of qualities not included among the criteria for approval, six men had been accepted and four rejected. That left them short one pillar. John Allin, Ralph Wheelocke, John Luson, John Frayry, Eleazar Lusher, and Robert Hindall were safely in. Edward Allin, Anthony Fisher, Joseph Kingsbury, and Thomas Morse were out.

Before nominations were reopened, the surviving six reviewed the cases of the rejected four, with the sequel that Edward Allin, being cleared of certain "Offences" that had held him back, was finally approved as Pillar Number Seven. Not speedily, however, as satisfaction waited upon the arrival of friends from England who could testify in his behalf. The other three, who had failed the first tests, fared no better by this referendum. For a time Anthony Fisher's case looked hopeful. He seemed to be in the way of repenting his "rash carriage and speaches savoring of selfe confidence", which had kept him out in the first place, but repentance faded and he was required to wait a further process of humbling and the decision of the whole church after it should be gathered. He waited. Joseph Kingsbury, left out in the beginning because he was "too much addicted to ye world", still remained "stiff and unhumbled" and could not clear himself to satisfaction. Finally, after what would seem to have been dire provocation indeed, he exhibited such a "distempered flying out" upon the brother who was examining him that they gave him wholly over until such time as the whole church might judge of his fitness. He waited also. Thomas Morse, who had at first been "darke & unsatisfying" as to the work of grace in his heart, could still produce no clear-cut evidence of saving grace, and he too was left to the further decision of the whole church. This second rejection must have been particularly galling to Anthony Fisher and Joseph Kingsbury, since they had previously been named by the town as members of a committee to "contrive the Fabrick of a meetinghouse", which was to stand on Joseph Kingsbury's lot. But holding up a "spiritual house" was a different matter from carpentry. Pillarhood was not for them.

These second trials had called for many meetings, many days of fasting and prayer, much inquiry, observation and hearing of testimony. The summer was now gone as well as the spring. The main project had gone forward, however, as soon as the approval of Edward Allin brought the number of pillars to the required seven. A town meeting had been called, the seven names propounded, and a time and place specified for the hearing of objections against any one of the seven. On this specified day Edward Allin was again in trouble, and for the same "Offences" that had first blocked his acceptance. Once again he was able to clear himself, however, and to remain (though precariously) Pillar Number Seven. He was fortunate in this second reinstatement and probably knew it. The twelfth man in New Haven was unable to get back after he had been once dropped. His misstep had been exceeding the ceiling price for meal. He had "sold to one of Pequonack in his need". The fact that he had duly repented this profiteering act and restored the money made no difference. He was not fit for "foundation work", although the record that he was dropped "with grief" by the other eleven may perchance have afforded a shred of comfort.

Meanwhile in Dedham, John Hunting had come to town and had quickly been approved as Pillar Number Eight, thus providing a comfortable margin against future dereliction by any one of the seven now approved by the town. Two things remained to be done; first, to review all their "professions" for the benefit of John Hunting who had missed the first recital, and then to declare, each in turn, his judgment as to "all ye Heads of Christian religion". They went at this latter appalling task as though it were merely another detail in this lengthening process. One man spoke his thought on "one point of religion", after which the seven others followed in turn, the whole group ironing out differences as they advanced.

Quite aside from the dreary repetitiousness of this eight-fold Act of Conformity, such emphasis on agreement in the matter of belief presaged ill for a new order in religious life. The zeal of these men for independence in matters of church government brooked no shadow of interference from any outside authority, and yet within their own ranks liberality in matters of belief was a totally different story. Here they were, a little company of men who had come across the world to be free (as they said) from ecclesiastical authority, and yet they were making letter-perfect agreement in belief a foundation stone in their own structure. They did not call it conformity, a word in bad odor, but rather "a sweete consent of judgment", which, as John Allin said, increased their love one toward another. We can only believe him, and remember that tolerance as to religious belief is a plant of slow growth in any soil, and that in the soil of seventeenth century Dissent it had one of its distinctly poorer chances. As religious leaders saw it, tolerance had made the world anti-Christian and they would have none of it. No one who reads with sympathy and imagination any considerable number of records containing items such as these in the Dedham story, or even as few as a year's worth of sermons such as men of John Allin's stamp preached, can doubt the depth of spiritual experience underneath them, the never-flagging loyalty to an unseen perfection, the sure conviction that God was near enough to be talked to and heard in reply. To think only of the inhospitality of these men to the views of those outside their own closed circle is to do them an injustice. Tolerance takes time.

As soon as the "sweete consent" had been reached by the eight pillars, a covenant was drafted, a date was announced for the gathering, and plans were made for inviting neighboring churches. There were still snags ahead, but at least first steps had been taken. They had the supports for the house. Nearly a year and a half had been spent in finding them. Uncounted hours had gone into many score of meetings, but not more than similar groups had taken in other towns. In the following year New Haven distributed a fourteen-month period in almost the same proportion: first, the small house to house meetings, given essentially to the same questions and answers, then the long "scanning" process, as twelve nominees shrank to the required seven. As the "saints" saw it, so important a business was not to be hurried, and though hazards stalked on all sides and another winter was always just ahead, they had more time than Americans have ever had since.

To say that all this concern, all these deliberations, all this fasting and prayer involved only a small group, even in a village of thirty families, is of course true. By no means all the adult population cared so deeply or would have paid so high a price in time, effort, and sleep. At the same time this small group was acting representatively and everyone in the village had an acknowledged stake in the outcome.

On the date announced, Nov. 8, 1638, the town of Dedham assembled, visitors came, the church was gathered. It was a solemn day. The reception of members was now in order. John Allin and Ralph Wheelocke were appointed to screen applicants once a week until such time as the church officers could be elected. These two men assumed their duties with much awe and humility. "It was meete", said John Allin, "yt we should be very watchfull, especially in ye first beginnings of ye church".[6] And watchful they surely were. Two angels with flaming swords could not have guarded the doors more vigilantly.

The proof of their vigilance was that although at these weekly hearings many testified to the "breathings of their souls after Christ", by the end of the winter only four men and six women had been received, hardly the number needful to exercise the "mutual watch" church membership required. John Allin's notes indicate the various levels of grace which were considered acceptable and the various degrees of warmth with which these ten members had been welcomed.

Margaret Allin, his own wife, the first member received, gave "a clere and plentifull testimony of ye gracious dealings of ye Lord with hir".

Henry Philips showed himself to be a very "tender and broken hearted Christian" (apparently a very superior kind).

The wife of John Luson (a Pillar) was "sufficiently humbled and constant in hir affections to ye Lord Jesus", so that the church took satisfaction in her and received her.

The wife of John Frayry (another Pillar) gave good satisfaction both in public and in private.

The wife of Joseph Kingsbury (rejected Pillar) appeared a "tender harted soule full of feares & temptations but truly breathing after Christ", and they took her.

John Dwite, after some scruples "wherein ye Church waited a good while for satisfaction", was finally received.

Robert Kempe seemed to be "a plaine harted Christian", although some objections to his private life had to be cleared before he could be received.

Daniel Fisher, "a tender harted & hopefull Christian young man", was easily and gladly received.

The wife of Eleazar Lusher (another Pillar), after various dealings in private, appeared much humbled and was received with great satisfaction.

The wife of John Hunting (eighth Pillar), in spite of scruples "sticking in some of ye Church", gave good satisfaction and was finally received.[7]

Sometimes the scruples were on the other side, as when Jonathan Fairebanke, some time later, "stood off fro' ye church" for a long time because he objected to the publicity of the "confession" exacted of him. He finally succumbed, however, and after "divers loving conferences" was gladly received by the whole church. Brother Hinsdell's wife, "being fearfull & not able to speake in publike", fainted dead away at the sound of her own public voice, and after much deliberation was allowed to speak her "Relation" in private and then confirm it on the following Sunday morning. Other churches soon found that they must make similar concessions to the "more fearful and bashful Sex", who were unequal to the strain of a public accounting, but they did so reluctantly. When it came to determining the visibility of the saints, merciful exceptions must not be allowed to go too far. Reticence as to one's soul's health was not among the virtues, and the excuse of stage fright was no excuse.

Not all congregations were equally strict, even at the outset. When the Milford group set off through the woods after their gathering, it included among the ten "Inhabitants" several "very valuable" applicants, who could not give satisfactory evidence of their change of heart. They were too "valuable" to leave out. Besides, they would be co-residents in the new settlement. What would be the relation of this small minority to the civil government, if they were left out of the church fold? How should they be classified? Let them stay out, said John Davenport, minister at New Haven. We came to get a pure church. Let it stay pure. Milford heard the arguments and was duly impressed. The unregenerate did not sign their names on gathering day. Nevertheless, the journey on foot through the woods was long and John Davenport's arguments grew dimmer with each mile, with the result that when the site that was to be Milford was reached, the "valuable" applicants were safely inside the little bundle. Compromise had come at the very beginning and it would make trouble for more than the Milford quota of Christians.

Examination of the Dedham book for the fate of the ill-starred Pillars reassures one. An applicant's case was never closed beyond all hope. Decision was merely postponed until one was ready for another chance. Three years after his rejection as Pillar, Thomas Morse, he of the dark answers, the doubtful state of grace and the unsubmissive "Carriage", grew sufficiently innocent in his conversation to be received. Almost a year later Joseph Kingsbury, on whose lot the meetinghouse stood and has continued to stand for more than three hundred years, was adjudged sufficiently humble to pass muster. Anthony Fisher's "improvement" took longest of the three. Despite all efforts to "reduce him to order", his symptoms were not favorable until 1645, almost seven years after he failed to qualify for Pillarhood. He was finally brought to "a penitent co'fession" and "comfortably received". His persistence under repeated humiliations and also the tenacity of the covenant members to test his visibility to their complete satisfaction are equally eloquent as to how much it mattered on both sides. Unanimity as the condition of acceptance was given up under protest, but it presently had to be given up, for the simple reason that it was impossible. The few who remained unsatisfied as to a candidate's eligibility were given a full chance to speak, and if they could not convince the majority, they were required "to sit down in their votes". The rejected Dedham trio would have had a better chance fifty years later.

By the end of the second April membership hearings were temporarily halted while the small group already inside proceeded to elect a pastor and teacher. Their dilemma was that they had only one candidate but two offices to fill. To which one should they elect John Allin, as it was a foregone conclusion that he would be chosen. Which office did he prefer? When he continued to have no preference, an advisory committee was called in, and when they professed neutrality, John Allin himself finally had to decide. He chose to be pastor and in this choice the whole membership formally concurred. Plans were set on foot for his "solemn ordination" in case nothing contrary intervened. Something intervened at once. In their great zeal to elect him, they had forgotten that only a Ruling Elder could lay ordaining hands on a pastor, and they had no Ruling Elder. All right; they would produce one.

Once again many meetings were needful, and when these were at last accomplished, they found that they had two candidates for the office instead of one. John Hunting and Ralph Wheelocke were both Pillars, both acceptable as Ruling Elders, but neither one was good enough to be inevitable. What to do. Before debate had gone too far to continue amiable, they solicited advice from Roxbury and Dorchester, with the result that John Hunting was presently chosen. John Allin, pastor-elect, informed Ralph Wheelocke of his defeat and he behaved so well under the blow that the whole church was "more intirely knitt unto him in respect thereof". John Hunting, when informed of his victory, was not to be outdone in good behavior and he too carried himself "with great circumspection", accepting the honor with "much modesty feare & trembling & many teares in respect of his owne insufficiency". Nevertheless he accepted, and the path was at last clear to the double ceremony of ordination.

When the great day came, John Allin preached half of his own ordination sermon in the morning, and then after solemn prayer put the question as to whether anyone objected to John Hunting as Ruler in the house of God. Blessedly no one objected, whereupon John Hunting made a trembling speech of acceptance, and waited. Three men, previously designated, came forward, placed their hands on his head and gave him a solemn charge to be "faithfull and dilligent" in his office among them. He rose up a Ruling Elder. In the afternoon John Allin preached the second half of his sermon, and was in turn ordained as pastor.

Now it was all finished. More than two years had gone by, but at last they were a church. On the following two Sundays the "Ordinances" were celebrated for the first time in Dedham. On the first Sunday five children were baptized and on the second all those who had thus far "laid hold on ye covenant" partook of the Lord's Supper together. The occasion was described as "very sweete" to all the church and to one sister in particular who "had long bene full of Doubtings". For the moment all doubtings were hushed, and in the fulfilment of their long and earnest hope brotherly love was triumphant. The little collection of "visible saints" in Dedham was closer to sainthood than they would ever be again in this life.

The near-millennium could not last, nor could the spontaneous freshness and intensity of these earliest gatherings survive numerous repetitions. First days must pass. Foundation stones lie deep beneath the surface. Later generations assume them and build their structures with more assurance. These men of Dedham in their day and generation knew the importance of such beginnings as they attempted, and if they strained at gnats in their zealous struggle to lay a right foundation, it was with the conscious awareness that they built for later times.

"It is better to settle our *Foundation* right at first than to have it *to mend afterwards*",[8]

John Eliot wrote, although he penned this neat epigram not of the beginnings of church and state, but of his own studious attempt to make a proper alphabet for the Indian language. Briefly, whatever men did of "foundation work", they did with the awareness that they were doing it for the first time. Theirs was a rare chance. Every page of this off-stage Dedham record encourages one to think that men of such high purpose could be trusted to take it.

CHAPTER FOUR

"Our Meetinghouse"

Dᴜʀɪɴɢ all this long, slow process of organization sermons were being preached every Sunday and town meetings held once a month on Monday; sometimes oftener. Someone's "goodly parlour", a barn, the shade of a tree still sufficed as meeting place. Often the meetinghouse had been voted before the church was gathered or the minister chosen; in fact, work on the building might be well under way before these long-drawn-out negotiations were completed. If not, the fact that the town was now "raised to church estate" quickened the eagerness of those both within and without the covenant circle. Barns, parlors, "Pulpit Rocks", and wide-spreading oaks would no longer do. The town must have its own place of assembly, and speedily.

The dual purpose of the projected meetinghouse was fully understood, as the typical phrasing of a town vote authorizing its construction is likely to show. It would be voted "for the town's use in public worship and in open town meeting". All records, public and private, bear out Cotton Mather's statement that even as late as his day no one called it a church.

"A MEETING-HOUSE is the Term that is most commonly used by the *New English* Christians",[1]

he wrote, and for what was to him the very good reason that there is "no just ground in Scripture to apply such a trope as *church* to a place of assembly".[2] On Sunday it was always "going to meeting" or "going to preaching"; never going to church. In the town mind, as well as on the Town Book, this was not God's holy temple; it was an all-purpose place of assembly. In typical phrase which expressed the current view for more than a century it was

"our meetinghouse, built by our own vote, framed by our own hammers and saws, and by our own hands set in the convenientest place for us all".

Accordingly, no particular sacredness attached to the building itself. On Sunday the town assembled here for preaching; on town meeting Monday essentially the same group met in the same place to vote "fence repairs", convenient "Horse Bridges", rings for swine, bounty on crows and wolf heads; to specify more trees for the "shade of cattle" or to vote penalties for those who had "deaded" trees contrary to order; to grant one applicant "liberty to set his house upon a Knole", another "liberty" to move into town or to depart; to elect chimney viewers, hog-reaves, surveyors, constables or other officers, and to learn "the mind of the town" as to various other imperatives of their daily lives. Each of the multiple other uses of this central building was likewise a response to some urgency of neighborhood life. In the earliest days the Dorchester settlers had brought their plate and other valuables night by night to the palisadoed little structure on the hill, where a sentinel stood guard until morning. Other first settlers did likewise. The drumbeat at any other time than the accustomed hour on Sunday morning was a signal to assemble here at once for some purpose that brooked no hesitation. All paths led to this spot of "rising ground"; all distances to other towns were measured from the front door. The meetinghouse was the center of life, even in a literal sense. While Sunday preaching was going on, solemnity was fitting. The knob and fox-tail of the tithing-man and the vigilant eyes of the deacons took care of that; but there was no reverence for the place itself, any more than for the previous places of Sunday preaching. The congregation entered without awe, banged the hinged seats of the sheep-pen pews, and continued to bang them as they punctuated their prayer and praise by rising and sitting at proper intervals. Such unholy clamor shocked no one, except perhaps the latest comer to the town and he would soon get used to it.

On Communion Sunday the drop-leaf table back of the deacon's seat held the communion cup; on town meeting days it held the gavel. No meetinghouse was built without this convenient shelf, but it was no holier than anyone's kitchen table.

Had building taken place immediately upon arrival, as seldom happened, such casual attitudes toward a place of worship might have appeared unseemly to the worshippers themselves, but after the lapse of weeks and months, perhaps even the three years permitted by charter stipulation, old Sabbath ways were far in the background. Besides, any thought of the place of preaching as a sanctuary, with the altar its holy of holies, had been deliberately banned along with other Romish survivals. By what amounted to an official pronouncement, oft-repeated,

> "There is now *no place* which renders the Worship of God more acceptable for its being there performed",[3]

nor is any part of worship now confined to special places. Keep the place of preaching repaired and in order at all times, treat it with fitting respect while worship is in progress, but use it freely and lawfully for "Civil Service" at other times. Above all, avoid setting it off with a "Theatrical gaudiness", which does not "savour of the Spirit of a true Christian simplicity".

No doubt on first view the Dissenting version of "a true Christian simplicity" within and without was a shock to English eyes, accustomed to Lincoln, Peterborough, Norwich, Salisbury, or some other noble pile of stone on their daily skyline, such richness of beauty once they stepped inside, but if so, it was a shock of brief duration. Adjustment to newness was necessarily swift in all directions (if one would survive) and, besides, plainness was a deliberate expression of protest, as well as a necessary compromise with pioneer scarcity. Once again the spirit of religion had begotten a new style, this time plain to severity, solid, durable, and utterly useful. Early worshippers accepted the substitute their protesting temper had wrought, and they accepted it pridefully. So did their children and grandchildren, most of whom would never see a cathedral. Cotton Mather spoke for the third generation when he wrote, in 1726,

First Meetinghouse in Middletown, Connecticut, about 1652.

An imaginary drawing (now lost) of the building voted Feb. 2, 1652. This was to be a twenty by twenty by ten foot structure, enclosed by palisades. From a cut appearing in the *Centennial Address* of David D. Field, Middletown, 1853.

THE OLD TUNNEL MEETINGHOUSE IN LYNN, MASSACHUSETTS, 1682.

Built in the center of the Common, where it stood until 1827. It took its name from the octagonal, funnel-shaped cupola, *tunnel* being obsolete for *funnel*. From a print appearing in Clarence W. Hobbs, *Lynn and Surroundings*, Lynn, 1886. A line drawing of this structure, with side dormers added, is owned by the Lynn Historical Society. Another print, showing two front dormers, is owned by the Lynn Public Library.

"and every Town for the most part, can say, . . . They have modest and handsome Houses for the Worship of God, *not* set off with Gaudy, Pompous, Theatrical Fineries, but suited unto the Simplicity of Christian worship".[4]

It was a "modest and handsome" ideal which had allowed common sense to dictate many a decision, particularly in the beginning. If the intersecting point of lines drawn to the four corners of the town failed to coincide strictly with the "knowl with a grate many pines on it", for which they were aiming, the "Center committee" forgot the precise measurements and let the knoll and the pines win. If specifications as voted did not match materials as the axe left them, the axe won. All measurements were "thereabouts". "Voated", said Longmeadow, Massachusetts,

"that the meeting hous should be built Thirty Eight foots square, if the Timber that is already gotten will allow it, or If this Timber be too scant to make it sumthing less".[5]

That was the spirit. Each town was a law unto itself as to all structural details. The general agreement which prevailed was due in part to essential unity of purpose, in part to both conscious and unconscious imitation, and most of all to the fact that early builders had learned the hard way to achieve a house and barn for themselves, but that their knowledge and experience stopped short at this point. When they came to "contrive the frame of a meetinghouse", the result could hardly be called architecture, nor was it meant to be. At the same time these earliest structures are as good an illustration as one could hope to find of the truism that architecture is a mirror held up to a time in spiritual as well as physical ways. Almost any one of these all-purpose little buildings, exposed to the worst that weather could do and yet equal to the strain, is an embodiment of what William Bradford had in mind when he wrote of the steadfastness of his own Plymouth people and called their courage "answerable". Answerable courage and other such-like qualities of mind and heart were pegged into the "modest and handsome" meetinghouses of the first generations, just as they are written on and also between the lines of interleaved almanacs, private journals, and town meeting records. Were it possible to show in a purely pictorial history the long succession of early meetinghouses turning into churches, successive chapters of what, for want of a better term, we call spiritual history would be plain to see, as well as improved skills, increasing abundance, and suitability of materials.

Whatever the dimensions of the first meetinghouse in any town, they were likely to be scanty, and accommodated to the size of the original congregation, as though growth were hardly to be expected. By what seems a strange lack of foresight (surely not a lack of faith) no first meetinghouse was large enough to take care of the unborn children of the founding families, and this in spite of the fact that protecting their posterity from English corruption was acknowledged as one of the more urgent reasons for removal. The 1634 meeting-house in Salem (probably the second structure) measured 17 by 20 by 12; the first in Dedham (1638) 20 by 36 by 12; in Milford, Connecticut (1640) 30 by 30; in Hartford (1640) 40 by 40; and in New Haven in the same year, 50 by 50. It is not likely that any of the meeting-houses built before 1640 (for most of which specific data are lacking) were planned more amply.[6] The record of a great storm of wind which in 1643 "lifted up the meetinghouse in Newbury, the people being in it", no doubt does honor to a very great wind indeed, but it also calls to mind a day of very small things. Even after galleries were added in some meetinghouses, it was often possible to pass the collection box from one side of the house to the other at the pulpit end.

Dimensions, however, were no index to importance in the town mind. From the day the structure was voted, more than a generous half of the subsequent items on many a Town Book would concern it in some way, either as a building or as an institution. For church members and non-members alike it was a community responsibility of first magnitude, and for the very good reason that every resident of the town was a part owner and had a financial stake in its affairs. Once the vote to build was taken, every townsman would share responsibility for the plans and perhaps also for the work itself. A committee of three or five men would have the project in charge. They would first "lay out" the building "after such manner as they shall judge most convenient for the public good". If the town wished "bowed rafters", they must be weighted for at least a year; if not, work might begin as soon as the "lay out" had been approved. A master builder would then be appointed. He would be one of themselves, a villager, known for his "skill and courage", and he would greatly need both. There would be no blueprints to guide him. His special equipment would consist of no more than a scribe rule and a ten foot pole, but these would be sufficient. He would know in advance the amount to be expended and also that he would be expected to render an account to the last nail. When the Salem meetinghouse was repaired in 1647, exactly five hundred nails were provided and exactly five hundred were used. When the Cambridge congregation decided in 1676 to seal the hall and hall-chamber of the parsonage and to lay a second "floore of bords" in the "chichin-chamber", they used exactly three thousand five hundred and sixty nails at a cost of 8s.10½ d. Every nail was accounted for. All allotments of materials were similarly precise and had better be. When a building was finished, the same committee of three or five men would "judge the work" and if it were thought satisfactory, the master builder would be "paid to his content", perhaps with a "cow-pasture", or more or less, according to his initial bargain. Goodman Elderkin of New London, Connecticut, was satisfied with a cow. He had undertaken in 1651

"to build a meeting-house about the same demention of Mr. Parke's his barne [the previous place of worship] and clapboard it for the sum of eight pounds, provided the towne cary the tymber to the place and find nales. And for his pay he requires a cow and 50s. in peage".[7]

It took him three years to complete the work.

Invariably these new style temples would face south, so as "to be square with the sun at noon"—in the idiom of the day, "sun-line houses". Until long after the first generation there would be no spire "to smack of popery"; instead a turret, suitable for watching; no stained glass, obstructing and discoloring the light of heaven; only the single window back of the pulpit to admit honest sunlight, unadorned. Other windows were luxuries; they could wait. Instead of the cross surmounting the turret, there would be a weathercock to remind Christians that even Peter had once slipped from grace, and also to answer the early morning question of every farmer-freeman as to wind and weather.

The interior would be planned for preaching sermons and hearing them, not for adoration. There would be an elevated pulpit with its hourglass and sounding board, but no altar; a deacon's seat, from which the psalm could be tuned, but no choir-loft. The supporting posts would be in full view; the walls unplastered. In the beginning seats would be no more than planks laid across the floor. Later when it came time "to pue the meetinghouse", the floor would be "lotted out" and bids taken. Pews would then be built at individual expense and according to individual taste, but only after the town had heard each case individually and given permission. Except below the pulpit, where there would be "free seating for venerables", all seats would be assigned by an elaborate scheme of privilege and consequent obligation. In the beginning, however, all seats were free and with little respect paid to rank and station, except that magistrates must sit high and have a "cushin". A middle aisle divided men and women. The bench for the "guardsmen" directly inside the one door spoke eloquently of the perils which fringed the lives of those who dared to come to preaching.

So also does the vote on many a town record, documenting seasons of special danger. From Meriden, Connecticut, in 1675, this memorial to King Philip,

"Also that evrie man bring his armes and amunition compleat on the saboth day that he may be able in a fitt posture to doe service if need reqire".[8]

Ministers wrote in their diaries, "I took my gun to meeting", as naturally as they recorded the weather, the fact that a cow had calved, or "This day a bluebird sang". It was a part of life.

Within the meetinghouse there was of course no provision for heat. Not until Hawthorne had grown to young manhood would a stove be generally considered lawful in what he called "the frozen purgatory of my childhood". Comfort was thought to war against attention to doctrine. A town vote in Nottingham, New Hampshire, as late as 1729, decreed that there

> "shall be no fire Kept on the Lord's Day to Disturb the people In the public Worship in the Block house".[9]

On the exposed hilltop worshippers enjoyed the privilege of sermons at seasonal temperatures, meaning the outside maximum, summer and winter. From November to April the minister preached in great-coat and gloves; the male worshippers stamped their feet; the females took what comfort they might in foot-stoves, if they were lucky enough to have them. During the noon interval between preaching periods those who had come from a distance warmed themselves at some neighbor's house, or around the chimney "of sufficient bigness" at the Sabba-Day or "Nooning-House", if the town had seen fit to provide one. Otherwise they accepted one more bodily discomfort as the natural price of the inestimable privilege of sermons. The black tassels of the cushion on which the pulpit Bible rested waved freely as the wind blew through the cracks; the water in the baptismal bowl froze; there was "great coughing" in the congregation, but the hourglass was turned twice as usual. Judge Sewall thought to record fact, not to suggest parable, when he wrote of his seven-day son, Stephen, presented for baptism on a February Sunday in 1686, "Child shrunk at the water but cryed not".[10] This same child would live his whole life in that spirit, but seven days seems a tender age for his initiation.

In due time there would be windows and "shuts" for them, although even then, when winter came, the glass would be removed and the windows boarded up. For a six month space the congregation listened and sang and prayed in darkness as well as in cold. The deacon often had trouble seeing what came next as he "lined out" the psalm; likewise the preacher in reading the Scripture and explicating it line by line. A frequent winter item in ministerial diaries parallels what William Brinsmead wrote (in Latin) of a certain September day in 1688, "The pulpit was so dark this rainy day I could not read the text".[11] As for the sermon itself, it must be memorized word for word or the preacher was lost.

Along with the windows came the "porch" or enclosed projection beyond the outside door, by way of rendering this draughty entrance less intolerable to those who occupied the back seats. The expense of this improvement, however, would usually be for the back-seat occupants; not for the town. If one would have comfort, let him pay for it himself. Winter regulations, doubtless aimed at protection against cold, make no mention of it. There is a record from Woodstock, Connecticut, in 1725, requiring that doors be kept shut in very cold or very windy weather, "according to the lying of the wind",

> "and that people in such windy weather come in at the leeward doors only, and take care that they are easily shut, so as to prevent both the breaking of the doors, and the making of a noise".[12]

Not a word about the inrushing mighty wind upon worshippers already chilled to their bones. There was no excuse for not complying with this order, since two years earlier Manassah Horsmor had presented the town with an iron bolt and staples for the purpose and been duly thanked on the Town Book for his gift.

In due time also there would be "Horse-sheds" or a "Horse-house", a "covenient Horse-block" and perhaps also "a causeway to the door". The walls would be lathed and "daubed over workmanlike"; the thatch on the roof would be replaced by "good sedar shingles", although if proposed too early in the story, this particular improvement would require much voting time and perhaps many adjournments without a decision. Likewise the proposal that "Some pinakle or other ornament be set at each end of the house". A gallery would eventually provide for the increasing lean-to population up and down the street, and thereafter many items on the Book would attest propping it, flooring it, seating it, and then for a lifetime thereafter adding new "gice" under the floor, frequently repairing or rebuilding the stairs which led to it and then deciding who might lawfully sit on them. Sometimes on crowded ordination or revival days this gallery would fall. Men and women might die in this by no means infrequent accident which would then supply fresh warrant for grim sermons, warning of worse than falling galleries. In the body of the house long seats and short seats would be added wherever there was room, and always "three or four short Seats nye the Pulpit stairs for Antiant Parsons

[Persons] to sett in". Pews of all sizes and sorts would turn the central area into a crowded patchwork of designs, but each addition would have its separate permission and justified use.

The pulpit itself would be the earliest invitation to ornament, if not the earliest challenge to beauty of design and skill in workmanship beyond the requirements of solidity and elevation. A canopy, usually turnip-shaped, would be a major improvement, born of long consideration and debate. A cushion for the Bible had come far earlier. Almost from the beginning this one detail of interior elegance had graced even the smallest and barest meetinghouses. Custom had early decreed that this cushion should be of green velvet or plush, with long tassels hanging from the corners. It sometimes took as much as four yards of velvet, ten yards of silk, and much voting time to achieve this mark of prideful elegance, but eventually it was always achieved. Even the length and color of the tassels (should they or should they not match the velvet) were important enough to be mentioned in the minutes of the precinct meeting which finally took action toward such improvement.

The pews in turn would profit by the example of the pulpit; the high backs and the doors would invite carving, spindle railing, corner posts. The crowded patchwork look would give place to a design in which the several parts had relation to the whole; the meetinghouse interior would take on a quiet dignity, orderliness, and even beauty. But that is a story in itself. Such changes came slowly and in many chapters. Far hence there would be a bell; before Paul Revere's time imported from England, and "hung fit to ring", even though we have "to sell the Little Boggie Meadow and improve the money" to afford it. If the meetinghouse burned (and many did) the bell would have to be sent back to England to be recast; but before that time came many things would be different.

Early congregations went to meeting by the drum beat or the flat, nasal drawl of the "kunk" and asked no more musical summons. In every town some member had his rates cancelled and perhaps a few bushels of corn added to his annual budget, or possibly a pound of pork from every family in the town, in exchange for "blowing the horn for half an hour before meeting on Lord's day", beating the drum or "sounding the kunk" perhaps for a lifetime. Richard Pinkham of Dover, New Hampshire, beat the drum for thirty years and had six bushels of corn and immunity from rates per year for so doing. When in 1660 the town bought a bell, he was henceforth unemployed. For another lifetime someone else would be slightly more highly paid for "ye wringing of ye bell".

In every town also someone escaped total oblivion (except on his gravestone) by record of payment for sweeping out the meetinghouse once a week, taking care of the "cushin and glass", "attending to cobwebs", hanging out the flag after the first "kunk" and taking it in after the second, supplying water for baptisms, and possibly digging graves, extra, "for such as have occasion from time to time", eighteen pence per grave or more, "according to the nature of the digging, frost or the like". "Old Goodman Cumstock" of New London, Connecticut, had forty shillings a year for ordering the youth in the meetinghouse, sweeping it and beating out dogs. He also made all graves, four shillings for adults, two shillings for children "to be paid by *survivors*". Benjamin Morse of Newbury was engaged "to winge or rub down the principal seats the day after sweeping". Worshippers assigned to "common seats" took the week's dust along with their social rating. Brother Towne of Cambridge was voted a twelve shilling bonus in 1639 "for paynes taken more than ordinary in making cleane the meetinge house in the time of its repayreing". In Longmeadow, Margaret Cooley agreed to do a year's sweeping for "17s/ if there be no work don in the meetinghouse, 18s/ if there be any considerable". John Nuttin, a selectman of Groton, swept for 14s. There was no minimum wage.

Towns took frequent action against dogs in the meetinghouse; the dogbeater sometimes being a separate employee, somtimes the sexton. "It is an indecent thing", says a York, Maine, record,

> "for dogs to come into the Place of Publick Worship, in Time of Divine Service, & is often the occasion of great disorder & disturbance by their Quaraling and fiting".[13]

Understatement, one might say. A 1673 record of Dedham, Massachusetts, combines various services in one office. It reads,

"Agreed with Nat Heaton; to whip doges out of the meeting House: and to goe upon Arands for the reverand Elders: referring to the church: and to take care of Cushin and glass, till further order be taken and for his paynes herein he is to receive of the Towne ten shilings for on whole year".[14]

Anyone who "suffered his dog" to get inside on Sunday, in spite of the vigilance of the Dog-pelters, advanced rapidly from a one shilling fine in the earlier years to five, which became almost standard for most towns. Not to pay the fine meant to lose the dog. Sheep lying down on the meetinghouse steps in time of divine service were another nuisance which called for town votes in many places. In fact, one Newbury worshipper found a large sheep in her pew one Sunday morning and recorded the difficult eviction in her journal. For some reason Hampton had found it necessary in 1661 to vote an order

"yt if any person shall discharge a gunn in the meeting house . . . hee or they shall forfeit five shillings for every such offence nor shall any person ride or lead a horse into the meeting house under the like penalty".[15]

More understandable orders decree from time to time that the "several Passways" into the meetinghouse should not be "encumbered with people". One stepped lively in exit and exchanged news elsewhere.

Such items, many hundreds of them, document the day of small things, but small things which expressed values. The "Lord's Barn", as one humble first meetinghouse was labelled by a neighboring company which worshipped under a steeple, was something more than a building to the average freeman, although he could not have told why. It represented a focus of interest which had no precise parallel in his thought, and a panorama of activity which provided a central unity to his life.

To achieve it, even as a building, took time—years of time. Children grew up between the first "enclosing" of the walls and the later 'daubing" them. First covenanters became too deaf to hear sermons and died before the "deaf Pue" was provided against their infirmity.

Towns paid as they went and delay, long delay, was neither a reproach nor a calamity. Danger from without dwarfed the importance of many an improvement. The Amherst, New Hampshire, entry of 1744,

"And in case there is not an Indian war the next fall, to laith and plaster the walls and ceiling, as the committee shall think fitt",[16]

balances the alternatives for one frontier town in one instance, and supplies one reason why twenty or thirty or even forty years may have gone into the completion of one small building. Falmouth, Maine (now Portland), voted to build in 1719. The frame of the meeting-house was raised in 1721; it was enclosed in 1722 and finished on the outside in 1725. The seats were voted in 1728; they were first occupied in 1740. The structure was finished in 1756 and painted after the Revolution. This record could be matched many times even so late in the story.

The sequel of course was that when the last major item toward the completion of the building had finally been accomplished, it was almost time to rebuild. The first structure was outgrown and outmoded, if not decrepit. But it could still be patched and repatched, and probably would be for another lustrum or two. Year by year a day's work for every man in the town could "preserve the underpinning from foundering by blowing away of the sand", supply new "gice for the gallery floor", "stop the leaks for the present", patch the "Ruff", mend the putty, prime the sashes, provide a "convenient Lock & kee" for the door, build stairs into the "Bell-chamber", perhaps a "Bell-Coney", clear the bats out of the sounding board, provide a frame for the "Baptism Bason"; and otherwise add, repair, refurbish against the weekly need, until presently there would come an end to patching and the town must start over.

"Voted", says the record of Bridgewater, Massachusetts, in 1671,

"to build a new meeting-house, and granted four score pounds and no more for falling, squaring, framing, enclosing, covering, flooring, glazing, and seating, and whatsoever belongs to the finishing of the same, excepting the galleries and ceiling: the dimensions to be forty by twenty-six feet, and fourteen feet studs".[17]

To read between the lines of such a record is to see a new focus of interest, a new panorama of activity, involving every family in the town for another long stretch of time. Every voter would share not only in the responsibility of the new decisions to be made, but very probably in the labor itself at some point.

Many "dwelling houses" and many "handsome barns" were raised in every town by the coöperative strength and skill of one's friends and neighbors up and down the street, but unless a man lived a very long life, there would be but one or two raisings of a meetinghouse in his memory. Consequently, it would be an event and something of a gala day. As many men as were thought "convenient for the raising" were chosen by the selectmen. Others were named to "provide vitls & drink" for workmen and spectators. Someone else was appointed to "Dool out Drink" as was convenient, perhaps "two or three barrels of licker", "20 Gallons of Rhumb and 20 pounds of Sugar to go with the Rhumb", according to the expected size and thirst of the crowd. The women provided the feast. Everybody came. At the proper moment the master builder "gave the word to lift". When the ridgepole was in place, it would be "wet down with rum", and if the town boasted a young six-foot acrobat, he would then stand aloft, raise a two-gallon jug and drink to the safe completion of the job. If he were equal to the more perilous feat of standing on his head at this high perch, so much more the gaiety. Each town varied the story according to its resources in kind.

But gaiety was only a very small part of the story at its more triumphant moments. The town records report instead the deep sense of obligation and individual concern which had punctuated every step of the long process. Two feet subtracted from the length or width, one more or one less window, "sedar shingles" or not; such details had been worth "heat of spirit" or worse, as townsmen struggled toward unanimity on almost every point in the construction, convening, adjourning without agreement, voting, declaring the vote null and void, and meeting again after a hard day's work, or if the "heat of spirit" were very intense, at ten o'clock the next morning at the expense of their work. The voting of any single item took little space on the Town Book; accomplishing the reality sometimes took many weeks, first in mutual agreement and then within the pattern of busy private lives from sunrise to sunset.

In recalling the story of the first century meetinghouse as a building, it is easy to make too much of the details which suggest its plainness and crudity. It is easy also, too easy, to remember only the details which spell physical discomfort, even a two-hour torture, if one balances it against one's own "eleven to twelve" seated comfort on a modern Sunday. These details, if one would be fair, deserve to be made only as important, or rather as unimportant, as they were to the men and women to whom this building, and what it represented, was central in their lives. What it stood for meant more to many of them than their own personal prosperity in this yet unconquered and hopeful new land. It was not an isolated fact in a picture challenging to the point of grimness. It belonged to a time when bread had to be "cut very thin for a long season", and willingly so.

The record on the Town Book (any Town Book) for the decade of the 1640's, as of meager dimensions, of committees appointed to "fall the trees", square the timbers, mow the thatch, should be read along with the 1644 record for almost any Massachusetts town then in existence that "By an agreement each family in each colony gave one peck of corn or one shilling to Cambridge college". It should be read along with a record in a private diary intended for no eyes but those of the writer, Captain Roger Clap of Dorchester, who had come in 1630. He wrote,

> "I do not remember that ever I did wish in my Heart that I had not come into this Country, or wish myself back again to my Father's House".[18]

Or again, in an entry recalling an early, perhaps an icy Sunday morning, watchmen in the turret, "guardsmen" on the rear seat, and the future as well as the present about as insecure as imagination could paint it, when he wrote,

> "God's holy Spirit in those Days was pleased to accompany the Word with such Efficacy upon the Hearts of many; that our Hearts were quite taken off from Old England and set upon *Heaven*".[19]

The values underneath such statements merit respect, for they were the values by which strong men and women lived. Life was hard enough, but it was also filled with deep satisfactions. It was hard to grimness, but it also offered more in terms of normal human enjoyment and happiness than has often been supposed. We sometimes forget that these New England Puritans were Elizabethans, and sons of Elizabethans, adventurous, by no means scornful of hearty human pleasures; men and women who laughed, sang, loved, and had a full-bodied concern for their success in this world as well as for their safety in the next. The "Lord's Barn" on the hill was the center of much that mattered and mattered deeply; but in their acceptance of the regimen of life which it imposed, they were by no means pious recluses.

As to the building itself, considered as a building, it is unimpressive enough. Even the "rising ground" on which it stood could hardly make it look important. Its significance to later times, as to its own, is that somehow it embodied fundamental loyalties and created a state of mind in which these loyalties took on reality. In some way, not easy to understand perhaps, it stood for "the good of the whole", the "mind of the town" and "holy walking". In some way it teased the thought of village men and women beyond village boundaries and the Here and Now of their lives. It stood for the eternal against the transient. In such terms small things are not small.

BOOK TWO

"ZION IS NOT A CITY OF FOOLS"

CHAPTER FIVE

"Our First Good Men"

I T was just as well that the first generation ministers who set sail in the *Lion's Whelp*, the *Mary and John*, the *Griffin*, the *Ambrose*, the *Talbot*, and all the other "tall ships" of Winthrop's and the later fleets which brought them hither did not know what was ahead of them. The wilderness formula for what might correspond to priesthood had no precise parallel in the pulpit annals they knew, and whatever they might have conjured up in imagination was likely to be different from the truth according to life as they were to discover it, and far easier. Even so, their resourcefulness, as well as their courage, was still "answerable".

Nothing in their whole story does them greater credit than their speedy adaptation to the grim urgencies and unimagined readjustments which awaited them. Once they had stepped ashore and seen the New World with their own eyes, they promptly laid aside the pulpit-worn analogy of a land flowing with milk and honey, manna dropping as the gentle dew from heaven and themselves, Moses-like, at the head of the march. They straightway became realists, put on their old clothes and proceeded to grow their own manna, planting each his own corn and beans at the first favorable time of the moon and thereafter choosing texts of seedtime and harvest to match. Most of them had come as students, men of the cloister and lamp, skilled in the "Tongues" and in the subtleties of theological argument. "So Big Study Man", as an admiring Indian once called John Davenport of New Haven. "So Big Study Men" most of them remained, and to their own very great honor, but they also (and perforce) took on a new character with their first winter woolens. In this particular Promised Land they would not only live a totally different kind of life, but in so doing they would lay aside their deeply inherited notions of the priestly calling and turn into a new order of men.

"Who and of what sort were they?" It is Cotton Mather's question, asked half in pride and half in pique, as though to say, How can anyone alive not know who and of what sort they were? In reply he opened the ministerial chapters of his *Magnalia* with a crisp anouncement.

> "*Reader, thou shalt now see, of what sort they were.*
> Zion *is not a* city of Fools. . . .
> Here, *behold* them, of whom the world was not worthy, wandring in desarts!"[1]

Waving an early American flag was not Cotton Mather's main intention, or even a conscious minor one, but the whole of his book is eloquent proof that the leaven of patriotism was already at work on American beginnings, glorifying first migrations, first settlers, first leaders, to fit the proportions of something resembling a golden age. By 1702, when the *Magnalia Christi Americana* first appeared, every village Hampden on every town list of first settlers was already a great man, if for no other reason than that he had come before other men. Naturally enough, first generation ministers fared unusually well in this hero-tale, particularly as it was told by the grandson of one of them. Patriotism and family loyalty aside, however, the men Cotton Mather elected to honor in this "Not Fools" category were in some ways greater than he could know, and for reasons not included in his criteria of praise.

According to his count there were one hundred and five of these first generation ministers whose record of service was established in time for inclusion in this first *Who Was Who in America*. Obeying his flair for classification he divided them into three groups: those in the active service of their ministry before leaving England making a *First Classis;* the younger men whose training was not yet completed, a *Second Classis;* and those who later sought refuge in America a

Third. He treated all three groups with honor, but it was the seventy-seven men of the *First Classis* whose memories he sought to "embalm" most imperishably. There is some justice in his emphasis, although his caption, "Our First Good Men", no doubt nettled some of the grandsons of early civil leaders when they opened the *Magnalia* in 1702. One hopes it would also have nettled the seventy-seven ministers upon whom it was bestowed, but by that time the last of them had "died well" and entered, more or less belatedly, "into the Heavenly Society".

Except for the notables and near-notables among them, theirs is largely a lost story. Were their lives long or short? Often we do not know. Some of them survive as little more than names on town and church records. Their tombstones have long since crumbled. They came too early for portraits. Their diaries are mostly lost. What of their personal quality? Of this, most often, no hint; they had no Boswells. Only a teasing clue survives as to the daily lives they led up and down their own village streets. The few who "outlived their deaths" by writing books or pamphlets, or by leaving so much as one sermon in print, have had one more chance for doubtful remembrance, albeit a slender one. The account of one single hour by hour day in each of their lives might tell us more of the shape and color and rhythm of colonial village life than has come down to us from many other sources combined. Failing this, we can only seek to discover the truth according to fact underneath Cotton Mather's easy superlatives and fictional embroidery, and in such other records as remain.

Of what sort were they? At least a part of the answer is that, allowing for individual variations, this "man of God", New Style, was closer to the yet unborn Daniel Boone than to St. Boniface, St. Severinus, or all the saintly kind already in print. He would be a man who dared boast of his biceps, and well he might; an outdoor man, indifferent to weathers; a traveller, who would spend weeks of his year in the saddle, make a hundred mile journey on snowshoes where his horse could not take him, find a path through the woods where there was none, use a gun in self-defense, ford a river, steer his course by the sun and stars and pass the night under a tree when he must, even in December. He would be a jack-of-all-trades who could clay a chimney, build a stone wall, run a sawmill; a six-day farmer, wielding his scythe, shearing his own sheep, making cider, threshing peas, grafting apple trees; a pioneer villager, who instead of mortifying the flesh thought he served God better by using his strength, his physical endurance and his wits, and who proceeded to use all he had of each, with results no doubt sometimes startling to himself as well as to posterity.

If Thomas Hooker, for example, during his eight-week voyage in the *Griffin*, had caught a prophetic glimpse of himself on the Old Bay Path three years hence, heading a cavalcade of men, women and children, their servants, their cattle, their sheep, through the wilderness, he might for all his bold courage have called himself a fool indeed. It was one thing, under the passion of the moment, to declare in his farewell sermon to his Chelmsford congregation that

> "England has seen her best dayes, and now evill dayes are befalling us, . . . Our God is going, and do you sit still on your beds? . . . God is packing up his Gospel, because no body will buy his wares, nor come to his price";

even to go so far as to say, "the poore native Turks and Infidels shall have a cooler summer parlour in hell"[2] than England, once so exalted in God's sight. It took courage of a quite different stamp to break his own personal career in half, relinquish the fame which was beginning to be spoken beyond St. Mary's borders and, perhaps hardest of all for him, to forego the chance to lead in English church reform which at that moment seemed to be his. Nevertheless he left it all behind him, gambled with the unknown and began over. He was forty-seven years old, and as men thought of their life span in those days he was already old. Why not, after all, he might have asked, the semi-retirement of Little Baddow, with its quiet business of school-keeping as a livelihood? If Laud would not let him preach as he must, there were other ways of being heard. But he had turned the page, and however unwillingly he had made his decision, there was conviction as well as expediency back of it. There was also vision.

Whatever made his two-year sojourn in New Towne a restless time (and that still remains something of a mystery) Massachusetts was not his answer. He was preaching to the Mt. Wollaston congregation, "a joyful and affectionate people", numbering some of his former English congregation, and they were well satisfied with his ministry. He was living in a comfortable house within the confines of what is now Harvard Yard. Here he had daily intercourse with men who spoke his own language. Magistrates consulted him. His chance of being one of the "Big Men" of the colony was bright. The contrast between his two flights from London and his escape to America in disguise, when placed beside his New Towne honors, is dramatic. Why did he wish to leave this hopeful new life behind? Was it that the lure of "a long, fresh, rich river" gave concreteness to a vision not to be satisfied in Massachusetts, or was it (as is more probable) that life in the orbit of John Cotton was less free than his nature and his powers demanded? Did one walk a chalk line even here? As to all this, he kept his own counsel, but petitioned to remove with a substantial number of his congregation. The General Court said No. He repeated his plea and then despite the repeated denial, the resulting schism in the Court and the noisy debate—despite even the "melting sermon" of John Cotton and the apparent peace it brought—he and his people persisted in their plea until it was finally granted. Then when spring broke in 1636, they sold their houses and were off toward the deeper wilderness.

Their fortnight in the woods reads like a chapter out of *Pilgrim's Progress*, except that they were not fleeing from the wrath to come. Theirs was a pilgrimage toward a freer life. Ten miles a day was their pace. Says Trumbull, their earliest historian:

"They had no guide but their compass; made their way over mountains, thro' swamps, thickets and rivers, which were not passable but with great difficulty. They had no cover but the heavens, nor any lodging but that which simple nature afforded them. They drove with them a hundred and sixty cattle, and by the way, subsisted on the milk of their cows. Mrs. Hooker was borne through the wilderness upon a horse-litter. The people generally carried their packs, arms and some utensils. They were nearly a fortnight on their journey. This adventure was the more remarkable, as many of this company were persons of figure, who had lived, in England, in honor, affluence and delicacy, and were entire strangers to fatigue and danger".[3]

They would never be strangers to it again while they lived. Their share in the founding of Hartford was in part their exchange for comfort and safety.

For other ministers whose lives were split apart between the call of a pursuivant and the sailing of a ship, it was likewise a new kind of test, physical as well as moral. The dangers and rigors to which their bold speaking had exposed them under Laud's espionage were the dangers and rigors which come to intellectuals in a fevered time. They had spoken out with the full knowledge that in so doing they invited the need for disguise, concealment, even flight; else imprisonment. The New World dangers were of an entirely different sort. So also the nature of their participation in pioneer life. Very little if anything in their previous training and experience had given more than the barest hint as to the untried areas of resourcefulness, not to say stark endurance which would be required.

"I have not been dry, night or day, from the third day of the week unto the sixth",

John Eliot wrote on what for him was a typical weekday page,

"but so travelled, and at night pull off my boots and wring my stockings, and on with them again, and so continue. But God steps in and helps".[4]

John Eliot had arrived aged twenty-seven, young enough to become inured to physical hardness and though he later admitted that he "was forced to be more wary", years of such exposure did not rob him of an eventual eighty-seventh birthday and vigor to preach until his last earthly Sunday. For others who were in middle life when they arrived, such hardships sometimes proved too stern; but whether their pioneer chapter was long or short, the best of them made history while they wrote it.

In terms of what was ahead for them, aside from physical hardships, they were fortunate not to come as unseasoned schoolboys. For many of the more forceful among them life in America began in their early or full maturity. John Wilson, first teacher of the Boston church, was thirty-nine years old when he arrived in Boston. So were Richard Mather of Dorchester and John Allin of Dedham. John Davenport, one of the founders of New Haven, was forty; Francis Higginson and Hugh Peter of Salem were forty-two; John Cotton and Ezekiel Rowley were forty-eight, or a year older than Thomas Hooker; Charles Chauncy, second president of Harvard, was forty-nine; Peter Bulkeley of Concord, fifty-four; Nathaniel Ward, drafter of the Massachusetts Body of Liberties, fifty-six. The list no doubt could be much longer, if Cotton Mather had not claimed immunity (on biblical grounds) from searching out more of their birthdays. The Bible contains the birthday of no single saint, he announced; why should he be at pains to discover the hidden birth dates of these men?

There were other founders of cities among them. One thinks of John Davenport, "a princely preacher", and also a practical colonizer with a program. His plans, like Thomas Hooker's, called for space and remoteness and he would take nothing less. During his year in Boston he had been urgently entreated to throw in his lot with Massachusetts. Generous grants of land were offered him; in fact, the General Court gave him what amounted to a *carte blanche* choice of any location which pleased him, but he said No. He had already taken significant part in Massachusetts affairs, both civil and religious; new opportunities were opening, but he still said No. He too felt the lure of the "long, fresh, rich river", the challenge of open spaces and what seemed to him a second chance to establish "civil Government according to God". Accordingly in the spring of 1638, like Hooker, he headed south with a company. If they went by boat and took their nightly rest on something softer than a stone pillow, "such as Jacob found in his way to Padan-Aran", their glory is not thereby diminished. The founding of New Haven was in part the sequel to their pilgrimage.

One thinks also of John Lothrop, setting out on foot from Scituate in 1639, en route to the "hay grounds" of Barnstable, forty miles away, his congregation with him. The road was a mere trail, sandy, swampy, hilly, through dense woods and along the shore; their destination a town of some dozen houses. There is Peter Bulkeley, who "carried a good number of planters with him up further into the *woods*, where they gathered the *twelfth church* then formed in the colony and called the town by the name of Concord". There is also Peter Prudden whose preaching in New Haven and Weathersfield made of one mind the "free planters" who in the same year went with him to settle Milford. There is Samuel Newman whose restless desire for room and more room led him to migrate twice after first settling in Dorchester, taking with him each time a portion of his original congregations. He went first to Weymouth and then five years later to Rehoboth, a name which according to local tradition (recently challenged) he borrowed from Isaac, declaring as he did so, "for now the Lord hath made room for us, and we shall be fruitful in the land".[5] Again and again one hears a similar echo from John Cotton's farewell sermon, as pastor and people time after time in response to the urge for larger spaces headed out toward the moving frontier. Stephen Bachiler, doughty ancestor of Daniel Webster and John Greenleaf Whittier, founded no cities and was no path-breaker in kind, but he was made of pioneer stuff physically as well as mentally. He was seventy-one when he arrived in Ipswich. Five years later he set out on foot to walk eighty miles to Barnstable "in a very bad season", and thence during the next twenty years, scandal pursuing him successively, he migrated from Barnstable to Newbury, from Newbury to Hampton, from Hampton to Portsmouth, and then finally, aged one hundred, back to England and a fourth wife.

For Abraham Pierson, more than for most, America also meant "no continuing city". He migrated four times after his first settlement in Lynn, taking a portion of his congregation with him each time, first to Long Island, west end; thence to the east end; thence to Branford, Connecticut; and finally after twenty-five years there, to Newark, being firmly persuaded, as he said, "of the everlasting welfare of my soul's estate". Surely he had earned his peace. Of course these ministerial Daniel Boones did not do it alone, but more often than not they were the magnets in the successive migrations they led, giving unity to the purposes of the group. They were also realists, enlarging the "man of God" tradition to include something of the hard business sense and sharp foresight of the large investor. Some of them also were minor statesmen in their own right.

Even when migration was a penalty rather than a choice, great things sometimes came to pass, notably when Roger Williams accepted exile rather than submit to thought control of the early Massachusetts variety. John Wheelright, brother-in-law of Anne Hutchinson, was another premature liberal, whose exile belonged to the same upheaval, during which he too had courage to protest against "that which is usual among us". In return for his "erroneous opinions" he found himself judged "guilty of sedition and also of contempt". His property was confiscated; he was disfranchised and banished from Massachusetts "forever". The season was November and he was given only fourteen days to quit the colony. He refused the invitation of Rhode Island, where he might have had measurable comfort, and struck off through the snowdrifts to New Hampshire, with a few of his loyal parishoners. Partly by land and partly by sea, they finally arrived at Exeter, already the seat of a logging camp. Here Wheelright built a meetinghouse and on a prophetic date, July 4th, 1639, he was the leading spirit in the founding of Exeter colony. When Massachusetts was about to take over, he moved on to Wells, Maine, where he began over again, built another meetinghouse and also a sawmill. He stayed here for fifteen years, preaching and ministering to people with whom he had little in common except a religious fellowship. Aged seventy, he accepted pardon from Massachusetts and began his fourth and longest pastorate in Salisbury, where after seventeen more years he died, a stormy petrel to the end. For him the right to think his own thoughts had meant twenty-five years of exile and intellectual loneliness.

If the temperament of these adventurous, strong-willed, stout-hearted minister-colonizers inclined them to meditation and lonely quietness, they fought for the privilege, even on the edge of the frontier, for theirs were days of varied and ceaseless activity. If there were a single white-handed recluse among them, his name has not been preserved. Cotton Mather would have it that Thomas Hooker, wherever he came, "lived like a stranger in the world", but if so, it was an achievement that does not show on his New Towne or Hartford record. As he himself once said of ministers, "Little good will they do if they doe only explicate". His American chapter is a fourteen-year example of the precise opposite. He also spoke for others of this *First Classis* who did far more than explicate. To some degree and in different ways his pronouncement would take in most of them.

The new "man of God" pattern made room also for the rôle of the energetic and controversial Hugh Peter, who, according to report, left behind him in Salem not only the memory of a powerful pulpit voice but, as tangible testimony to his seven years of tireless week-days, a water-mill, a market-house, a salt works, a "glass-house", substantial encouragement to fisheries, ship-building, hemp growing and other local industries. It includes what sounds like a Boston myth (and probably is one), namely, the rôle of John Wilson, teacher of the First Church, perched in an apple tree electioneering for John Winthrop in an acrimonious political campaign. To make a better myth, Winthrop won the election. In the same connection it includes Thomas Parker of Newbury, walking forty miles to cast his vote for Winthrop and against Harry Vane, and doubtless making more votes for Winthrop as he travelled. It includes John Warham of Windsor, Connecticut, scholar in the pulpit and also six-day' foreman of a corn-mill. In this frontier outpost to which he had somewhat unwillingly followed his migrating congregation, John Warham, if given his choice of gift, might have asked for books and more books, but when his congregation elected to honor him with a corn-mill, he accepted the gift, learned how to run the mill and, furthermore, made it pay. It was the first corn-mill in Connecticut.

Perhaps most significantly, in terms of a far future, these men among their extra-curricular interests, concerned themselves with government in theory and in practice. This is a story which has never been fully or realistically told, and perhaps cannot be, except in only a few scattered examples that are sufficiently documented to be trustworthy. In any representative list of such services, Thomas Hooker's 1638 sermon in Hartford is a natural first. It survives in outline only.[6] Presumably delivered before the General Court in adjourned session, it reduced to clear aphoristic statement the essentials of civil government as already practiced in the Connecticut elections of the preceding year. He chose as his text, *Deuteronomy* 1, 13,

"Take you wise men, and understanding, and known among your tribes, and I will make them rulers over you".

As is now well known even to casual students of American political history, he argued for principles which to later times are the very commonplaces of democratic practice, but were not yet commonplaces in 1638.

Government should be by universal suffrage.
In the choice of magistrates, the "people" must rule.
Franchise is a trust.
The foundation of authority is laid in the free consent of the governed.
Those who appoint can also set a limit to power.
It would be a good thing to commit both the powers and the limitations of power to writing.[7]

A year later these principles were written, presumably by Thomas Hooker, minister, Roger Ludlow, lawyer, and John Haynes, onetime governor of Massachusetts, into the Fundamental Orders of Connecticut. This was the first written constitution in history.

That these ideas were neither original with Thomas Hooker nor unique in Connecticut practice is well known; also that they were neither new nor startling to those who listened to this sermon. Every self-gathered church from the beginning had elected officers from among themselves, practiced consent of the governed, and in all their doings proceeded on the assumption that all power needful for the functioning of the society was vested in the membership alone. Every incorporated town had run its own affairs, elected its own officers and its representatives to the General Court. Thomas Hooker on this occasion (and it was an important thing to do) was reducing known practice to clear-cut axiomatic principles as basis for civil as well as ecclesiastical government. In so doing he voiced one of the most deeply shared convictions of Puritan Dissent, and gave self-government a wider basis and a deeper significance, as well as a Scriptural warrant.

One need only qualify the praise so often accorded him for this sermon by remembering that the basic principles of self-government, as he asserted them on this occasion, were not so democratic as they sound to later ears. Like John Winthrop, John Cotton, and other early shapers of opinion in such matters, Thomas Hooker put certain limitations on the word "people". He did not mean all the people, acting directly. Even in his own Hartford circle of church members, he did not mean all the people. He believed that

> "The debating matters of difference, first before the whole body of the church, will doubtless break any church in pieces, and deliver it up unto loathsome contempt".[8]

Therefore, if he feared debate on some action to be propounded, he saw to it beforehand that the elders were informed as to the action he desired, so that when the meeting was called, they could move quickly to bring it to pass before the lay opposition could be vocal one way or the other. Such a court-packing scheme was what Samuel Stone, Hooker's successor, had in mind when he uttered the much-quoted aphorism that a congregational church is a "speaking Aristocracy in the face of a silent democracy". Such a notion made trouble, plenty of trouble, even in Hartford's long-drawn-out "Scandal of an incurable breach". Luckily, however, the principles which Thomas Hooker had so clearly asserted had already been put into practice in many places, and as soon as they were better understood by the rank and file and had been ventured by a few more recalcitrant laymen in critical situations, it would be forever impossible for the pulpit to control the meeting or foreordain the result by any such manipulation as Thomas Hooker had sanctioned. But so to say is not to minimize the importance of his justly famous sermon at this early date.

Furthermore, when a hundred years later timid ones among the clergy and worried magistrates in the pew were arguing whether or not the minister might justifiably bring affairs of government into the pulpit, it would be precisely a hundred years too late to admit the matter to discussion. Before the first election preacher had solemnized the annual voting day with a two-hour sermon on what makes a godly ruler and how the people should behave toward him, the first principles of a working democracy had been written into village history. Thomas Hooker in his early Hartford days had been one of those who had written them most legibly and also most indelibly. "3rdly", as he put it, among the "Uses of Exhortation" on this 1638 occasion, "to persuade us, as God hath given us liberty, to take it". He and his congregation had already taken it when they set off through the woods in the spring of 1636.

During this same critical and strategic decade of the 1630's Nathaniel Ward, better known as the "Simple Cobbler of Aggawam", was applying himself to the task of a code of laws for Massachusetts. He had come to preach; but when forced by ill health to give up his Ipswich pastorate, he had accepted the commission of the General Court for the formulation of a code of laws for the colony. He was well equipped for the task, having been trained for the law before he began to preach. Like Thomas Hooker, he was distrustful of the "people", meaning *all* the people, although he had firm convictions as to their rights. He would have preferred to withhold suffrage from those of the "inferiour sort" until he was sure it was of God that they should have it. "I suspect both Commonwealth & Churches have discended to lowe already", he wrote; "I see the spirits of people runne high, & what they gett they hould".[9] Therefore, in his view, it was well to be sure before the vote was granted.

Nevertheless, the Body of Liberties which resulted from his two-year labor represented a liberalizing of English common law both in principle and in details, and also a definite reshaping of its provisions to fit conditions in the New World. One liberalizing detail that has caught the eye of modern readers of the code concerns marital life. No longer might a Massachusetts freeman beat his wife, not even with a reasonable instrument, as was permitted by English law, except in self-defense. In other words, except on presumably rare occasions he could not beat his wife. In the words of the code, provision No. 80 states the case positively.

"Everie marryed woeman shall be free from bodilie correction or stripes by her husband, unlesse it be in his owne defence upon her assalt."[10]

There is also a section "Off the Bruite Creature", which makes unlawful all "Tirranny or Crueltie towards any bruite Creature which are usually kept for man's use". Conversely, when a man is driving his cattle to a far off place, it is lawful for him to "rest or refresh them, for a competent time, in any open place that is not Corne, meadow, or inclosed for some peculiar use".[11] The cornfield makes this provision American.

In its firm declaration of "the free fruition of such liberties Immunities and priveledges as humanitie, Civilitie, and Christianitie call for as due to every man in his place and proportion without impeachment and Infringement",[12] this Body of Liberties deserves to be called the first American Bill of Rights. The phrasing of the preamble looks directly toward 1792. As finally adopted after three years of discussion, revision and amendment, both the preamble and the code itself remained essentially as Ward had written them. No clergyman's "meddling with the things of the world" during these early years was more important or more far-reaching in its results. "Much have I seen in my almost eleven years abode in this Wildernesse", Ward wrote on his return to England. Much also had he contributed, and though he was still unconvinced that all men could be trusted with the vote, he went so far as to concede that "A house is like to be well governed, where all are Masters".[13] The eventual choice of the Body of Liberties he had formulated—rather than the one John Cotton had formed, using the Mosaic code as his model—shows the wisdom of the lay mind of 1641, as well as of Ward's own.

If the full story of first-generation participation in the affairs of government could be told, it would probably include many names among these seventy-seven, and many special services which are not listed in either civil or ministerial annals. There is record of those who were sent back to England on special missions or as agents for the colony; likewise of those who by appointment of the General Court served on various committees from year to year. The list is long and impressive. But these were special services, remembered and recorded because they were special. In addition to these, and solely in his relation to government, there are the services of the village minister in his own parish. He was a leader without office save that of pastor. In colony affairs he had a vote but not in the affairs of the town. He came to town meeting by invitation only. In spite of these restrictions, or more probably because of them, during the first two generations and well into the third he exercised more power locally than has ever been possessed by any elected American in a comparable sphere. He used this power in his rôle of *ex officio* counsellor in matters of large and small import, and the fruits thereof were determining in far-reaching directions.

Nor was this all. Contradictory as it may seem to be, considering all the practical services from these men who studied maps, sought out harbors, bargained with Indians, led migrations, counselled with magistrates, drafted laws, pled cases before the General Court, concerned themselves in large ways with agriculture, commerce and other secular needs, they were also men who lived the contemplative life (according to their own specifications) perhaps as successfully as any later generation of their own sort has ever lived it. In differing degrees and by their own special definition they were all students, "hard students", as the saying was, men who normally spent more hours of each day in solitary pursuits than in active ones, and this in spite of all the other duties which crowded their days from candlelight to candlelight. For a minister not to begin his day in the study as early if not earlier than his farmer neighbors began theirs in the barn and field betokened an unworthy softness in his make-up. To rise at four in the summer and at five in the winter was standard practice, and there were those who for life bettered even this stern record. Ordination sermons counselled young ministers to be "morning students" and to count that day lost which did not net them more hours in the study than in bed. Only a few lived up to the record of the pace-setters, but a fair number approximated it on a fair number of days.

Some ministers thought a little discomfort added to their efficiency, perhaps also to the virtue of such Spartan application. Peter Hobart of Hingham, a "morning student", always "obeyed the rule to study standing" and recommended it to younger men. Not until extreme old age and decrepitude caught up with him did he know even the moderate comfort of a hard-seated, stiff-backed chair, while he invited his thoughts. John Davenport, the original "So Big Study Man" of New Haven, made it his custom "to sit up very late at night at his lucubrations", although he counselled younger men not to emulate his example. Each minister set his own goal, but for all of them the study was the most important room in the house, both for private devotion and for diligent application to books.

The two went together, with safety in the mixture giving the margin to devotions. Without devotions, study was an unsanctified performance; a self-indulgence, in fact. Henry Dunster, first president of Harvard College, confessed that as a young man, "the greatest thing which separated my soule from God was an inordinate desire of humane learning".[14] He conquered the temptation. Thomas Parker likewise, as a young man, forced himself to give up the "profound and knotty study of school divinity", which had so deeply engaged him, lest the "ensnaring temptations" of which it was full should lead him astray. Charles Chauncy, we are told, customarily rose at four o'clock summer and winter, spent the first hour in prayer, and then after some private study went to the college to expound a chapter out of the Old Testament, having first read it aloud in the original Hebrew. Home after this early exercise, he repeated the performance in his own family circle, only choosing a different chapter. At eleven o'clock and again at three he was at prayer. After supper he returned to the college, read and expounded a New Testament chapter and, returning home, again repeated the performance before his family. The day ended with more study and more prayer, prayer always coming last. A minister would no sooner go to bed without a session on his knees than he would lay another book on top of the Bible. By such a daily program, allowing for whole days out for fasting and prayer, this Harvard president set an example for the young scholars under his care which (it is said) was "hardly followed" by them, at least not in their chrysalis stage.

Such a private régime continued through a lifetime would produce either something queer in human kind or something rather special. It produced both; and for some of the early men who were able to take it and keep their equilibrium, and also for some of their sons after them, it enlarged the ministerial rôle rather than restricted it. In a sense erudition as well as piety was their business, and their lives were consecrated to the marriage of the two. Paradoxically, although some of them, as was said of John Davenport, were "never out of the study unless duty called them forth", they were also "acquainted with great men and great things". Somehow they struck a balance, and it saved them.

How far personal inclination was responsible for all this studious busyness, it is hard to know. Behind these men lay a long tradition of specialized learning associated with their calling, and they accepted it along with their white bands. So did their congregations. That the resources of this pulpit culture at points of sharpest emphasis bore little relation to village life as it was being lived, troubled neither the minister nor his lay hearers. Even after the general level of culture dropped so woefully in the second and third generations, congregations still demanded a scholar as their minister. It seemed incongruous to no one that in order to qualify as a preacher to thirty families a man must be proficient in five or seven languages, all of them ancient. What if the members of the committee appointed to find him were barely proficient in one? No matter. To the unlettered or half-lettered pew this was not dusty erudition. It gave authority to Scripture mandate when the preacher "opened his text" on Sunday morning, even though the "Plain Style" preaching to which he had been trained demanded that he hide his knowledge under a bushel. Sufficient unto his congregation was the fact that he possessed it.

In its main intent this ministerial erudition began and also ended with the Bible. No matter how wide-ranging their other interests these were men of one Book, and in their allotment of daily study hours it had foremost place. A standard program called for reading it through several times a year, so many chapters a day, and when *Revelation* 22 was reached, the next day's quota would begin with *Genesis* 1. Progress in this marathon was slowed by what was also standard practice of reading a portion of the daily stint in the original Hebrew or Greek, by way of a perpetual refresher course. Even so, George Phillips held the record for six times annually. For "recreation work" they collected "Instances", parallel passages, passages showing the same word after another same word. How many times

OLD-TOWN MEETINGHOUSE, NEWBURY, MASSACHUSETTS, 1700.

As voted in 1698, this structure was to be fifty by sixty feet, with twenty foot studs. A later vote lengthened these to twenty-four feet. The building stood until 1806. From a cut appearing in Joshua Coffin's *Sketch of the History of Newbury, Newburyport, and West Newbury*, Boston, 1845.

THE FIRST MEETINGHOUSE IN WEST SPRINGFIELD, MASSACHUSETTS, 1702.

This was four years after the inhabitants living on the west side of the "Great River" had been granted permission to call a minister of their own. The dimensions of the building were forty-two by forty-two by ninety feet, the imported weather-cock making the last four feet of height. The building stood until 1820. By courtesy of the Connecticut Valley Historical Museum.

are the "holy Angels" mentioned in the "sacred Oracles of Heaven"? Is it two hundred and sixty, or more or less, and how may these various entries best be sorted into categories?

For all such tallies and computings the "Tongues" were a first requisite. "Elegance in Latin", always first on the list, was a basic accomplishment, to be pridefully noted for those who excelled. In the extravagant phrase of Cotton Mather,[15] Peter Bulkeley wrote it "with great Ease and Elegance"; John Norton, a "most accurate Grammarian, with uncommon elegance"; John Cotton both wrote and spoke it with "great facility and with almost a Ciceronian elegancy"; Samuel Whiting was "accurate in Hebrew, elegant in Latin". The "Tongues", however, were not his first love; he "employed his vacant hours in History", and notwithstanding the "Plain Style" requirements, he sometimes sprinkled his sermons with ancient personages not of biblical lineage. Samuel Danforth, more exemplary in this respect, kept his allusions within the covers of the Bible, often indulging his abilities as a "notable Text-man" to the extent of crowding as many as forty or fifty verses in a single sermon. For such lavishness he was highly praised. James Noyes excelled most in Greek, but the writings of the fathers and the schoolmen were his special delight. Henry Dunster and Samuel Eaton were "great Hebricians"; John Eliot was "a most acute grammarian, and understood very well, the languages God first wrote his Holy Bible in"; Richard Denton "small of stature" had a "well-accomplished mind in this lesser body" and was indeed a veritable "Iliad in a nutshell". Ezekiel Rogers was a "tree of knowledge from which the apples fell off in the children's mouths". Some of Thomas Thacher's "hard study" mornings went into the making of a Hebrew lexicon. He was also proficient in Arabic and Syriac and for recreation often copied the script in these tongues. This same delight in fine work led him occasionally (one hopes not guiltily) to indulge his "mechanic genius in the ingenuity of clockwork wherein he did things to admiration". Restless Samuel Newman somehow found time between migrations and the founding of cities to complete the *Concordance of the Bible* which he had begun before sailing. One would like to believe that he did so by the flickering light of pine knots, but this pleasant detail is doubtless merely decorative. John Sherman, "that golden-mouthed preacher", was famous for his uncommon proficiency in mathematics and astronomy, wherein he lectured at Harvard College once a fortnight for over thirty years. And so their "Big Study" accomplishments multiply.

Cotton Mather, to whom we are too much indebted for all this, would have us believe also that the piety of these early men should be rated higher than their scholarship. Possibly, although the specifications he offers make piety a lean thing at best. For example, John Eliot, in his own private strivings, lived on "ill terms with the devil—that old usurping landlord of America", "was perpetually jogging the *wheel of prayer*", "kept the beast in him ever tyed with a short tedder", was an "enemy to idleness", and never in all his eighty-seven years knew what it was "to feel so much as a noxious fume in his head"[16] from any wines or drams stronger than "good, clear water". These five sample virtues (several of which are subject to vigorous contradiction) hardly encourage one to expect a very complete man or a very likeable one—as portly John Eliot seems to have been among his Roxbury people or among the Natick Indians and others of their kind, for whom he did more than any other missionary of the first generation. Samuel Whiting, we are told, counted his natural passions as at least a dozen, but he did not allow himself to "be hag-ridden with the enchantments thereof". He grew more "holy" as he grew older, until "in a flourishing old age, he was found fit for transplantation". "That elect vessel", John Bailey of Watertown, once tortured himself with the knowledge that on a certain day he had spoken "two unadvised words", that on another he had been "too forgetful of God and exceeding in tobacco", and that on still another he had been "too chearful". For all of these lapses he had found himself successively "almost in the *suburbs of hell* all day". Gentle Thomas Shepard, perhaps the most truly pious of them all, was once "in despaire", so he himself tells us, lest (thanks to pulpit-incited fears) he had committed the unpardonable sin. Something of the quality of his piety is suggested by the list of "Good Things" he had received of the Lord, in which No. 1 reads, "He is the god of my being, who might have made me a woorme".[17] Out in the fields whither he went to listen to what God had to say to him, he "was eased of a woorld of discouragements" by such thoughts as this. Of a more literal and usual sort was that "mighty man" Richard Mather, who recorded as Vow No. IV, to "strive against carnal *security* and excessive *sleeping*".[18] Excessive sleeping was a real enough pitfall for any of them, but as for "carnal security", he need not have worried. Security of any brand was not for him or for anyone in his pulpit generation. Nor did they need it, "solid men" that they were, concerned above all else for their soul's health and to that end holding themselves to a standard of personal integrity to the inch mark. Men of affairs, intellectuals, the "Big Men" of their day, in their own private review of their day by day record they were as simple as little children saying, "Now I lay me". It is a relief and also adds a flavor of credibility to their alleged saintliness to hear a funeral elegist once in a while slipping in the phrase, "with faults, even as others".

We see a few of these same men in what were probably characteristic attitudes, which further hint at their personal quality. Samuel Whiting, for example, leaving the delights of history behind for an hour while he walked in his orchard "to enrich his mind" at meditation, "hand, and eye, and soul, often directed heavenward". He was a learned man, an overseer of Harvard College, a man of power and wisdom beyond his own borders, but to his Lynn congregation he and his assistant Thomas Cobbett, also "a very praying man", were "a sweet pair of brothers" . . . "two angelick men", who gave each other as "little jostle, as the angels upon *Jacob's ladder*".[19] We see Thomas Parker, also a very learned man, the voluntary thirty-year schoolmaster for the boys of his congregation without a cent of pay, sitting in his doorway at twilight singing duets with his colleague James Noyes, one of the best scholars of them all. We see Samuel Stone, a noted wit, trying out his sermon before his family on Saturday night and struggling "to compose himself unto a most heavenly frame in all things, and not let fall a *word*, but what should be grave, serious, pertinent".[20] A single sentence preserved from the "learned and worthy Mr. Henry Dunster", "a man pious, painful and fit to teach", is at least one index to his character. Known as "one who differed somewhat from his brethren", he probably did not surprise many of them greatly when at the height of his career he "fell into

the briars" of anti-paedo-baptism, one of the most seditious and subversive of all un-American opinions in his day. When convicted of
holding these "erroneous opinions" and deposed from his office as
president of Harvard College, he replied quietly, "I am not the man
you take me to be".[21] Silence would have saved him, but he spoke out
and lost all. Thought control was not for him either. His successor
in office was also in his own private convictions on the wrong side
of the infant baptism fence, but he kept his heretical opinions to
himself and prospered.

In his essay on "The Preacher," Emerson was later to say of his own
contemporaries of the cloth, "The clergy are as like as peas". He
could not have said it of his first American ancestor's generation.
Nothing about these men can be run into a mold. They were individuals, often so thorny in their individuality that they could not long
walk the same path in amity. Their small kingdoms must perforce be
separate. John Cotton and Thomas Hooker, looked back upon by an
admiring eye, may indeed have seemed the "Luther and Melancthon
of New England", but they could never have played such rôles side
by side in Cambridge. No town was big enough for the two of them
at once and fortunately one of them had the good sense to know it.
Fortunately also, the wilderness was wide and they separated in time
to avoid the explosion which would certainly have come had they
continued to pitch their tents in adjoining fields along the Charles.

In lesser examples as well as in greater it is folly to speak of a New
England mind.[22] Except for the main postulates of a theological system, the quite easily traceable pattern of a common University education, and essential unity of purpose in a common cause, there is
much diversity in their thought and their ways of thinking. Had the
Cambridge men among these first seventy-seven (and that would include more than half of them) migrated before they lost their University accent, they might have borne the stamp of their training less
individually; but with enough practical experience as English pastors
behind them to try their mettle, they had the courage to go their own
way and to go quickly.

As a group of men with a program, they were singularly fortunate.
Few religious leaders at any time in history have had the stage set for

them so favorably. In their own particular realm they had almost a free field. They faced no competition from any other priestly class. They were in essential agreement as to the fundamentals of their purpose and plan, and could therefore present a united and forceful front on all major issues. Civil leaders were almost unanimously party to their plans and their counsels were urgently solicited. From the hour they arrived on the American side, their training and abilities put them in great demand. Not a settlement so small or so new that it did not quickly claim one of them as monitor and guide; and once claimed, they had a weekly hearing from the whole settlement by legal compulsion, as well as by majority wish. For these and various other reasons they had possibly the best chance any seventy-seven men ever had to impress their deeply shared convictions and values upon a civilization which as yet possessed little character of its own; in fact, for the first comers, did not yet exist. Had they stayed at home and fitted comfortably into the pattern to which they were born, possibly not five of them would be known by name three hundred years afterward nor deserve to be. Instead, they refused security at the price of conviction, took risks, made sharp, irrevocable decisions, and grew visibly taller in the process.

Nor were they heroes in their own eyes. In the next generation it would be possible for Joshua Moody to say grandly of himself and his fellow-clergymen (and mean it):

> "We are like soldiers landed in a hostile country whose commander has burned the ships behind them and told them they must either eat up their enemies or drink up the sea".

So to say and so to believe of one's self is to feel very noble indeed. It is also to be unacquainted with even the fringe of uncertainty, as these first men knew it. They had to make the path before they could see themselves walking in it. They were a race by themselves. Their assets were mainly three: an untenanted wilderness, a handful of men and women framed for hardihood, and an idea. It was enough. Nor would their chance come again.

Their sons and grandsons would follow with vastly more ease. Some of these younger men would still find the parish to which they had been called, on foot and by the aid of blazed trees. They too would flounder through snowdrifts and be lost in the woods for days. Arrived at their lifetime station, they too would carry guns to meeting, build sawmills and perhaps operate them; but long before John Ward went tardily to heaven, thus bringing up the rear of this first generation, it was already broad noon of a new day.

CHAPTER SIX

The Power of the Unprinted Word

Sᴇʀᴍᴏɴs, thousands of them. Two per week, one hundred and four per annum from every minister until his last earthly Sunday. No sermon was less than two hours long and usually it was longer. "Do not pinch them with scanty sermons", said the ordination preacher among his advices to the young incumbent. There was no danger. "We know not how to conclude", said one of the long-winded himself. "Wee make many ends before we make an end. The fault is in the Climate; we cannot helpe it, though we can." So confessed and exonerated, they kept right on turning the glass. Urian Oakes had once been seen to turn it four times and there were others equally generous.

For pulpit and pew alike, the resulting totals are appalling. In every New England town "pious, plaine-hearted Christians" spent weeks of their waking lives, year after year, seated in the pew, listening. The obligation was largely self-imposed; they wished to listen.

"It being as unnatural for a right-N[ew]-E[ngland] man to live without an able Ministery as for a Smith to work his iron without a fire",[1]

Edward Johnson had written, and *unnatural* was precisely the word for it.

To assess the conquences of a man's lifetime exposure to such a quota of sermons is of course impossible. To assess it for a church-going society is even more so. Such an assessment would call for many chapters in a complete cultural history. For the rank and file, in addition to ministering to their religious needs, these Sunday and Thursday sermons took the place of the newspaper, the magazine, the radio, the lending library, the lecture platform, the school and college education. In fact, for more than a century they were almost the whole intellectual life of small village communities and only to a lesser extent of Boston, Hartford, New Haven, Northampton, and other larger centers. Part of the aura around the minister's head came from the learning with which it was supposedly stuffed, and to hear him making use of this learning in the interest of man's most important earthly quest was one of the privileges of life. Besides, it was a privilege for which every freeman had paid his "Rate", and to enjoy what one's own money had purchased was only good sense. Sermons were the customer's half of the bargain, and even without the legal requirement or, later, the long obedience to a Sunday habit, well stiffened by conscience, the pews would have been comfortably filled. Perhaps no other adult education program has ever served its own day so completely or so successfully.

It goes without saying that the printed sermon record does not tell this story fairly or fully. Despite the impressive number of sermons that rolled off Boston presses, particularly after John Foster made the path to the printing house an ocean shorter, few laymen profited greatly by this form of broadcast. Boston editions, like the earlier London ones, were usually small, and sermons so honored were correspondingly rare except in ministers' libraries. It was probably just as well. Second and third generation sons had not been born to the educational privileges of their fathers and grandfathers, but perforce had become farmers, tradesmen, mechanics, woodsmen, shopkeepers, men who rose early and worked late, and in whose lives books, aside from the Bible and the almanac, had little place. Their education had usually gone little further than the somewhat doubtful ability "to reed and right", as an early Groton plea for a schoolmaster "to come up" has it; possibly also to "sypher" for everyday purposes. To spell out a sermon by candlelight after the day's work was over would have afforded little pleasure and less profit. To the average layman the minister was a voice, not a printed page, and he had better be.

Incomplete and perhaps unrepresentative as the printed sermon record is, however, with a few reservations one must judge the unprinted by it. Obviously, it was the "big name" output that was welcomed at the printing house—"big" sometimes being equated with merely prolific. A few men, who were extraordinarily so, beat an early path to John Foster's door in 1675 and continued to walk it year by year thereafter, sometimes several times. Others followed them and the annual flow of sermons widened accordingly. Obviously, also, it was the sermons for special days which had the best chance of being "embalmed" in print: Election and Artillery, Thanksgiving and Fast, Ordination and Funeral days—days on which a "vast Concourse" of people assembled at the meetinghouse to hear what they had heard before on many similar occasions. No minister would disappoint them; instead, he took pains to step carefully in the tracks of those who had been similarly honored before him. The result was a stiffly patterned, highly conventional sermon, far different from the common garden variety, fifty-two Sundays in the year.

It is this common garden variety we should prefer to hear. What, one may well ask, did a remote country congregation hear on those unstarred Sunday mornings when no Indian deliverance was immediately behind, no threatening danger immediately ahead, no "Pillar of the world" to be mourned, no election impending or successors in office to be installed, no criminal to be hanged, or militia encamped for training? What did the average farmer, shopkeeper, housewife, young boy or girl clad in homespun, hear on a Sunday morning that was like the fifty-one others? What did the "honey-mouthed preacher", who would never be invited to preach an election or artillery sermon, say to his own people when no strangers were present? The answer is hard to come by, except in scattered manuscript examples and notations in almanac margins and private journals. Wherever available, it is an answer which tells more than it says.

Not that the record of an obscure minister's mental life is of any particular interest for itself, or that one may hope to discover some forgotten intellectual giant. Such were rare in the colonial pulpit, and even so-called "stars of the first magnitude" have a way of winking out under a critical modern appraisal. The sermon record is significant for a simpler reason. Sermons, whoever preached them, are a mirror held up to the thought life of the generations. If one would listen in, as it were, from a sheep-pen pew, to the history of certain early American ideas unfolding Sunday by Sunday, here it is. The home-made, tightly sewn, closely written manuscript booklets, nesting in the open crack of the pulpit Bible, were the contemporary mind speaking, and in the perspective of many generations, speaking plainly.

Here are the overhanging ideas by which men lived and wished to live, the deeply imbedded assumptions from which their thought proceeded. Here also, decade by decade, are the newer, seminal ideas, planted one scarcely knows when or by whom, but which on finding soil take root and are presently strong for the hour which needs them. Here are the more transient frames of men's thought, ideas perhaps of scant significance for themselves, but helping to change the intellectual climate as they pass. The turnip-shaped sounding board caught them all, as the minister's voice reached the dark corners of the meetinghouse.

Fortunately, ministers sometimes yielded to what they would have us believe was the "urgent entreaty" of their people to let this or that "Savoury Sermon" be "Extorted for the Public" from them. Their modest apologies were a convention. "You made me do it", said Peter Bulkeley (in effect) in the preface to his *The Gospel Covenant Opened*, in 1651, and you must bear part of the censure. "Ears are better than eyes for the entrance of truth", said Samuel Moody sixty years later, in his similarly apologetic preface to *The Doleful State of the Damned, Especially such as go to Hell from under the Gospel*, and this because, as he saw it, on the printed page the preacher's flaming zeal has no chance to kindle a fire in the breast by the "Spirit's in-breathing". Reading a sermon is lawful, however, he conceded, since through it God's "elect" may possibly be aroused. In fact, the printed page had one advantage over the sounding-board in that "Written Sermons vanish not in the Air"; They "abide in our View";[2] and by frequent perusal we may understand them better. He was right. Thanks to the relatively few which "abide", we may also understand some other things better.

To begin with, one's respect for the unlettered or half-lettered mind increases as the sermon record is unrolled. The fare is solid, the reasoning close, the tight-woven texture of logic unrelieved by light moments. There are no anecdotes, only examples from sacred and sometimes from profane history. Typically, even these are in scant supply and then only to point warning or confirm faith, never for themselves alone. Those who sat in the pew must be at home with abstractions, vast abstractions. They brought their minds to meeting and were instructed and edified according to their several capacities.

Broadly speaking, all early colonial sermons in one way or another and whatever their subject or occasion concerned what was called SALVATION—the commonest of all sermon words; to the rank and file layman the be-all and end-all of the religious life; in fact, the goal of one's entire earthly pilgrimage. Why else be here at all? Salvation—the Scripture promise of it, the plan of it, the wonder of it, the way to get it, the first signs of it, the tests of one's possession of it, the peril of losing it, the bliss of gaining it in this world and in the next, and then the eternal enjoyment of it: first in the heaven of the birds, then in the heaven of the stars, and finally in the highest heaven—the heaven of God Himself.

There was nothing new to say on the subject. Every child in town knew all the answers in catechism terms. Every adult had known them from his own childhood up. It was the preacher's task to traverse the familiar track, putting the successive steps into simpler and ever simpler terms, alarming "sleepy sinners" who had not yet acted on their knowledge, putting doubts in the minds of those who already felt secure, and giving an edge of urgency and excitement to something as familiar as the order of the seasons. Not for a full century after the founding were ministers trying to save sinners. Instead, they were trying to interpret the divine will to the "elect", and the method was by line and verse. For all the familiarity of the "plan of Salvation" in large outline, in its intricacies it was a lifetime puzzle. Over and over the preacher detailed the steps and as many times was eagerly and hopefully heard. To the pew this was a subject never stale. To the preacher it was a perpetual challenge. Maybe he could say it still more simply.

In his "Preface to the Christian Reader", introducing twenty-six sermons on *The Plain Doctrine of the Justification of a Sinner in the Sight of God,* Charles Chauncy remarked that it might seem strange that anything "should be further adventured to the Presse about such a common Theme or Argument". He had tried in these sermons, however, "to condescend (as God hath enabled mee), to the meanest capacity", and to adapt what he had to say on this familiar subject to the "Capacity of the Weak and Ignorant". Perhaps because he was president of Harvard College, he dared be simpler than other preachers who were "too polemical, too deep, too obscure"; at any rate, in this series of discourses he mounted the pulpit with the way-faring man as his particular target. This was in 1659. Nearly three centuries later one may humbly suggest that if the Massachusetts hearers in this bracket found these twenty-six sermons sun-clear to their feeble understandings, then the more honor to the "Weak and Ignorant" of Charles Chauncy's day. Their posterity may be justly proud of them.

Contrary to a persistent but very misleading assumption the preaching emphasis on eternal burnings in these heavily doctrinal salvation sermons was not disproportionate; certainly not during the preaching lives of the first generation ministers. Later, particularly in revival seasons, the tortures of hell fire invited the preacher to do his realistic best, but this was distinctly a later emphasis. Very little lurid sensationalism was spoken from the early colonial pulpit. To be sure, hell was a real place and all easy ways to heaven led directly to it. Every sermon that a man heard, as Thomas Hooker had declared, put him nearer either to heaven or to hell; there could be no guarantee which. When he was "shot into the other World", he would discover his destination, but then only. Meanwhile, be not over-confident, Jeremiah Shepard cautioned:

"There are many in Hell, that have had a Presumptuous Confidence that they should get to Heaven".

When their eyes are opened, many more will be due for a surprise.

"Many that are Ear-mark'd among Christ's Sheep here will be found to be Goats."[3]

Certainly, said Charles Chauncy, there is room enough in hell for all that do evil, but do you say then,

> "If I go to Hell, I shall have company,—and will bear it as well as I can? Wilt thou bear it, O heap of dust? Hast thou an Arm like God?"[4]

Such assumptions of would-be certainty are fairly frequent, possibly sufficiently so to make a sinner change his direction, but they were presented flatly as part of "sound doctrine" and with little help from the roaring of the flames.

Even the execution sermons preached to criminals after the sentence of death had been pronounced upon them were neither so harsh nor so sensational as they may sound to later ears. It was merely a case of greater urgency, as these unfortunates were carried in chains from one meetinghouse to another on their last three or four Sundays on earth and importuned with all the preacher's persuasiveness to seize their last chance, their very last. If these execution sermons sound unbearably personal, it is because of the preacher's sense of responsibility for a soul in the balance.

> "You are yet a young man and according to ordinary Course, might have lived many years in this world. Instead, you have yet but four more days. Oh chew upon it, dwell upon it, that a few hours hence you shall surely die."

This from Joshua Moody to a poor soul who had already had to listen to another execution sermon that same day.

> "Unto thee may it be most truly said, 'Now or Never'. . . . Hell followes Death hard at the Heels. [But] . . . notwithstanding all that has been spoken, there is Hope.—Beg hard for a *broken Heart.* —All the sins that ever thou hast committed shall not damn thee, unless thou add *Unbelief* to all the rest: viz. *the willful rejecting of a tendered Saviour.*"[5]

Later execution preachers were usually less restrained. Even without a hanging to provide urgency as his motivation, Samuel Moody in 1710 tried to find words to tell the respectable sinners before him, who were going straight to hell "from under the Gospel", how it would feel to

> "lie Frying in the Hottest Fire, World without End. It must needs be Dreadful",

he announced, and then tried to enforce his statement by shrinking hell to a "Kettle of Boiling Tarr in the Shipwright's Yard", and hurling men, women and children into it alive. Not content with these proportions, he enlarged them.

> "Suppose the Water of some Large and Deep Pond were turned into Boiling, Flaming Brimstone"; [and visible devils were to drag our neighbors and friends, one after another] "and cast them Alive into that Boiling Pond, . . . And suppose further, that God should keep them Alive in this Fiery Pond, from one Year and Age to another; and we could walk safely by the Sides of it, and Round it and see the Poor, Undone Creatures Swimming about in the Midst of the Flames, and hear their Fruitless Cries for One Drop of Water."[6]

Cotton Mather, equally clumsy in metaphor, hurled the "Pirates" of 1726 ill-fame through the "Trap-door" of death "into the place of *Dragons*, a place of Torments". "*Every Sinner is a Fool*", he told them, and if a man die without wisdom,

> "he must be lodg'd where he shall *gnaw his Tongue for Pain*, and know no *Language* but that of Roaring and of Blasphemy".[7]

The title of the sermon, however, is *Wisdom in the Latter End*, and it was preached to remind the pirates that they still had a chance. Whether because of this sermon or some other, two of these pirates repented; in time (as was thought) to prove themselves wise.

> "Be suitably affected with thine own Condition, and the Awfulness of that Eternity thou art so near unto, and must quickly be in",

said Samuel Checkley to the notorious Julian—an Indian who had run away from his master, had been recaptured, escaped again and, on the second recapture, had killed his master with a jackknife. "I can't assure thee that thou art now hearing thy last Sermon", the preacher went on, not meaning to be hopeful. There was still Thursday to provide yet another warning, but

> "This Sabbath is thy last Sabbath. Thou has seen the beginning, but shalt not live to the end of this week. Thy Coffin will be made, and thy Grave opened, and thou be laid in them before another Sabbath. . . . Say thus within thy self, I am now going to die for my Sins. . . . And am I ready for all this?"[8]

Like all others of its sort, this sermon was preached in order that "Poor Jullyoun" might get ready and promptly. The preachers did not mean to be harsh, nor were they, as they went day after day to the prisoner's cell to pray with him, and then walked beside him to the gallows. It was the publicity of these ghastly occasions which made their words seem intolerable. Whatever prison chaplains still say to condemned men on their last day, their counsels are at least mercifully private and newsmen content themselves with report of the last meal.

Few colonial children grew up without hearing an execution sermon; perhaps several of them. Young men at Harvard went to executions and noted the occasion in their diaries, almost as they might have done for a fast or thanksgiving occasion. Children also heard their quota of sermons on the untimely deaths of their brothers and sisters, victims of open wells, upsetting canoes, Indians, and the dread "throat distemper". Perhaps the pulpit warnings, grounded on such disasters, invited cruel nightmares in tender ones, but if so, such was not the preacher's intent. As he saw it, all such occasions were heaven-sent reminders to parents and children alike that salvation was desperately important. As the "keeper of souls" he must let no such occasion slip. Besides, children knew long before they had learned it from the pulpit that death was a fact of life.

> "In the burial place may see
> Graves shorter there than I",

was not only in the *Primer* to be memorized and repeated sing-song fashion, but the grim reality back of the words was already household reality to most children before their *Primer* days. These warning sermons, reminding them as well as their parents that salvation might be missed even by the youngest member, were powerful not because they made sensational new pronouncements, but because they reminded young and old of the unchanging verities of which they were already aware. In the familiarity of the warning, as well as of the supposed truth upon which it was based, lay much of the power of these sermons; as in fact, much of the power of any sermon in any day.

Broadly speaking also, every sermon, whatever its specific content, carried its freight of counsels on any everyday level of personal integrity and righteousness among men. Pay your debts, love your neighbors, tell the truth, defraud no man, watch your tongue, keep the Sabbath, be a godly example before your children, come to meeting, revere your minister, have charity for the poor, "guard our land from the onrush of vice". The list was as long as man's varied duties and associations and it touched the far corners of his life. It would seem that nothing was left out. However abstruse the doctrinal part of the sermon, before the hourglass was empty the second time, the *Uses* and *Application* had caught up with life on a six-day level.

Although no representative list can be made, nor can any single sermon be called typical, the sampling of any minister's record of titles as it may be reconstructed over a few months' time will show the same broad paths of choice, the same persistent stress upon practical virtues for everyday living. Sermons

to Promote Mutual Love and Peace among Christians
to Prevent Murmurings and Promote Patience
to Dissuade against Tavern Haunting and Excessive Drinking
to Caution against Idleness
to Teach our Children
to Advise the Sick and Well
to Commend Frugality ("a Dutch frugality")
to Condemn Fraud and Injustice
to Practice Economy
to Warn against Bad Company
to Reform Manners

to Get out of Debt and Keep out of Debt [avoid instalment buying]
to Improve Mirth[9]

In some form all of these topics will be in almost any minister's list
over the months, together with sermons on the local fire, the eclipse
or the comet, the earthquake, the drought or flood of the month, the
capture of pirates, the judgment of God in the death of a "prophane
swearer", (perhaps in happier vein, on the birth of twins), and other
front page news items from week to week. The smallpox inoculation
warfare of the 1720's entered the pulpit in a spate of sermons. Benjamin Colman and others took issue with Dr. Mussey of London, who
had attempted to prove by Scripture that Satan was the first inocula-
ter. In this warfare, as in all others, the Bible was newly searched for
appropriate texts which astonish by their aptness.

Ministerial diaries tell a similar story of timely practical counsels
on an everyday level:

"I admonished for drunkenness."
"I preached on the sins of the town."
"I spoke to the people to come sooner."
"I preached against sleeping."
"I encouraged the people to build a New meetinghouse."
"I exhorted the church to attend ye Church meetings more care-
fully."[10]

Perennial sermon topics for any age; certainly. No minister misses
them or their everyday equivalents; and because they are inevitably
recurring choices, the stamp of one time as distinguished from another is plainly upon them. Read in sequence decade by decade over
a hundred years or more, the individual subjects become less important
than certain persistent directions of emphasis which suggest that the
basic chart of colonial preaching was far simpler than its swelling
bulk might indicate.

Among these practical counsels no note recurs more persistently
than the social. It is not by accident that the Plymouth sermon of
Robert Cushman in 1621, the first of all New England sermons to see
print, was strongly social as well as almost desperately practical. It

was a plea for immediate and complete coöperation in building up a common store of provisions for the winter which was already upon them.

"Let no man seek his own; but every man another's wealth", was the inevitable text, and the application plain to bluntness.

> "And what doth this shifting, progging and fat feeding, which some use, more resemble anything than the fashion of hogs? . . . That bird of self-love which was hatched at home, if it be not looked to, it will eat out the life of all grace and goodnesse. . . . May you live as retired Hermites? and look after no body? Nay, you must seek still the wealth of one another; . . .
> Will not a few idle drones spoil the whole stock of laborious Bees: so one idle belly, one murmurer, one complainer, one selfe lover will weaken and dishearten a whole Colony.
> Lay aside all thought of former things and forget them, and think upon the things that are . . . be thankfull to God, it is no worse. When *Job* was brought to the dung-hill, he sat down upon it."[11]

The immediate application of such plain counsels is not always so clear as in the Plymouth urgency, but the note of social responsibility is always there. It had begun with John Robinson's parting injunction to the *Mayflower* travellers, that they

> "be truly bente upon ye generall good, forbearing all private respects of mens selves: and those not sorting with the generall conveniencie".[12]

It had also been emphatic in John Cotton's Southampton farewell.

> "Goe forth, every man that goeth",

he had said,

> "with a publicke spirit, looking not on your owne things onely, but also on the things of others".[13]

Such was standard counsel. In a broad sense the accent of Puritanism was intensely individualistic. Salvation was a personal affair, almost frighteningly so, but the "care of universall helpfulnesse" was also part of the legacy of the primitive church and therefore incumbent on all its successors. Fraternity in the scriptural sense was the common denominator of many hundreds of Sunday sermons and of sermons for special days particularly. None more so than the annual Election Sermons of which "Be truly bente on the generall good" was the doctrine, no matter what scripture verse the preacher might announce as his text.

In pulpit interpretation this oft-repeated injunction widened in meaning through the years. The "general good" included far more than Robert Cushman's sermon had intended in the Plymouth crisis; presently it was large enough to take in all of New England and to reach far beyond any immediate need. It meant legislate wisely in civil affairs, administer justice equally to all, provide for the teaching of our children, develop our local industries, prepare for our defence. In a stricter sense it was an ideal of government; in fact, the chief reason for the existence of government among men.

> "That for which God hath appointed and set up civil government in the world is the *common good* of man."

> "The Welfare of the People—This is the *Compass* that Rulers are to steer by, and the *Touch-stone* of Right and Wrong in all their Motions—What is for the *Common Good*, that and that only are you to do.—It is impossible that anything should be truly right, that is destructive to the common good."[14]

In this broad sense the common good was preached as the cornerstone of all government; and thanks to iteration and reiteration from the pulpit, one generation after another grew up with this conviction firmly fixed in mind, along with the practical applications thereof. The nature and ends of government, Abraham Williams declared, are not so mysterious,

> "but a Person of *common sense*, with tolerable Application, may attain a competent Knowledge thereof".[15]

At least after a lifetime of exposure to Election Sermons or the echoes of them in remote parishes, he would have been a dull clod indeed who did not know without knowing how he knew it that

All civil power is from God in the root,
The common good is the end of all civil government,
Magistrates are God's ministers, and their power is delegated power,
Office is a sacred trust,
Power has its foundation in compact.[16]

The management of his own affairs in town and church turned these familiar preachments into concrete reality. Both circles were small enough to put *power*, the *common good*, and in a sense *liberty*, as he understood them, within the reach of every voter in the circle and to make his guardianship of them to some extent personally felt. The accusation which awaited Joseph Hills one Sunday morning in Malden, "Mr. Hills is not fit to be a Rouling Elder, for hee took part with A Thief",[17] together with its many analogues on many other Sunday mornings, owed something to pulpit tutelage as to the obligations of rulership and the responsibilities of those who conferred it. Hold office; be above reproach. It was an equation for which the election preacher was in large part responsible.

Year by year also in the Election Sermons preachers put their hearers to school as to their earlier history and built up traditions which would presently not be subject to willing change. The freedom to worship God tradition has roots in these annual sermons, usually in answer to the "Why did we come?" question.

"Why came we here?" said Thomas Shepard, son of Thomas Shepard of Cambridge, in his once famous *Eye-Salve* sermon of 1672.

"God's people came hither for Liberty; i.e. Liberty in the way of Holiness."

They came so that they might

"enjoy freedom from those pollutions, and *freedom to follow the Lord fully in all his Ordinances, and appointments* . . . (not by halves; . . . but *fully*)".[18]

"*Why came you into this land? was it not mainly with respect to the rising Generation?* And what with respect to them? was it to leave them a rich and wealthy people? was it to leave them Houses, Lands, Livings? Oh, No; but to leave God in the midst of them."[19]

This from Eleazar Mather in his *A Serious Exhortation* in 1671. John Wilson's *A Seasonable Watchword* in 1677 put it almost identically.

"You came hither for your Children, Sons and Daughters, and for your Grand-children to be under the Ordinances of God."[20]

Before these same grandchildren were old enough to join the "vast concourse" in the election day procession, the tradition would lie deep in men's consciousness. Cotton Mather himself, who was one of these grandchildren, quotes from an early sermon with the full confidence that he was repeating unassailable truth. The question was often put, he said, why did we come.

"We came because we would have our posterity settled under the pure and full *dispensations* of the gospel; defended by *rulers that should be of our selves*."[21]

It was the official answer.

To this end the "godly Household" sermons were chiefly directed and in a plenitude of examples. No colonial preacher left the "rising Generation" alone for very long at a stretch, as would of course be a natural enough program for any day. These colonial "godly Household" sermons belong to their own day in very special ways; none more so than in the blend of family pride, Mosaic code equity, and judgment day certainty which they exhibit.

"Consider and remember alwayes",

said William Stoughton in his *New England's True Interest* of 1668,

"that the *Books* that shall be opened at the last day will contain *Genealogies* in them. There shall then be brought forth a Register of the *Genealogies* of *New-England's sons and daughters*. How shall we many of us hold up our faces then, when there shall be a solemn rehearsal of our *descent*, as well as our *degeneracies?* To have it published whose Child thou art will be cutting unto thy soul, as well as to have the Crimes reckoned up that thou art guilty of".[22]

The humiliation would work both ways: whether parents failed their duty, or children disregarded parental counsels. Either way, the family scutcheon was smirched.

As men (at least in the Election Sermons) grew increasingly "All in a hurry about the world", every man for himself and less care for the *common good*, preachers spoke heavy lamentations for the lost Golden Age, which as it was publicly recalled year by year became ever more golden. As they itemized present sins and "heaven-daring wickedness", in comparison with earlier godliness, they built up a sense of history and of New England's noble beginnings which later preachers would one day use as basis for appeals to patriotism, a word which has no place in this earlier preaching. As early as 1660 American history lengthened backward until the pious beginnings were spoken of as *ancient* and the picture of that piety made almost mythically extravagant. Now "New England has forgotten her errand into the wilderness", and "We are become like the rest of the nations", they said. "When Indians came", or crops failed, or "thunder fell", or a ship was lost, or a great man died, this was a "frown of God" for "our Backslidings".

> "When our Heavenly Father is thus spitting in our faces, shall we not be asham'd and humbled?"[23]

one election preacher stooped so low as to say. He will continue to chastise us until we mend our ways. "When the house is swept, He will lay away the broom", John Eliot promised early in the story, and preacher and pew alike believed it literally. But a year later the house was still unswept and someone else said it again.

The greater the calamity, the more strained the eloquence. When the "Timber Town of Boston" burned in 1711, and when God shook all of New England in 1727 so violently that they knew they had been shaken, it was because both the wise virgins and the foolish ones had been asleep and their lights out. Look out that God does not do worse.

> "He has His Mines and Trains in the Earth under us, and His Bombs and Fire Balls over our Heads, and Hosts of Angels to attack us."[24]

He who "Holds the Wind in His Fist" has horrors yet unlaunched. His resources for punishing "our wickedness" are limitless. Let us repent before worse comes upon us. Sinners may lose their memories, but God will never lose His. He keeps an exact account, and will have His "Reckoning-Days".

These accusing sermons, aside from building up a myth of earlier and better days, have significance in the long view, because they made New England one, if one only in wickedness. Though the itemized sins were local enough to be recognized, even to have names and addresses pinned on them, election preachers gave them a wider base. God was angry not only with Boston or Charlestown, or Hartford, or New Haven, but with all of New England for the sake of the town that had offended. In pulpit handling, local sins became

"the sins of our Land".

Unrighteousness in Boston could create floods along the Connecticut River. What affects one, affects all. It was John Winthrop's

"that every man hath need of other",[25]

in reverse, as the preacher's excoriation pushed the thought of the "vast Assemblage" beyond their immediate horizon and made each representative present feel responsible for all. This indirect and doubtless unconscious suggestion of unity would in time bear a quite different fruit from that which the preacher had intended in his plea for immediate reform. The words *we* and *our* were the most important words in the election preacher's vocabulary.

Fast and Thanksgiving sermons through recalling earlier deliverances in kind (from fire, flood, Indians) built up expectations for a far future. Why has God saved us so many times? There must be a reason. This reason changed with the years, but not the slope toward something greater (one may as well say "bigger and better") than had yet been realized. The future was in the eye of these pulpit men, and

"For the benefit of them that shall come after",[26]

a persistent motivation of their counsels.

For all of their preaching, whatever the subject or occasion, the Bible was their secure anchorage, and their sermons were powerful precisely in proportion as this anchorage could be proved. The preacher invented nothing, proclaimed nothing on his own authority, but thanks to his knowledge, particularly of the Tongues, back of his words lay the split-hair accuracy of God's word for word dictation. There was no doubt about it; only if he could get back to the original text in which "God wrote it", was he on safe ground. It was then his business to amass the Scripture proofs of the doctrine and the instances in which it had worked during the something more than six thousand years since (according to Samuel Stone)

"God made the world of nothing very good in six dayes",[27]

and then (by William Adams' addition to the marvel), hung it "upon nothing". The authority of the Book was the one absolute, inviolable, incontrovertible certainty in the universe. Locked up somewhere between *Genesis* and *Revelation* lay the answer to all the questions men had ever asked or ever could ask. The authority of the Bible was a certainty not open even to debate.

"The truth is, the most wise and fam'd Philosophers, either stole all their wisdom from the Books of divine Revelation, or borrow'd it from those that did; though they had not the courage or honesty to own it; nor to preserve it so pure or simple as they received it."[28]

This from learned Solomon Williams as late as 1741, and though most of the brethren might have said it more courteously, when they came, one and all, to the authority of the Scriptures, doubt was a world they did not enter. Wherever they opened the Bible, they heard God speaking in His own voice. Furthermore, they could prove it.

Once pulpit and pew had accepted this inviolable certainty, many things were settled: a sense of God in the world; in fact, "at your very elbow", as one preacher uncomfortably put it; a sense of the inescapable and irrevocable consequences of man's life on this earth; the possibility, however slender, that he might do something about it all, if only he acted in time. In some form these certainties are the very spine and ribs of every sermon, no matter what the text or how painstakingly the preacher saw to it that he never wandered out of the sight of it. No wonder men went to church in all weathers.

As might be expected, biblical authority could be called in on low levels and Scripture texts be debased to abysmal literalness. It happened frequently. Should one hold up his hand in taking an oath or not hold it up? Should he kiss the Bible or merely lay his hand upon it? Are veils lawful, and if so, where may they be worn and where not? May a man wear a wig? Because conflicting Scripture could be produced on most of these questions, controversy flourished. It was a battle of the erudite against the erudite, and sometimes a battle in which wigs and veils became less important than the nicely balanced arguments they had caused. On the mental level of such a man as George Weeks of Brewster, Massachusetts, I *Corinthians* 11, 4,

> "Every man praying or prophesying, having his head covered, dishonoreth his head"

was the biblical rule, and biblical examples proved it. Why not?

> When God clothed Adam, he did not provide a wig.
> Elisha, who being bald, might have had a reason to cover his head, wore no wig.
> Jesus did not cut his hair.
> There is no warrant in Scripture for so doing, except in extraordinary cases (not specified).
> After the Resurrection, no one will wear a wig.
> After that date, all clothing will be superfluous.[29]

In making such a judgment against George Weeks and his kind as such contentions merit, one remembers that to some men of affairs likewise and to certain intellectuals in the ranks of the clergy God abominated wigs and that they too could prove it by Scripture. So could the opposition who wore them. Samuel Sewall was a man of flat-footed sense who for reasons of his own covered his head, but he had time and interest to record what the pulpit had to say on the subject. He once expressed surprise at hearing "a vindication of Perriwigs in Boston Pulpit by Mr. Mather". So far, so good, but he puts himself with the literal-minded when he adds, "however, not from that text", and then joins the preacher in literalness by praying "that my Heart and Head may be his [the Lord's]".[30] Elisha might have saved much argument had he declared himself on this issue; but even without his help ministers who needed wigs could open their Bibles to the purpose. Within his large sphere of influence Solomon Stoddard of Hampshire County proved to his own satisfaction and that of the bewigged within range that "God does allow Man, by *Art* to Supply the defects of *Nature*",[31] that is, provided man does not cover up his deformity needlessly, "Ruffianly", pridefully, that he does not choose a wig "of unreasonable length", or pay more than he can afford in its purchase. These many wig arguments make an amusing chapter in the sermon record, but not a very important one. Nor is the colonial age unique in making oracular soundings of Scripture concerning such trivia. The best that can be said for all such dull seriousness is that by means of it Sunday preachments touched life on everyday levels.

Thanks to the "Plain Style" ideal, colonial preachers also spoke a language the pew could understand. Their power in the pulpit owed much to this common-sense discipline. Erudition—they had been trained to think—although necessary to their calling, was a minister's private possession, and any ostentatious display of it was not cricket. Plainness was imperative and for the best of reasons; the preacher had in his keeping the souls of educated and illiterate; all must understand the doctrine. Plainness was also the fruit of training.

> "I have accounted it the chiefest part of judicious learning, to make a hard point easy and familiar in explication",[32]

said Thomas Hooker, and no one ever expressed this early pulpit ideal better. One of the greatest compliments a preacher might hope to earn (in his funeral sermon) was that his way of preaching had been so plain that "the very *lambs* might wade, into those discourses— wherein elephants might swim",[33] although so paradoxical a virtue was hardly within easy reach of all who strove to attain.

The "Plain Style" meant, first of all, plain language. "Silken language, gallant language, embroidered language never did God's work." As Giles Firmin put it, "Silken Language sutes not those who are cloathed in Sackcloth",[34] although as currently understood *silken* was a word of devious application.

Next to simple language the preacher's best chance of bringing abstruse doctrine down to the level of "unlearned" comprehension was by analogies to familiar things. Homely similitude has of course been the resource of the pulpit in all ages. Colonial pulpit training sought to develop a technique for its greater effectiveness, although even without his Harvard or Yale training in this direction the colonial preacher might have found it convenient for the enforcing of spiritual truth to use heavy timbers, hammer and nails, haycarts, ice jams, sudden frost, obedient oxen, spinning wheels, copper pots boiling on the fire, and other farm and household equipment convenient to his hand. Houses can be built and furnished and the whole routine of daily life reconstructed out of the figurative items these sermons supply, along with the biblical rivers of water, bows in the heavens, laborious ants. So Thomas Shepard:

> "I am in want of outward comfort", [says a poor soul] "It may be God dealeth with thee in this", [says Thomas Shepard] "as a mother with her children, who takes away the victuals from the children for a while and puts it in the cubbord, but afterwards she giveth it them again. So sometimes God taketh away these outward things, locketh them up for a while in the cubbord."
>
> "I am afraid of death" [says a poor soul]. "I answer" [says Thomas Shepard] . . . "make death itself a ground of comfort and joy to thy self. If a child be at boord from his fathers house, tho he be at play with his fellows, yet if he see horse and man come to fetch him, he is glad, and leaves his play and companions to goe home to his father willingly; So here we are at boord in the world, and we are at play, as it were, among the creatures, but when death comes, which is as horse and man, we should be willing to goe to our Father's house, which is best of all."[35]

"Give me leave to use this similitude, because it is very fit", says Thomas Shepard again, as in *The Soules Invitation Unto Christ* he built his thought around the figure of a "Suter" who comes to speak with one whom he loves and will not be denied. Not all his brother ministers might have approved his application to Christ, who as a "Suter", "desireth to be a real speeder", but Thomas Shepard felt safe in the example of *Canticles* 5, and he pressed the similitude still further.

"If a man once sets his mind upon a woman, he will have her, no body shall scarce withstand him."[36]

So it is with "Christ, the Suter".

There were other sides to Thomas Shepard. He could be adamant against Anne Hutchinson, with whom temperamentally it would seem he might so easily have been in sympathy. He could refuse to sanction the gathering of a church because he thought not all of its Seven Pillars could give satisfactory evidence of their regeneration. He could split doctrinal hairs with the rest, in dusty wise, but he was also something of a poet. One cannot read far in any of his extant sermons, of which there are far too few, without coming on metaphors which win by their very simplicity; likewise his language.

"The deepest sorrows run with least noyse."

"I have thought it not unusefull, but very comfortable to a poor passenger, not only to know his journey's end, and the way in general to it, but also the several *Stadia* or Towns he is orderly to pass through."[37]

Though he too occasionally stumbled in metaphor, he could never have been guilty of such comparisons as Charles Chauncy was likely to invoke in his clarification of doctrine for the "unlearned". Said he,

"When your Parents are gathered to their Fathers, . . . the Lord will wipe *New-England* as a man wipes a dish; wiping and turning it upside-down. You have more to answer for, than the Indians have."[38]

"See how many in your Families, Towns, and Neighbour-hood, goe clattering up and down in the bonds of iniquity, in the fetters and chains of the Devil. Pitty these poor prisoners. Give them a lift to help them out."[39]

"Now if this weight that Christ bare, had been laid on the shoulders of all the Angels in Heaven, it would have sunk them down to the lowest hell. It would have crackt the Axel-tree of Heaven and Earth."[40]

"When Christ was shaken [as water in a glass], there was no mudd in the bottome, which rises in us, when wee suffer extremity."[41]

"The breath of God's displeasure is the very bellows of Hell."[42]

"There are none that attend a faithful Ministry, but have many a pull from Christ. . . . The Devil will also have a pluck at you, [but Christ] pulls with all his might and main."[43]

John Norton saw "God applying a plaster to the wounds of Zion", and "David's tears falling into God's bottle"; Thomas Thacher found it "hard work" to awaken "a people that are rocked a sleep in sin", and warned them not "to be sealed up under the Tomb-stone of a hard heart".[44] William Stoughton recalled New England's founding as the time "When God first began to keep House in this wilderness". At that time He had "the choicest Household-stuff, much Plate and Jewels, and other precious things. Shall we now rise up to fill his House with *meer Lumber*, worthless cumbersome sorry stuff?"[45]

Cotton Mather, guiltiest of all, though admitting that he was the least poetical of men, guessed not how widely he missed port, as he continued to strew his hundreds of pages with painful images. His attempt to make Thomas Cobbett a man of prayer above all others is a fair sample of his double vision. Said he,

> "*That golden chain*, one end of which is tied unto the *tongue of man*, and the other to the *ear of God*, . . . our Cobbett was always pulling at".[46]

So be it, if the life of prayer is thereby made desirable. A close second comes in his *Things for a Distress'd People to Think upon*, the Election Sermon of 1696, in which as he laments a land "full of dead souls", he asserts in sober earnest,

> "If thy Grandfather had imagined, that ever thou wouldst have become, such a pittiful Thing, he would have swum in his own Tears, unto his Grave upon it".[47]

Thomas Prince thought to compliment that "wise Master-Builder, Mr. Shepard", in a late edition of his *Diary* by the prefatory remark that it was no disparagement of him to say that he was wont "to labour sometimes by the Hammer of the Word, to fasten these nails of Truth in a sure place, even in the heads and hearts of Infant-Christians".[48]

One hopes he was not misunderstood.

The specifications of the sermon pattern also made for clarity. "The parts of this text are two: 1. A *Dehortation*, 2. An *Exhortation*", said Robert Cushman in 1621. "In handling of which I will first, open the wordes. Secondly, gather the Doctrine. Thirdly, illustrate the doctrine by Scriptures, experience and reasons. Fourthly, apply the same, to every one his portion."[49] Every New England preacher, until George Whitefield broke the pattern in 1740, followed a similar track. Without these captions the hearers would have been lost; perhaps betimes, the preacher also. They were themselves a language to the colonial pew. The Text is God Himself speaking; hearken. The Doctrine is deducible from the Text and therefore authoritative; believe it. Here are the Scripture proofs; remember them and mark them in your own Bibles. Doctrine has a relation to your own life; here are the Applications; find the one that belongs to you. Is it Instruction, Exhortation, Warning, Consolation, Admonition? Act upon it.

Instead of interrupting the thought these elaborate divisions and subdivisions within the familiar framework were station identifications along the way; green lights and red lights to be obeyed automatically and then quickly forgotten in favor of the scenery. Those who had brought their notebooks (and many had) in order to outwit the drowsy tempter recorded the preacher's thought by these familiar signposts as he inched along. Even the "meer Highway Hearers . . . restless till the Tiresome Glass be run out and the Tedious Sermon be ended", found the "Wild fowl of roving Thoughts & carnal Affections" brought back with a jerk by the announcement of a *Curve* immediately ahead. Children who stayed to catechising gave the preacher his thought back again by the same outline. It was all a familiar road map and a sure-fire pedagogical device. Again at home on Sunday evening those who kept the Sabbath by code recalled the morning preachment and prompted each other by the same scaffolding of Uses, Reasons for the Doctrine, Objections raised and Objections answered. By comparison with this social practice around the kitchen fireplace the printed page would have been baffling indeed. A sermon-taster like Samuel Sewall also found them convenient. In his own private log-book, continued through forty-one years, he not only seldom failed to record a "pithy and pertinent Discourse", but made frequent cross-references to previous sermons by the aid of these same captions. On October 22nd of one year he recalled Thomas Thacher's "Answer to the objection under the 2nd Reason" of his sermon for the preceding December 10th, Mr. Shepard's 3rd Use of December 15th, and Mr. Thacher's Direction 9 of December 17th. Of this last item he remarked, "which I am sure was spoken to me".[50] Such was the preacher's intent, and directly in line with his own best concept of his priestly office. Samuel Sewall's *Diary* is rich in suggestion as to how much sermons mattered in the life of a man of affairs, utterly practical, and standing at the extreme opposite pole from one who could be called to any degree spiritually minded. On one occasion he recorded annoyance because an old man,

> "Jno. Maryon, the Father, faints in the Old Meetinghouse, in time of Worship, which obstructs Mr. Allen, and makes considerable disturbance".[51]

Obstructs was not a strange word for Sewall to use. To him it was the sermon which was important and whatever interrupted the thread of its logic was clearly a *disturbance*. On the other side of the desk, obscure country ministers wrote out their weekly sermons before sundown on Saturday with as much care as though the Sunday congregation would be made up of their peers. Once after having been "grievously afflicted with the Toothache" for three days running, Ebenezer Parkman reported triumphantly, "My Toothache continues, but I finished my sermons".[52] Sunset on this occasion was but one hour away, but at least he had touched base in time.

As one plays the sermon record backward through the founding years and well into the generations of those who were beginning to forget these years, much of the endless iteration and reiteration cancels out, leaving a fairly simple residuum. The total impression is more positive than negative. From the pulpit side sermons were mainly friendly, utterly plain reminders that the world to come was more important than the one we live in, and that man's only hope of gaining infinite bliss in that world depends on what he does about it while he is still in this one. With this motivation sermons were also sensible and workable counsels on the plane of everyday living. Religion, said the preachers, is "Man's true Interest as to both Worlds", and Sunday by Sunday they tried to make it so.

From the side of the pew sermons were light thrown on the mysteries a man could not even state for himself, much less unravel, though they were part of his daily consciousness. Once a week for two hours his thought was lifted above the interminable chores of life, and his destiny linked to something vaster than he could immediately know. His daily performance was tested by a great idea. In the midst of manifold uncertainties he was given a North Star. He needed nothing so much.

Colonial preaching is not preaching in the way of the prophets, except in its desperate earnestness. A theological system was made more important than that which impels men to construct theological systems. Always the system itself, its logic, its immensity and comprehensiveness, not the urge behind it, is in the sermon foreground. One looks almost in vain (though happily not quite) in all this vast sermon library for preaching which attempts to make articulate the passionate striving toward perfection that has belonged to great preaching in all ages. Colonial preaching is of a different order, and its virtues and strength are measurable by a different standard—the standard of its own day. These "great, grim, earnest men" knew what they were about, and their satisfactions were commensurate to their zeal. Said Charles Chauncy, the First, who was one of them, "The rewards of a painful ministry are not regarded by covetous earthworms". In the fraternity for which he spoke, *earthworms* were few.

BOOK THREE

"NOISES ABOUT THE TEMPLE"

CHAPTER SEVEN

"Where to Set"

IN spite of the annual election day emphasis on "the good of the whole", up and down the village streets townsmen found this particular golden mean hard to translate into local terms. When election day was over and shops were again open, for church-members and non-members alike *our* preference meant *my* preference and *our* convenience *my* convenience. Shall we buy a new bell, "imported from England"? No, said the deaf members of the congregation. Why pay for an improvement from which we can reap no benefit? Shall we levy a special tax "to build a deaf-pue just below the pulpit"? No, said the non-deaf. Why should one in full possession of his ears pay for such a convenience before his time to use it? Let the deaf Christians foot their own bill. The sequel on all such issues, major and minor, was what the Town Book called "warm debate"; possibly worse.

Ministers did their best. They kept up a steady flow of sermons enjoining Christians to love as brethren, but despite all their efforts "heat of spirit" was chronic, both within and without the fellowship. It was not only that every town was a divided company, with an ever increasing majority on the side of those not included in the "gospel covenant"; more often than not it was the godly lined up against the godly, and for reasons deep-seated in human nature. In pulpit language, "the Devil" had gone to work "to stir up the corruptions of the children of God". He was uncommonly successful. Almost before anyone residing within the prescribed half-mile of the meetinghouse quite realized what had happened or how, the "little bundle of eternal life", which the founding members had thought to tie up so securely, had begun to fall apart. The harmony of first days had been of brief duration. Instead, and very early in the story, one reads, and not once only, such a news item as Thomas Lechford wrote of the Rev. John Wilson of Boston in 1641,

> "*Master Wilson* did lately ride to *Green's Harbor* [now Marshfield] in *Plymouth* patent, to appease a broyle".[1]

Certainly, and so did many another gentle diplomat with a known talent for peace. To be able "to sweeten, compose and qualify exasperated spirits" put one in a special bracket among the brethren, as month by month, upon urgent invitation, the few so endowed rolled up their horseback mileage in the interest of harmony among God's children. They had their hands full. Worse still, while a minister was absent appeasing some distant congregational broil, the devil often went to work in his own home territory. If a few Sundays after his return he announced as his text, *Genesis* 13, 8, "And Abram said unto Lot, let there be no strife, I pray thee, between me and thee", or *Exodus* 4, 27, "and he [Aaron] went, and met him [Moses] in the mount of God and kissed him", there was still hope; but if he chose *Proverbs* 18, 19, "A brother offended is harder to be won than a strong city; and their contentions are like the bars of a castle", the battle was either lost or else moving swiftly into a critical phase.

Over and over it was the same story and to belabor the fact was not to discover the remedy. Contentions were legion and they had come to stay. Covenants were broken and new covenants pledged time after time, for, alas, brothers forgiving and forgiven could again offend, and "a lapse after the pacification" could put the village into a worse uproar than ever. Old grievances motivated new outbreaks, most of them as definitely predictable as fire, flood or the seasonal storms of nature. Moreover, rifts within the fellowship meant alignments outside of it as well. Neighbors took sides against neighbors until presently the whole village was enmeshed. Division into "parties" followed the breach as the night the day, and was sometimes perpetuated long after the occasion for strife had been forgotten, even into the next generation.

While a battle was on, the Lord's Supper could not be celebrated.

Brethren were not in peace and harmony with brethren, and until at least a truce could be declared, this precious "ordinance" had to be postponed. Sometimes the postponement was continued for years together, by successive vote of the warring factions. The frequency and violence of these parish quarrels, even in the first generation, make one skeptical of the fabled state of "peace, love, and holiness" in which John Robinson's Leyden congregation is said to have dwelt together before their venture to America. No such Utopian calm ever gladdened the hearts of believers for long on this side of the Atlantic. Instead, the "new house was shaken with violence before it was well set and the Parts firmly knit", and if by good luck, or better, a minister escaped serious strife through a long pastorate, he was by that fact marked for special distinction. Many might covet but few deserve the record of the Rev. Grindal Rawson of Bellingham, Massachusetts, of whom it was written (one hopes truthfully), "He was a great peacemaker; in thirty-five years he had no considerable difference".[2] Unfortunately his secret died with him. Similarly with most of the other "blessed peacemakers" on record.

One of the earliest and also one of the bitterest quarrels to disrupt the peace of the community both inside and outside the covenant circle was the quarrel over where to set the new meetinghouse after the first one had become too small. Sometimes there had been "earnest controversy" over the placing of the first one. As early as 1640, while the Barnstable congregation was still shivering around Sacrament Rock on Sundays, the situation became so tense that they appointed a day of humiliation and invoked the Lord Himself "to finde out a place for meeting, & that we might agree in it". At the outset, however, new settlements were usually small enough and for safety's sake so closely huddled that a central spot agreeable to all had been fairly easy to find. Trouble usually arose after the half-mile limit for building a dwelling house had been relaxed and the "Street" had extended itself so far in both directions that there was no longer any "convenientest Spot for us all". Soon or late every settlement had this dilemma to deal with. The price of growth would be strife and whatever site was eventually chosen, not everyone would be pleased. As a result and almost unfailingly, when it came time to rebuild in any village, an era had plainly ended. Progressively, as the town continued to spread out, requiring in turn a third and fourth meetinghouse and then presently a division into distinctly independent precincts, rifts became wider.

In towns destined for rapid growth, rebuilding sometimes came as early as ten or fifteen years after the first settlement, sometimes sooner. Even then, a new meetinghouse was always overdue, for the families of the original founders had increased until their children numbered a small battalion to each household. Every lean-to on every private dwelling meant more pew room on Sunday. Every ship continued to bring new settlers who in their turn claimed the privilege of sermons. Every available inch of pew space was needed, and far more. The 12 by 20, 20 by 30, or 30 by 40 first meetinghouse could no longer accommodate the "throng" that assembled at "the sign of the kunk". Something must be done and at once. Almost any Town Book can supply a model for what followed. Merely to raise the question, "Where to Set", was tantamount to issuing a call to arms. If a congregation found itself with only two sites to choose from, it was fortunate, for usually there were at least three or four, if not five or six. The number of town meetings and their mean temperature increased proportionally with each additional site proposed. Let Watertown, Massachusetts, supply a typical, if somewhat more protracted example than most, of what lay back of a town clerk's cryptic phrase, "Some agitation there was".

After voting to rebuild in 1692, the town was split first into two and then three militant parties and the fight was on. At first all three groups agreed on what was meant to be fair procedure for finding out how the town stood on the matter and for resolving the disagreement if possible. In the words of the town vote for November 18, 1692,

> "Thos who are of the mind to buld [build] and set up a meeting hous on the hill betweene the pound and wedo [widow] whittnis, Let them folow Robert Herington, Saneer [Senior]; Thos that are of the mind to hould [hold] it whare it is, Let them folow Mr. Norcros;
> In case we cant agre among ourselfes, we will Refere it to men".[3]

They could not agree and their dispute was referred to "men" chosen by the Governor and Council of the colony.

A year and a half later the Council returned a compromise verdict calling for a meetinghouse to be erected within four years on a central spot designated as

> "A Knowl of Ground lying between the house of the Widow Sterns, and Whitney's hill; to be the place of meeting to worship God, for the whole town".[4]

Three weeks later, May 9, 1694, eighty-four men and women residing in the eastern part of town and thirty-three men and women on the farms in the western part signed an "earnest protest" against compliance with this Council decision. The stiff independence of their statement has a prophetic ring. It reads,

> "Because the Town, nor any part never desired any Gentlemen to say where we should Build a meeting-house nor when, and wee do absolutely Deny Ever to pay one peny towards any such Building at that place but if the Town shall see cause to Erect a place of meeting for the publick worship of God at the Westward part of our Town so as it may be convenient where the Farmers with such others that way as will be pleased to Joyne with them Shall think Convenient we shall be willing to be helpfull therein, as much as may be thought Necessary—".[5]

Although this protest was looked upon favorably by the majority who wished a central location, the party of the west (a minority) stood firm. Their degree of what is labelled "earnestness" may be inferred from the fact that in a town meeting alluded to as "riotous", the moderator "by advice" quickly called for adjournment, "to prevent such inconvenients as might justly be feared by Reason of the heat of Spirit" which prevailed. The party of the west promptly held a meeting of their own and passed votes which were in turn promptly declared "invalid" by the selectmen. Dissent and counter-dissent continued until by Council action the party of the west was officially declared separate and labelled the "Farmer's Precinct".

One might think this action would make agreement between the two remaining factions easier, but not at all; the fight was only beginning. After the meetinghouse on the central spot had been completed and duly accepted, the minister (Henry Gibbs) who had been chosen by the majority, but who was really inclined toward the party of the west, declared he would not preach "even so much as one day", until the dissatisfaction between the east and the center had been removed. He was of course asking the impossible.

More than a year later another minister was agreed upon by the center. He consented to come without qualification. At the same time three laymen from the center and three from the east were chosen to debate publicly

"thos matters of differance that did kep them from uniting in love and peace as to the worship of God in the towne".[6]

Unfortunately, no minutes of this session are preserved, but out of it three courses of action seem to have emerged.

Shall we have two congregations?
Shall we all go back to the old meetinghouse?
Shall we draw lots whether to go to the old or to the new?

Instead of any of these three choices they decided on a compromise, both sides agreeing to use the new meetinghouse with their respective ministers officiating jointly, Gibbs for the east and Angier for the center. Anyone might have known what would happen. It happened. At the hour appointed by the east for the solemn ordination of Mr. Gibbs, the "party of the center" got possession of the meetinghouse and refused to give it up. Not to be defeated by any such schoolboy trick the "party of the east" proceeded to ordain Mr. Gibbs in the open air, "though a cold day". Under such circumstances one may question whether this traditional "solemnity" was conducted with the "holy inner calm" appropriate to the occasion.

Henceforth the two congregations remained separate, although the tangle over "Rates", payment for the new building, repairs on the old, possession of the earlier records and other details dragged on for years. In fact, the boundary line between the two precincts was not established officially until 1720. This was twenty-eight years after the "where to set" controversy appeared on the records and even longer after it had first begun to ruffle the peace of this historic community of saints who in 1630 had taken the covenant to dwell together in brotherly love.

In main essentials this Watertown story is almost standard: the division into parties, their persistence, the warmth of contention, decisions made, decisions revoked, compromise, delay, and in the end secession of the aggrieved party. Habit was strong, however, and if the settlement were not yet large enough to support two ministers, more often than not, after months or even several years of futile argument, the town would vote to rebuild on the old site or as close to it as a new raising could be safely accomplished. Once this decision was made, opposition usually disappears from the record, although possibly not from the neighborhood. Typically also, on the Monday after the new frame was raised, the old building was pulled down, and if no one were hurt in this dangerous operation, God was publicly thanked and the old materials were prepared for use in the new structure.

One pleasant variant of this usual tale is the moving of the old building to a new site where it was to be the home of a widow who was a charge on the town. Sometimes it was sold "for what it would fetch" or given to someone who would take it away. Once in Stratford, Connecticut, it was "sold att an outcry". Generally, however, every timber and every scrap of lumber was salvaged for the new building and woe to him who helped himself to any of it in the dark of the moon. One of the charges against Deacon Abraham Merrill of Newbury in 1713 was for "acting illegally in disposing of a house, that you never built", and second, "for violently pulling down our meeting house and carrying it away contrary to our minds and consent".[7] He had had no "liberty" to do so. His action was not "decent".

Enlargement sometimes took a simpler course. This was to enlarge "by splitting of it In tow". Accordingly they sawed the building in two pieces, pulled the halves apart, filled in the middle and built a new roof over the whole. This method was followed many times with great saving of time, money, and sometimes of argument. There was abundant opportunity for disagreement, however, as to the direction in

which the sawing was to take place. Should the line run parallel to
the pulpit and the deacon's seat, in which case the pulpit would stay
where it was and the rear be moved back, or should the building be
bisected through the middle aisle, in which case the pulpit must be
moved. Many meetings and much talk around the Hill would eventually decide this vexed question, but never to the satisfaction of all.

Disagreement was sometimes given an edge of drama when after
long deadlock a divided congregation acted out its final vote by as-
sembling in person on the respective sites open to choice, with the
understanding that

> "ye biggest number shall have ye place".

Under such a plan lobbyists worked fast. Votes were changed at the
last minute and undue influence was no doubt rampant. But the
method sometimes worked. At Deerfield, Massachusetts, in 1729, the
town decided after long debate,

> "to move out and stand at 3 places discorst on",

and "upon Tryal they Concluded on ye Middle most of ye three".[8]
At Harvard, Massachusetts, according to tradition, it also worked in
1732, but not when it came time to rebuild again in 1773. If one may
believe the traditionary account of this later trial, when the case was
deadlocked indoors a fifteen minute recess was voted, during which
each man picked up a stone and deposited it on the spot of his choice,

> "with this restriction that there be but Two heaps, and that the
> heap which has the most stones in number shall be the place".

Cannily they also added the Yankee precaution that the selectmen
"inspect the heaps and see that no man lay more than one stone". Unfortunately, however, when the count was made, each heap had precisely the same number of stones, whereupon they voted

> "that the south cell of the meeting house be laid at the north heap
> of stones".[9]

It would be too much to hope that all were pleased by this compromise.

Derby, Connecticut, grew tired of its own dissensions, and after taking a year to think over their choices they voted in 1681

> "that the place near the tree where the town met and sat down shall be the place where the meeting-house shall stand, without any more trouble".[10]

The hill above Ephraim Smith's, which had been the opposing site, was dubbed "Squabble Hole" thereafter in local allusion. They also voted that the committee for "carrying on the building" had power

> "to call out the inhabitants as they see cause and when they please";

also that

> "In case any man neglect or refuse to work when he is called, he shall pay two shillings and sixpence to the work, having had two days warning".[11]

This would have been his wages. Thirty-seven years later, when this first 20 by 28 meetinghouse had been outgrown, there was more trouble; this time trouble born of an attempt to be strictly parliamentary. With the "pond party" lined up on one side of the meetinghouse and the "burial yard party" on the other, and the pond party showing a majority of three, one of these three votes was challenged. While this point of legality was being debated, "five others broke away", and the whole vote was lost. This mishap caused more disagreement, more delay. Two years later the town voted that a committee of three outside the town should decide on the location. This committee chose the "burying place", which was very near to the old site, and the work went forward without further delay. One sinister hint that the spoils system was actively at work comes in the notation that Henry Wakelee refused to pay his part toward this new 40 by 32 by 20 structure unless the town would hire him to keep the sheep again. Pressure groups also were learning the tricks. Doubtful majorities watched the weather and chose the day of a "greate snow" or slippery paths to ease the covenant and make "Holy Walking" more conformable to their desire, as well as to shorten the distance to preaching on Sabbath.

When a town could not iron out its own differences as to location, the General Court was called upon to "stick the stake", thereby making the site official. Everyone understood that the sills of the new structure must enclose "said stake or heap of stones" as officially placed. For many years the finality of such court action was respected. Those inconvenienced by the location either accepted their inconvenience with good grace or in time petitioned for withdrawal. In time, however, finality began to be questioned. Disgruntled minorities at first raised their objections timidly; then grew bolder. After all, wasn't this a town affair? Why bow to the outside authority of the Court? Why didn't they have a right, as a town, to settle their own disputes?

As unrest grew still bolder, counter-pleas were offered. Later still came frank opposition and then defiance. Let the General Court "stick the stake". It was a poor town which couldn't find someone who would dare to move it in the night to the spot preferred by the conspirators of one faction or the other, or, as was simpler, make off with it altogether, leaving things where they had been in the first place. Deacons might frown officially but, after all, the stake was gone, and next time opposition would be easier. Whole chapters in the long story of self-government are implicit in these manifestations of neighborhood defiance. Wanton mischief was not the motive. A philosophy of government was slowly translating itself into action. The "people" were learning who they were; and, as their identity slowly became apparent to themselves, it would be forever impossible to give the word Thomas Hooker's or Nathaniel Ward's intended slope toward a selected minority. This was *Everyman's* government and he was learning to sense his power to make it go his own way.

As the story moves into the third and fourth generations, a good many General Court stakes had been pulled up and vandalism or, in contemporary phrase, "damnifying the meeting house" had grown less timid and less rare. In 1721, after a majority vote had determined the location, and work had begun in Providence, the opposition came in the night and pulled the frame down. At Mendon, Massachusetts, someone cut off the corner posts; at Torrington, Connecticut, the "aggrieved party" shortened them by several feet. After the *North* farmers of Wallingford, Connecticut, had been made a separate society in 1725, those living in Milking Yard wanted the meeting-house in one place; those living in Dog's Misery wanted it in another. According to a tradition still current, after the Dog's Misery people had assembled materials ready to start, the Milking Yard people came in the night with teams and hauled them to the spot of their choice. It was no use; the Dog's Misery people were stronger, and on the fol-lowing day they had the satisfaction of seeing the Milking Yard peo-ple haul the materials back again.

In Hadley, Massachusetts, after ten years of voting and annulling the vote to set the meetinghouse first, "in the center of travel", and then in five different places successively, the party of the west finally won and work had begun. The party of the east chose this moment to come in the night, steal three corner posts and hide them in Pichawamiche Swamp. This loss replaced, the west proceeded once more and raised the frame, only to discover on the following morn-ing that the plates had been cut and that the frame was flat on the ground. A committee of five ministers was then called to determine whether the site chosen by majority vote was binding. They gave a verdict in the affirmative, on the authority of both Old and New Testaments. The lot was of a sacred nature and must be used. Their decision was accepted as final. The General Court then made a legal division of the parish, ordered the party of the east to pay damages and prosecuted the "damnifiers". The west spliced the plates and the work went on once more. Unfortunately, the neighborhood legend that three women of the east added gaiety to the scene of the first "damnifying" by sitting on the posts and singing while it proceeded would seem to be mere embroidery. Even this gay detail might prove milder than the truth, however, if town records preserved more than mere votes and penalties in such a case.

There would seem to be no doubt as to the truth of the Chebacco tale of three women, who took things into their own hands while their husbands had gone to a General Court session, bearing a petition to build the new meetinghouse. Hastily the wives went to the neigh-boring towns of Gloucester and Manchester, secured help, and brought the raising of the new structure to pass. This task accom-plished rejoicingly, the hostesses together with all who had approved their boldness feasted the helpful neighbors and all was gay. On their return the husbands were somewhat embarrassed, for the news had travelled; their wives were arrested, tried in Ipswich, and bound over to the next court in Salem. At their trial they were found guilty of contempt of authority. When the full story came out, however, the score was even, for the husbands, over-confident of securing a favorable decision, had gone further than the law allowed in laying the sills and placing the timbers in readiness for the raising before they had set out on their journey with the petition. A favorable decision in 1679 legalized the guilt for both parties and the meetinghouse work went forward.

Sometimes God Himself seemed to take a hand in these troubles. After the General Court had ended a dispute at Griswold, Connecticut, in 1717, deciding in favor of the minority wish to build "at the point of Country road where the path of Mr. John Brown turns off", workmen began to dig the well on this approved spot. All at once the well caved in, burying their tools. God had spoken, whereupon, General Court or not, they shifted to the rival spot, "ye knole—by the bridg on John Pray's land", and had no further mishap. Typically, a General Court interference merely made matters worse. In the end the people settled the dispute themselves, even though it meant defiance of a Court order.

The willingness of townsmen to be called out as many as forty or fifty times to vote, debate, annul, and start all over again is evidence of how much it mattered. So also the tenacity of the opposition and the No-concession policy of the majority. The record of one year of voting in Milford, Massachusetts, after what had the appearance of a final decision, can be matched many times. The record goes like this:

"Moved, that five feet be taken from the forty-five in width of the Meeting House, and also two feet from the twenty-four in height. Moved to "alter the situation of the New Meeting House *layed* out by the Committee". Negatived.
Moved to "erect the new House within twenty rods of the old one". Negatived.
Moved "to build two Meeting Houses". Negatived.

Moved "to repair the old house". Negatived.

Moved "to make a regular division of the Town". Negatived.

Moved to "set up the new meeting-house by the heap of stones made by the Committee". Negatived.

Moved to "set it within six or eight rods of the same place". Negatived.

Moved "to set it up at the west end of the Burying Ground, where the timber lies". Passed in the affirmative, with 13 voters protesting.[12]

The motion that the town provide "a Barrel of Rhum" for the raising was not negatived. Subsequently the new building was "damnified" in the usual way by the chopping off of the corner posts; but scars notwithstanding, it was eventually finished and some ten years later the party of the "negative" seceded. As the new century got under way, secession became fairly standard along with defiance of General Court decisions. Unanimity was no longer possible, no matter how many meetings were called.

Toward the mid-century, fire, supposedly accidental, but always in the night and always suspected of not being accidental, becomes frequent on the record. Those who wished to rebuild, as opposed to those who wished to patch, took this "wicked and hazardous" means of making patching impossible. At Needham, where a burning, supposedly attributable to the rebuilding party, had taken place, the rebuilders announced the "raising" for nine o'clock in the morning, but taking no chances of disaster from the "patchers", they assembled secretly at five-thirty and accomplished the raising, so that when an angry opposition arrived at the announced hour, they could do no more than "withdraw with many threats". At Hopkinton, New Hampshire, the party who wished to "move" the meetinghouse instead of enlarging it was suspected of a burning, but though the indignant selectmen constituted themselves a committee "to find out who Sot the meeting hous on fire",[13] and though several arrests were made, results were inconclusive.

Ministers took account of all these unChristian behaviors, preached many sermons about keeping the peace, but presently they too seemed to accept long-continued strife and even vandalism as routine accompaniments of a building program. About all that a minister could do was to plead repeatedly for peace and, when dedication day came, draw up a new covenant. "The Devil is a great enemy to settling ministers and building meeting-houses", Joseph Emerson of West Parish, Groton, had said, and he surely had reason to know. The Groton contention had been particularly feverish and undignified in the bargain. The General Court had given preference to the minority wish in this case, and when timbers were being drawn to the spot, the majority engineered a surprise attack, pricked the noses of the minority oxen and upset the carts, thus paralleling the better known ox-cart episode in the Yale College "battle of the books".

So it was. This is a story a century and a half long and always coming to the same end. Always the new meetinghouse was built, a new covenant was sworn, and shamefaced Christians started off once more. The drama even of a "spite meetinghouse" ended (at least on the surface) with gestures of peace among brethren. It was standard procedure that when dedication day was in sight, or sometimes as soon as work had begun, a committee of twelve or less would be appointed in town meeting to draw up resolutions to be presented to some later meeting and duly accepted, making the peace official. In what amounted to standard phrase these resolutions would recommend that

> "We do forgive each other wherein we have been instrumentall of grieving each other in word or deed,
> —that we will doe what we can to promote and increase love and doe nothing to break the peace now made,
> —that the whole towne shall go on joyntly together to finish the meeting house with all convenient speed, in the place where it now standeth, without any regret or reflexions one upon another".[14]

One hopes it was even so. Sometimes a town memorialized this peace-pipe ceremony by the purchase of a bell for the new house and voted to inscribe it, "Let us love one another", but even this reminder did not always work. The "forever" of the earlier covenant vows was now recognized openly to be of doubtful duration.

Once in a while what might pass for a happy ending came unsought. After much voting and then "nulling" and "voyding" of votes in Andover, Massachusetts, as to whether to build "at ye Oack by Capt. Benjamin Stevens, his barn", or at "the apel tree in Joseph Parker Senior his land", the apple tree won, for the very good reason that "the Bulk of the Timber lyeth for sd meeting house" nearer to the apple tree. Better still for the future peace of this divided house, the son of the minister chosen by the original company in time married the daughter of the minister chosen by the other half of the precinct, so that eventually harmony in the community became something of a family affair.

At Stratford, Connecticut, with five sites proposed, the one on Watch Hill was finally chosen because Israel Chauncy, pastor, made a bargain with the town to contribute more than a year's salary if they would build on this particular hill. Stratford was ready for this compromise on another count besides the financial, as they had had trouble enough once before when their contention had led to a General Court settlement. In 1669 when two factions could not agree on a successor to Adam Blackman (Blakeman), one of Cotton Mather's seventy-seven, and were attempting to carry on two separate preaching services on Sunday with two different ministers, Israel Chauncy and Zechariah Walker, the General Court set first a two-hour and then a three-hour limit to Minister No. I, and thereby invited something worse than the overlapping which had been the previous grievance. Minister I (Walker) filibustered past the three-hour limit and his followers went without their dinner in support of his trespass. The second congregation waited until their patience was exhausted, went to a private house, and eventually voted to "go and live by themselves and have no more dissensions". To do this meant to break the covenant which had originally made them one company "forever", and it was a step cautiously and sadly taken. In the many pages of the succeeding polite but resolute correspondence between these two factions for eight years, much more than one village quarrel is detailed. A sentence from one of the documents of the Chauncy side sounds like a far-off echo of Thomas Hooker's sermon of 1638, "5thly", they wrote,

"Rule forbids us, which gives a church power to choose her own feeders. Mr. Walker was never chosen by us to be our feeder".[15]

That settled it. In spite of the *forever* of their former covenant vows, those who wanted Walker to be their "feeder" could go and live by themselves, as they did.

The story of one Newburyport faction reduces many such battles to absurdity and in its ending was the beginning of "Toleration" in ways the "Simple Cobbler" had not even dared to fear. To those who battled, however, it was no affair of absurdity or of toleration. They merely wanted their own way. The seceders in this case had petitioned for division of the parish because of the distance to the meetinghouse, and having waited for five years without favorable action, they withdrew without permission in 1689 and built themselves a meetinghouse "on the Plains". Six years later the town decided that "Pipe Stave Hill" was the proper site, and eleven years later built themselves a new meetinghouse on that site. The "Plains" people objected to being taxed for this new structure, but their protest was denied, because they had withdrawn without permission. They waited their chance and when the Pipe Stave people voted to use the materials from the old meetinghouse to build a barn for their minister, the "Plains" people came in the night and carried them off. Twice the town ordered them to make restitution, but twice they paid no heed to the order. Instead they petitioned the town to let Artichoke River be the dividing line between the two parishes. Being refused, they became Episcopalians.

To make a better story, even this was not the end. Of strife came yet more strife. On one occasion the Pipe Stave people, having long waited their chance, found the Episcopal chapel vacant, broke in and carried off vestments and books. One fears that zeal against Episcopacy was not their sole motivation. Still later the "Plains" people had troubles of their own with these same "trappings of popery". Their rector, Matthias Plant, was too informal in dress and behavior to fit the offices he performed, they charged. He had officiated at the altar (so ran their complaint), with a colored handkerchief tied around his neck instead of a canonical band. In a dignified reply he denied the charge, declaring that he "never remembered wearing a speckled band", and that never, not even in the most "tempestuous weather", had he so much as buried an infant without wearing his band.[16] But this doubtless exaggerated charge was only one detail in the whole minor uproar, and when it became time to rebuild, a later Plains generation found the struggle too strong for continuance. They returned to the fold and became Congregationalists again. At least one wheel had come full circle.

And so the story runs on. Unlike most other village quarrels, the "where to set" controversy belongs to no specific period. It had a beginning but no end, perpetually breaking out anew as long as town and parish were one and all freemen were taxed for the support of church and minister. The duplication of this stormy tale is often so precise that except for names and dates a 1660 or 1670 account might be exchanged with one a hundred years later. Apparently one group of combatants learned nothing from their predecessors or even from their own previous battles. Were meetinghouses never peaceably erected? one may ask. Certainly, perhaps many of them, but peace called for brief record. It was the town clerk's business to record votes and nulling of votes, and in such totals trouble wins by many pages.

Let a record from Westford, Massachusetts, in 1763, balance the account. The town purchased a bell for twenty-seven pounds. One townsman went to fetch it. Ebenezer Stone, another townsman,

"in consideration of the Love and Good Will I bare on my mind to sd Town of Westford",

deeded a piece of land

"for a Bell-free to Ring Westford Meeting house bell on".

The town was pleased and grateful.

Ashael Wyman found the irons
Phinehas Hildreth laid the underpinning
Capt. Jabez Keep furnished "15 hundred of bords"
Benj. Carver a white pine tree
Abner Kent "an iron plate for the axel-tree"
Ebenezer Stone "nails and other things"
Joseph Boynton "claords"

James Dutton "477 feet of bords"

Thomas Comings Jr. "slit work and plank"

Timothy Underwood timber

The widow Thankful Chase "one crooked beam"

Joseph Dutton Jr. "for 4 days' works"

Capt. Samuel Fletcher "for work Nails and other Service"

Dea. John Abbot, Zechariah Hildreth, Amos Hildreth and Oliver Adams of Chelmsford "for work"

Capt. Jonas Prescott "for work planck & slitwork"

Henry Wright Jr. "for twenty eight days work"

Nathaniel Boynton "for work and stuf & painting and glazing and plastering 14 £ 10".[17]

The town honored Ebenezer Stone by making him the town Bell-ringer on a salary of one pound annually. One hopes that he felt rewarded and remained satisfied.

CHAPTER EIGHT

East Side — West Side

Comfort of a sort may derive from the fact that these many and various "Ruffles" over building a new meetinghouse are not all to be charged up to human contrariness as a first cause, or even to the devil. A number of them, including some of the most bitter, were caused by rivers. Obviously, no one was to blame. New settlers always seek out rivers, and as the settlement grows and spreads, the river presently divides them. All over New England this situation was multiplied: along the Charles, the Kennebec, the Connecticut, the Merrimac, and many other rivers. Original proprietors had usually taken up home lots on one side, meadow and pasture lots on the other. In time some of these first comers moved across, but more often it was their sons and daughters who began their adult lives on the opposite bank. For them the family relationship created a loyalty to the parent settlement. Newcomers, who had choice of either location, acknowledged no such loyalty. New interests developed. In time what had originally been one company, perforce became two.

Two companies but only one meetinghouse. Fifty-two Sundays in the year and more than half of them poor weather for crossing. For the tributary settlement with the meetinghouse in plain view, the river might as well have been a gulf. The homemade canoes, always over-crowded on Sundays, were a peril in all seasons, but when the current was swift and the river "broad-spreading" by reason of floods, they were sheer folly. Soon or late every river settlement wrote canoe tragedies into the record and usually they were Sunday tragedies. Yet for years these divided settlements struggled to maintain one minister and one meetinghouse.

The reason was chiefly financial. The parent settlement was unwilling to release the company across the river from its "Rates"; to do so would be to double their own quota in support of the minister to whom they were pledged. The tributary group chafed under the imposition of "Rates" in payment of benefits they were at such inconvenience to receive, or many times did not receive at all. They wanted to be independent both as a town and as a church. Worse still, their Sunday dilemma was acute. With a two-hour sermon both morning and afternoon on the one side, there were not enough daylight hours left for the minister to be ferried across to preach at some private house on the other side, although some ministers and some "other siders" tried this solution. The minister's "carrying fare" appears on various town books, adding one more argument to the protest of the tributary settlement. Even though they had been willing to pay it, however, not many clergymen were so hardy as James Wellman of Windsor, Vermont, who also served Cornish directly across the Connecticut River. In after times he was remembered for his liberal opinions, his willingness to lend his books, his record yields of maple sugar, and the fact that he often entered the pulpit dripping. No wonder, since transportation for him meant fording the river on horseback. Other equally bold but less hardy ones, "took wet" in such crossings and refused to continue.

The sense of deprivation of these across-the-river settlements was stronger than their resentment. They were not quarreling; rather pleading for a benefit without which life for them could not be happily lived. Over and over it is the same story; their successive petitions are eloquent of their extreme sense of need.

From the Bass River settlement in Beverly, Massachusetts, in 1667,

"the tediousness & difficulties over the water and other inconveniences";[1]

from the Oyster River people in Dover parish, New Hampshire, in 1669, "the intolerable inconvenience of our traveil many myles, part by land, part by water, manie tymes by both, to the public worship of God";[2]

from the Bath people on the west side of the Long Reach, Maine,

"a stretch of water—whereof the Ancient People, Women & Children can scarce Attend the Public Worship of God so necessary to their Wellbeing";[3]

from the Plainfield, Connecticut, people,

"a long labarynth of difficulties by reason of a tedious river" [the Quinebaug].[4]

From Hadley, Massachusetts, in 1667 come details that would fit them all:

"Sometimes we come in considerable numbers in rainy weather, and are forced to stay till we can empty our canoes, that are half full of water, and before we can get to the meeting-house, are wet to the skin. At other times, in winter seasons, we are forced to cut and work them out of the ice, till our shirts be wet upon our backs. At other times, the winds are high and waters rough, the current strong and the waters ready to swallow us—our vessels tossed up and down so that our women and children do screech, and are so affrighted that they are made unfit for ordinances, and cannot hear so as to profit by them, by reason of their anguish of spirit; and when they return, some of them are more fit for their beds than for family duties and God's services, which they ought to attend.

In brevity and verity our difficulties and dangers are to us extreme and intolerable; oftentimes some of us have fallen into the river through the ice. Sometimes we have been obliged to carry others when they have broken in.

There is about four score and ten persons on our side the river, that are capable of receiving good by ordinances, but it is seldom that above half of them can go. [We stay at home and "ward" by turns]. Further, . . . we leave our relatives and estates a prey to the heathen, when they see their opportunity. Yet, notwithstanding, our greatest anxiety and pressure of spirit is that the Sabbath, which should be kept by us holy unto the Lord, is spent with such unavoidable distractions, both of the mind and of the body."[5]

This plea was signed by twenty-five petitioners. They were answered in a document signed by forty-four of the east-siders, whose objection was that should they give consent to this separation, they should "sin against the Lord", because they had covenanted together as one body "forever". It was a case of forty-seven families against half the number, with the smaller group owning the larger share of land. One year later the west-siders were allowed separate preaching; two years later they "pitched upon a man", and in 1670 the town of Hatfield was incorporated. They had been luckier than most petitioners whose cases were analogous.

Immediate favorable action was all but unknown. Hence twice a year the petitioners in river towns renewed their plaint and twice more were denied, sometimes for three or four years or even fifteen. The importunateness of their pleas, as again and again they stated their reasons, pays a moving tribute not only to their zeal and persistence, but also to the reality of their concern for all that Sunday preaching meant in their lives. In the midst of Queen Anne's war, with Indian massacres almost at their very door and the nearest meetinghouse twelve miles away, a company at Dunstable, New Hampshire, could say of the Sunday privileges,

"after which Ark of God's presence our souls lament and the want of which, more than all other great hardships and hazards, doth discourage us, and threaten the ruin of this desirable plantation".[6]

The company at Lancaster, Massachusetts, in 1705, used these same Indian dangers as part of their argument for separate incorporation. Let us build the meetinghouse on the west or exposed side, they said, for if it is built on the east,

"the Enemy might come when the Inhabitants were att Meeting and destroy the whole Western part and secure the Bridge so that nobody should be able to resist them or Relieve ther Friends".[7]

Their fears were by no means groundless. Sometimes the enemy did come at preaching time, and the toll of little children and aged persons left defenceless under attack makes one of the grimmer and by no means infrequent pages in the pioneering story.

Even when there was no river to cross, division was sometimes urgent because of the distance between tributary and parent settlements. The inhabitants of Winthrop's Farms, Massachusetts, earnestly pleading to be "set off", gave as their reason the "unsupportable difficulties in attending constantly—as we desire to do".

> "In the extreme difficult seasons of heat and cold we were ready to say of the Sabbath, Behold what a weariness it is."[8]

The "west end" people of Newbury in 1693 requested the "pity and help" of the Council "to ease them of a burden of travel on God's day". Most of them lived four miles away, some six or seven. When they arrived after the long foot journey, the meetinghouse was too small for all of them to get in. When even this double grievance did not bring favorable action on their petition, they merely started on the long walk sooner, hoping to arrive in time to be at least within hearing distance of the sermon. The suggested picture of these weary "standees", crowding near the door in sun or rain, hoping to hear the Text "opened", the Doctrine defended and applied, and the Uses listed, before they faced the long walk home again, may look like a prose passage indeed, but read in the spirit of these importunate pleas for refreshment of soul on what was to them the day of days, it supplies more than one motif in that luminous epic of early American life which as yet no one has written.

For twenty years Shepaug (later Roxbury, Connecticut) went six miles on foot to preaching at the parent settlement of Woodstock, the men carrying guns. Then they petitioned for "Winter privileges", or separate preaching during the "difficult parts of the year". At first this meant four months, later six; and after twelve more years, incorporation as a separate society. In their thirty-two years of Sunday mileage some of the more faithful original members had walked across the continent several times.

If delay in such cases were meant to wear down resistance, exactly the opposite resulted. Tenacity was bred in the bone of these men and women and they would not be denied. It would be hard to find an "infant settlement" which ceased to renew their petition until they got what they were after; namely, "to be sett off as a Distink parish". Sometimes the bare record of this final triumph has an eloquence, even a romance that details would only weaken. Who would want to add a word to the item concerning the settlement at Killingly, Connecticut, "on the east side of a river commonly called Quinebaug, and bounded by the wilderness". When they were about to "raise" their first meetinghouse three years after the first settlers arrived, the town clerk wrote,

> "After the sills had been placed on their foundations every male person over twenty-one in the whole town seated themselves around on the sills and they just filled up the sills".[9]

The dimensions of the structure are not stated, but it is called *small*. So much the better for the suggested picture. The church had originally been gathered with eleven members.

The pioneer story of new towns, new meetinghouses, new beginnings, is not only the story of that which was less becoming greater, but of perpetual subdivision, whereby that which had become measurably safe and was even beginning to be prosperous, once again was divided. No sooner had a settlement around one Meetinghouse Hill learned to live together as a unit of hope and desire, than a little group, usually of their own sons and daughters, left it all behind and pushed off once more. Armed with axes, guns, and perhaps little else, they dared to put miles of forest or "a stretch of water" between themselves and the comfort of human companionship beyond their small circle. But "preaching" they must have, or life were not life.

CHAPTER NINE

"*Dooming the Seats*"

Oᴛʜᴇʀ battles were quickly brewing. No sooner had a town, new or old, accomplished the preliminaries and begun to build, than trouble broke out in another quarter. Once the raising had been accomplished and the new structure was beginning to assume the outlines of a building, the battle area merely shifted. How shall the "pew ground be parcelled out" was the next question. Where do we sit, perhaps for the rest of our lives? Where do our neighbors sit, and have they a right to sit there? Seating committees were duly appointed and went grimly to work, "lotting out" the space, receiving bids and making assignments according to dignity, age, estate, and "whatever else tends to make a man respectable". This was no matter of individual preference. It was a town affair, one of the touchiest on record. "Dooming the seats in any town as they shall continue for the future" was equivalent to issuing a new edition of the social register, and no matter how carefully any seating committee attempted to observe the "bester privilege" or "rule of proportion" as voted, they merely invited unpopularity up and down "the Street" for the rest of their natural lives.

Trouble arose not from pettiness or bumptious self-importance, although both were sometimes present, but from an honest desire "to seet the people orderly". The mistake was in the use of criteria not subject to precise measurement. Age could be ascertained. Estate was tangible. "Dignity" was not, except in military rank or office. "Whatever else makes a man respectable" was a veritable Slough of Despond to literal minded committee-men. Nevertheless, they did their best. Town Books attest their diligence and in so doing spell out a long, slow story of aristocratic privilege and a sense of democratic fairness jostling each other within an ironclad system hospitable to neither. During the early years the system itself appears never to have been challenged; merely the application of it in individual cases. Marvel it is that a laity, whom pioneer life had put on an equality of mutual need and dire peril, should not somewhere in this long story have seen the absurdity of running the whole community through a grading machine for Sunday purposes only. It would seem that one Seating Committee chairman with a broad sense of humor might have saved a hundred years of "uncomfortable Animosities", except that a society does not walk away from long-established customs so easily.

Any Town Book one may care to examine for the first generations shows that the system worked in the great majority of cases. At least men and women submitted to it through lifetimes, and Seating Committees likewise continued to take themselves as seriously as though they were Representatives to the General Court. The time consumed in the discharge of their duties is appalling, even when no complaints were registered. In 1662 the standing committee of elders, deacons, and selectmen which constituted the "constant and settled power" to regulate seating in Cambridge saw fit to put

"Mrs. Upham with her mother,
Ester Sparhawke, in the place where Mrs. Upham is removed from,
Joanna Winship, in the place where Ester Sparhawke was wont to sit,
Brother Ri. Jacksons wife . . . where sister Kempster was wont to sit,
Mary Lemon, where old sister Jackson was wont to sit,
Mr. Day, to sit in the 2d seat from the table,
Benjamin Crackbone, in the place where Richard Eccles was wont to sit,
Ens. Samuel Greene, to sit at the table,
Justinian Holden, to sit in the foremost seats,
Goode Gates [who was probably deaf], at the end of the Deacons seats".[1]

One may assume that they had good reason for each shift, and that each one was made only after due and serious deliberation. No appeals were heard from these assignments. This is a typical early entry of a routine sort.

Also typical are occasional cases of disobedience either from a sense of injustice or sometimes from mere obstreperousness. When Goodwife Randall of Newbury did not like her seat in 1667, and protested by sitting in the aisle, obstructing traffic, the selectmen thought to please her by assigning her to one "superior in dignity" on the west side of the meetinghouse and re-assigning her old seat to someone else. They miscalculated. Immediately her old seat became desirable to her and she crowded into it. When the pew door was shut against her, she climbed over, "it being four or five feet high". She was of course admonished for disorderly conduct in the meetinghouse, but the old Adam in her was not conquered. Her vocabulary of abuse merely improved under censure. Sometimes disobedience came wholesale. When a "Lentoo to the backside of the meetinghouse" in Marblehead had been built in 1672, those who had lost their seats by reason of "the new alley way through ye ould part" did not like their new assignments, and made such a stir that the selectmen finally decreed that those who did not sit where they belonged would pay a fine of "2/5 for *every* offence *every* Sabbath". In Milford, Connecticut, whoever "needlessly sat out of his seat" forfeited five shillings. Other towns imposed similar penalties in similar cases. Individual disobedience was always in full crop. When in 1714 Mrs. Mercy Marston of Salem "Removed Mrs. Osgood's Chair from the second seat and put her own in place of it", she received a stiff note of censure from the Town Clerk, "per order of the Selectmen", and was told to take notice of it at once, as her boldness was "Ill resented" by those who conformed to the usual order of seating. This was a preliminary warning. If she did not remove her chair at once, a fine would be imposed, and if it were not paid promptly, it would be increased. She probably complied, although by 1714 a sense of individual rights was stirring uncomfortably, and as the years passed, the Mercy Marstons would grow more numerous.

Had she seen fit to purchase a "handsome Velvet Cushin" for the pulpit Bible, her chances of favorable action might have improved. At least social elevation sometimes came as easily as that. When Madam Norton of Braintree presented the town with such a cushion in 1732, she was immediately rewarded by an invitation from the Seating Committee "to tak the upper end of the fore seet in the new Meeting-house". This was the seat of highest dignity in the Committee's power of gift. By the price of a cushion she had become an aristocrat, at least on Sunday. Otherwise, being a woman, she would have sat according to her husband's rate, even though she were better off financially than he. Ordinarily women sat on one side, men on the other. Wives fared better than "Ancient Maids" who along with "Ancient Bachelors" were usually assigned to the back seats on the side galleries. In some places wives were permitted to sit at the other end of their husbands' seats, but always in the same order as the husbands, so that wife matched husband or in Town Book phrase, "answerable thereto". Widows sat in a row by themselves; that is, transiently, for the personnel of this seat was always subject to quick change.

After the Seating Committee at Amesbury had used its "best judgment" in assigning "good wiffe Martyn to sett in the seat in the soweth west side of the metten house", her husband,

"Georg Martyn do enter his contry [contrary] desent [dissent] to the plasen of his wiffe in that seat".[2]

The designation "goodwiffe" meant humble rank, but even so her case would have received consideration, although higher rank would have foreordained such. When Major Johnson of Derby, Connecticut, was displeased with his assignment after the meetinghouse was enlarged, the town promptly voted that he should

"according to his desire, sit at the end of the pulpit in a short seat alone, and that the town be at suitable charge to make it handsome and convenient to entertain the Major honorably".[3]

They probably also gave him a cushion, for a military title was held in great esteem. A committee would wait on him to inform him of the town decision. Thus were things done "decently" and according to "Order". As late as 1759, the New Brick in Boston was inviting Lieutenant Governor Hutchinson "to set in the Fore Seat", and providing a cushion. When an assistant pastor was appointed in a parish, the town would take action to invite his wife "to sett in the Parsonage pew". The invitation would be conveyed by a committee in full numbers. Until thus formally invited, she waited, hopefully. Order was order.

Selectmen and Seating Committees were jealous of their powers in all this orderliness, however, and in punishing disobedience to it. They had no patience with any layman who took it upon himself to punish the intractables in his pew neighborhood. Certain young men of Newbury who broke into the meetinghouse and demolished a pew which had been built without permission were promptly punished by the town. The pew itself was reduced in dignity to a "common seat". Certain other young men were sentenced to be severely whipped and fined ten shillings apiece for demolishing a seat which several young women had been given permission to build "in the south corner of the women's gallery". Selectmen did not ask that piety be the motivation of such a request. Fourteen young women in Southbridge were favorably heard when they petitioned the town to let them build themselves a pew "where the hind seat is", because "the hind seat on the women's side is so low" that they could not see the new minister, Joshua Paine, who chanced to be young and comely. Besides, the other seats were "so full and crowded" [Joshua Paine no doubt being to blame] that it was "very uncomfortable sitting". In this case, youth, it would seem, won on both sides. Even so, there were limits. When certain young men of Hardwick, Massachusetts, built themselves a pleasant seat in the gallery on the women's side, the town took prompt action, but "Voted, that the same persons have liberty to build their seat on the men's side gallery".[4] Fortunately, there was no law as to eye direction during sermon time.

As unrest deepened in the 1720's and afterward, Seating Committees more and more took refuge in the tangible evidence of the account book. How much had a man contributed toward the new building? What was his "Rate" for the future? Was he eligible for pew space? If so, it was allotted accordingly. Inches counted. At Sutton,

Massachusetts, in 1723, when it was voted "that the Meeting House should be seated",

> Samuel Daggett got 5 feet front by 5.5 inches depth.
> Benjamin Willard, 5 ft. 2 by 5.4.
> Freegrace Marble, 4 ft. 10 by 5.6, "being on the south side of the front door".
> Isaac Farwell, 3 ft. 3 by 5.6.

Those not pleased "entered theire Decent" [Dissent]. The "pew ground" along the wall directly under the windows was usually given away, and with good reason, although the sturdy ones who dared sit there were still obliged to build their pews at their own expense. The "backer seats" were least in dignity and they went begging, except on special days. The common man's rights were growing increasingly important; but then as ever, no one wished to wear the label.

When it came to gaining permission to build a seat, all were on a level. Magistrates, deputies, even the minister had to ask the town's permission to enlarge their pews or build new ones as the family increased. In Braintree in 1697 William Rawson, Representative to the General Court, was granted the privilege of "making a seat for his familie between or upon the two beams over the pulpit, not darkening the pulpit". The result is hard to visualize. The family view from that elevation would probably have matched (in reverse) that from the "swallow's nest", or the seat over the gallery stairs, although the "dignity" of the pulpit position would have been far greater. In 1701, Moses Fiske, the new minister, was given permission, or rather "liberty to Build a Pew by the South-East window, in ye meeting house He leaving convenient passage".[5] Abraham Bishop and Stephen Bradley of Guilford, Connecticut, were permitted to "build a peu over the gallery stares, provided it haint a domieg [damage] to ye going up into ye gallerys".[6] If it had been a damage, they would have had short shrift. Action was taken against Joseph Fuller and John Burley of Ipswish in 1688 because they had built a pew which "hindered the light". They were promptly ordered to make a new window "at their owne charge", except for ten shillings out of the town rate, and to have it finished in fourteen days.

For a long time permissions, orders, punishments such as these, continued to be voted, and though unrest increased and sometimes reached troublesome proportions, the issues underneath it failed to declare themselves plainly. The inherited system remained the established order and selectmen merely stiffened their resistance to complaints against individual assignments or no assignments at all, for in spite of additions of all kinds or new meetinghouses there was never enough room for all. Because enlargement or rebuilding always meant re-seating, a crisis followed every such improvement. At Sunderland, Massachusetts, in 1736, a new "dignifying" of the seats brought such advance dissatisfaction that the town voted in what would seem to have been a fit of extreme exasperation, "that we will throw up all yt hath been done in seating the meeting house".[7] So saying, a new committee was appointed and a new basis for assignment agreed upon, this time "Two pound estate and one years age" were to be equal. The nine men, comprising the committee to achieve this result, stripped themselves for action and, as a first step toward what they hoped would be fairness, divided themselves into three groups: the three oldest by themselves, the middle-aged by themselves, and the three youngest likewise by themselves. Each group was to make "Locatings" separately, then to meet, compare results, and when agreed, to report their "Seatings" to the town to see whether they would approve. Unfortunately the record does not show how it all came out, but success to such a plan of action would hardly seem to have been foreordained.

So it continued for a century and a half and in some towns even longer. In almost the same words one despairing committee and then another, after all their months of work, had to see the majority in town meeting vote "To Intirely fling up and Set a Side the Seeting of our meeting hous", and start over once more. On the very eve of the Revolution and, in fact, during and after it, in some places committees were still at great pains to make the "bester privilege" work, estimating the fore seat beneath the pulpit equal in dignity with the front seat in the middle gallery, and deciding how many pound income were equal to one year of age. In the end the whole system would be swept away, nobody ever being able to tell how or precisely when. Like other more important amendments to an unofficial and unwritten constitution, it would be "flung up and set aside" without benefit of town vote. The experience of living would have rendered it obsolete.

CHAPTER TEN

Old Way—New Way

Unlike the "Where to Set", the "East Side—West Side", and seating controversies, the "Singing Quarrel" can be definitely dated. It hardly even simmered beforehand, but broke out explosively all at once in 1715. The immediate occasion was the publication of a sixpenny booklet written by a twenty-four-year-old minister-to-be of whom few except his Harvard tutors had ever heard. This tiny 3 by 5″ booklet had very soon initiated a widespread and violent controversy which reached its peak in the early twenties and then gradually faded out in favor of other front-page excitements. Trivial and benighted as this *fa-sol-la* battle appears to a modern judgment, it can hardly be passed over, not only because it was a sword in the fellowship, bringing schism in its wake, but because it underscored certain basic issues in group government which would soon go far beyond mere psalmody. Recalled in its more militant stages, it also holds the mirror up to a chapter of American experience when rural culture was at minus tide indeed.

The young author who set off this explosive charge was John Tufts of Medford, Massachusetts, a ministerial candidate with his Harvard degree behind him but as yet no settled pastorate ahead. His book was entitled *An Introduction to the Singing of Psalm-Tunes, in a Plain & Easy Method, With a Collection of Tunes in Three Parts*. In its first edition it included nine pages of instruction and twenty-eight tunes. Later editions raised this number to thirty-eight. There was also an Introductory Poem "On the Divine Use of Music". Everything in the book was wholly derivative, being taken with little change, poem and all, from an English Psalter published by John Playford thirty-eight years earlier, and another by Thomas Ravenscroft nearly a hundred years earlier,[1] but as neither Playford nor Ravenscroft was known in America in 1715, John Tufts' adaptation of their work had all the force of an original. His little *Introduction* was the first book of musical instruction to be printed in the colonies. As such it sounds innocent enough, but it soon proved to be far otherwise.

The elementary nature of these nine pages of instruction intended for adults makes the musical illiteracy of the day immediately apparent. He introduces *fa, sol, la, mi* as utter strangers, explaining in all but words of one syllable that their function is to show

> "the Distance of the Notes one from another, or to give you the true Pitch of every Note".

Sharps, Flats, "Cliffs", Repeats, and a few other musical terms are also briefly explained, as though for mere babes. Then follow a few Lessons to assist in "*Raising* or *Falling* of Notes, either Gradual or by Leaps". You may need help with these instructions, he says. Beginners ordinarily cannot attain the "Ground-work of all good Singing"

> "without the help of some skilful Person, or of an Instrument; But being attained, and observing the few foregoing Rules, you will be able to leap with your Voice from one Note to another, as they occur in their various Distances, and with a little Practice, to sing all the Tunes in this Book in any of their Parts, with Ease and Pleasure".[2]

As to the ease, no record; but as to the pleasure, the testimony of ten more editions of this little primer (five shillings per dozen) and a tide of interest which could not be stopped. In partial sequel, singing took its place among the arts, and psalmody, according to the "Usual Way", was doomed. But not if the Old Guard could help it.

Details of the current practice of psalmody which this little book interrupted are all but incredible to later generations. To sing the Old Way, or as its adherents chose to call it, "the Usual Way", was to sing without regard to the time and pitch of anyone else. One merely "took the Run of the Tune", as the saying was, and then added "little Flourishes" of one's own according to one's own vocal talents and the inspiration of the moment, clipping some notes or hanging on to them, singing some "too *high*, others too *low*, and most too *long*", performing "little Slidings and Purrings, raisings and lowerings" as the heart inclined. Thereby was the singing made individual and thereby was the Lord pleased. Naturally, on such a course no one came out at the same time as anyone else. While the singer in one pew was continuing to intone line three, possibly taking two breaths to one note, his neighbor in the next pew was halfway through line four and charging along to the finish. "Indecent jargon" resulted. In Thomas Walter's purposely exaggerated verdict, "In the Ears of a good Judge", it sounds "like five hundred different tunes roared out at the same time".[3] Increase Mather called it an "Odd Noise". No wonder.

More than mere inertia and ignorant conservatism lay back of the Old Guard's unwillingness to be instructed otherwise. As these oldsters saw it, to sing the "New Way" was to strip praise of all flavor of individuality and to return to the formalism from which Luther had delivered them. Sung "regularly", the Psalm would be a mere ceremony, without unction, without inspiration of divine grace. "The Papists do so", they said, and thought to close the argument. In so far as the battle concerned singing for its own sake, this phrase, so often used by the opposition, supplies the main motive for the whole uproar and the violence of it. Essentially the same issue lay underneath the "dumb reading" controversy, which concerned the pulpit reading of the Scriptures with or without the line by line annotation and explication. At root both quarrels were of course the old ritualistic battle in more modern dress, only grown narrower, fiercer, and now being fought with provincial weapons. Away with all innovations, said the Old Guard. The Old Way is best. It is also safer. As these rural combatants did not know, they fought a battle that had been won long before.

To the ever restless "young people" of the congregation fear of "Papacy" was a dead issue. They had had no part in fighting the ritualistic battle and they were not interested. Their eyes were forward. What is new in the world? Tell us about it, they said, as this new skirmish in the perennial warfare of the generations broke out in their neighborhood. Fortunately for them, the first leaders of the New Way were young men themselves and as such they captured first the curiosity and then the eager interest of the younger members of the congregation, to whom on first report the New Way seemed truly marvelous. To sing "by Rule", they were told, was to come out at the same place and at the same time as their neighbors. More marvellous still, when sung the New Way, the same tune sounded the same, though sung by different congregations who had never heard each other sing. How could such things be?

Ignorance of course provided a fertile soil both for the stubborn adherence to the old and for this eager sense of marvel at the new, and around the beginning of the century ignorance was plentiful. The general level of culture in the colonies was lower than it had been at any time since the founding and lower than it has ever been since. In most back country towns, "school keeping" was irregular, sometimes lasting only a few weeks in the year. "Hundreds of children in a Town, & scandalous neglects of them, *perhaps not a Tenth of them taught at Schools all the year long*", was John Danforth's accusation in a sermon of 1704. As a result, most children could "rede, right, and sypher" to some degree, but that was about all. Many adults could neither read nor write and merely made their mark by way of signature. As to music, the level of literacy was zero. Not, however, because music was disapproved. Contrary to a widespread modern notion Puritans on any social level were hospitable to music; and from the first settlements forward singing had a fairly large place in colonial life. There was daily singing of psalms in many homes and much enjoyment of it. In taverns and among the "ungodly" in other centers there were ballads and secular songs of many other sorts, frowned upon because they were secular, not because they were songs. But that there was anything to learn about music, least of all that music had laws, few rural singers would have guessed.

Sixty or seventy years earlier it had been far different, even on the frontiers. The "singing quarrel" would not have been possible during the lifetime of the first generation. However untrained musically, these first comers were familiar with psalmody conformable to literate standards, and however skeptical they may have been as to formal praise, in general they were not ignorant as to the "regularity" of music. In the earliest days music had been a subject of study at Harvard, and young ministers had gone to their first parishes with at least a modicum of knowledge with which to check the slovenly practices which presently prevailed in remote settlements. No doubt some of these young men had tried to reform the psalmody of their congregations, only to find themselves helpless against the ignorance and prejudice they encountered. Unchecked, the slovenliness increased; perhaps also the minister's hopelessness as to changing it. A few older men, "ripening for heaven", had lamented the sad decay of congregational singing. "I am of opinion that the singing of psalms in harmony is too much neglected",[4] John Higginson wrote as Counsel No. Seven of his *Dying Testimony* in 1708, but only a few of his fellow-octogenarians were listening to such plaints. It was already a new day and a very different one. Younger ministers had their quota of new problems.

Besides, leading the singing was the deacon's business, not the minister's, and few country deacons had been to Harvard. They were mostly older men, tenacious of their prerogatives and prideful of their very special dignities. "Lining out" the psalm called for very special talents. Other laymen might "guard the treasure" deposited in the collection box, provide the sacramental elements, listen to "Relations", but only a man with a "big and taking voice" and the courage to let it out could be elected a deacon. The method of his great moment on Sunday morning is an old story. When it came time for the psalm, he arose from his prominent front seat, directly under the pulpit, "set the tune", and then intoned the psalm line by line. The congregation sang it after him. Sometimes he sang one line and they repeated it after him. Sometimes he read two lines, sang the first, and they replied with the second. Sometimes he sang the whole line, and they repeated the second half as a refrain. Sometimes he sang each line in turn through the stanza and they replied only with the first, used throughout as a refrain. There were various other ways, all of them based on the principle of response, as in the early Christian practice or the earlier practice of the synagogue. The result need not have been "indecent"; quite the contrary. The method was shaped for tunefulness; only the ignorance prevented.

The deacon himself was not wholly to blame for what had happened. Even though he had been musically trained, his was a hard assignment. He had no instrument, not even a pitch pipe; only a psalm book, presumably a good ear, and confidence in his powers. Samuel Sewall, who had some skill in singing, more than once confessed his humiliation when he aimed at one tune and hit another. Once he wrote that he "intended Windsor, and fell into High-Dutch", and again that he "Try'd to set Low-Dutch Tune and fail'd. Try'd again and fell into the tune of the 119th Psalm".[5] At least he knew when he had failed, as other deacons who likewise set great store by their deaconing often did not. They introduced their own "Turns and Quavers", their "Little Flourishes of the Voice", their "Slidings and Purrings", thus licensing similar variations down the aisle. The congregation picked up where the deacon left off, sliding and purring their way along, each singer advancing on his own speed and no two men "quavering" alike. The congregation was seated, complaisant, relaxed, each worshipper adrift on his own musical sea. The deacon, in semi-control only, was adrift on his. He did not really lead and they did not really follow; he merely blazed the trail, but they were helpless without him. When the deacon was absent, there could be no psalmody. Forgivably enough, he felt his importance and let out all the voice he had to prove it. Those who had elected him did likewise. Who could doubt that a modern recording of their joint adventure would deserve to be called an "*Ungrateful Jarr* in the Ears of those who can well *distinguish Sounds*". Those who could not well distinguish them were having a thoroughly good time, and whoever disturbed them in their complacent enjoyment would get no thanks for his pains.

John Tufts' little volume of dynamite set things going and quickly. The "Usual Way of Singing" would henceforth be a decision in every parish, not an unthinking perpetuation. As soon as his book was in print, he began to give personal emphasis to the new pleasures it promised by taking the stump in their defence. He first chose the

Greater Boston Area, travelling between Sabbaths from town to town and giving what soon came to be called a "Singing Lecture". His brother ministers, young and old, were almost solidly behind him. They too began to give Singing Lectures. Singing masters all at once landed from every ship as though by prearrangement. They put their qualifications in the Boston newspapers and were on hand to organize singing-schools in the wake of the lectures. Town by town, they were met by eager, if incredulous enthusiasm by the young people, and by stern reproach of foregone dissent from their elders. Music, pro and con, became the talk of the town—every town.

As might be expected, the Singing Lecture was really a sermon with a Text, a Doctrine, all the usual paraphernalia of proof by Scripture authority and examples—Reasons, Objections, Answers to Objections, and Application. The laity of the early eighteenth century could not have been expected to adopt such an innovation as the New Way merely as a melodious "concord of sweet sounds"; less still as a pleasant pastime. From long habit they must first face the doctrine underneath it, examine the scripture evidences in their own Bibles, and then either join the singing classes or join the opposition. Patiently the ministers in the campaign attempted to match remonstrance with biblical precept and example, in the hope of effecting a peaceful transition from the old to the new, adding also reasons dictated by good sense. Always their intent was to persuade, not to criticise. But peace was too much to hope for. This was a revolution, and as rural parishes became aware what was going on, every Singing Lecture became a call to arms, every lecturer an invader and disturber of the peace. "These that have turned the world upside down are come here also" (*Acts* 17, 6) was Josiah Dwight's text for a Singing Lecture at Framingham in 1725.[6] He could not have searched his Bible for a better one to serve also as a rural news item at that hour.

"Polite Boston", blessed with many more of these preachments than rural towns, made the transition from the Old to the New for the most part peaceably, and became thereby a bright example for the lecturer's use in country places. Self-styled Philomusicus Thomas Symmes, an early evangelist in this crusade, replied to the objection,

"There are many speak against it",

by saying, Certainly, but not everywhere.

"It is not so, at *Boston* (that I can learn) nor at *Cambridge*, where People have as much Ability & Opportunity surely, to know What's what, as at *our Town*, and some others in the Country."[7]

Even in the dark, fearful days of 1721–22, with the smallpox raging and soldiers being recruited for a new outbreak of the "Eastern Indians", the new way of singing shared space in the *New England Courant* with the "New Way of Receiving the Small-Pox", and abuse for the inoculators was not more extravagant than for the singing masters and those who aided and abetted them. For a brief time only the *Society for Promoting Regular and Good Singing and for Reforming the Depravations and Debasements our Psalmody labors under* abandoned their weekly meetings in the interest of public safety, but only briefly. A notice in the *Courant* for December 18, 1721, announces that since Boston is now "almost free from Infection", there will be a meeting on Thursday evening next

"to consider whether it may not be proper to begin their Weekly Meetings, for Improvement in this delightful and heavenly Exercise".

Thomas Walter's Singing Lecture preached before this society on March 1, 1722, presents music precisely as this epithet describes it. He called the sermon *The Sweet Psalmist of Israel*. It was a young man's sermon, disarmingly so. Delivered in a hospitable atmosphere and before those already convinced that music in its very nature is "sweet and pleasant", the young preacher let himself go in its praise. Even birds, "those Idle Musicians of the Spring", please us by their singing, he said. Why is this so, and for a minute he permitted himself a little "wading in the depths of *Philosophy*" to explain what happens in the striking of a chord. But he caught himself in time and proceeded to the music of David, with incidental rhapsodizing as to the nature of music considered, as he said, theologically. He attempted to prove that

"Music is congenial to the soul;—

It creates a most blessed Serenity and quiet Calm in the Soul of the Worshipper;—

It is of good use to suspend and cure the evil and malign Influences of Satan on the Soul;—

It serves to fix the Mind upon religious Objects;—

Our Prayers are sweetly and gloriously conveyed to Heaven in the Chariot of Music and Praise;—

It collects the scattered Powers of the Mind, and so unites them, that the Soul . . . mounts as on the *Wings of Eagles,* . . . is raised and transported beyond the Limits of Time and Sense, and is seated in the Lap of Eternity;—

The Church of Angels looks down and rejoices at our efforts to imitate their *Hallelujahs* and bring them as near as possible to the same heavenly Perfection;—

What a pity and what a shame is it to abuse so sweet and heavenly an Art". [8]

Those before him had no disposition to abuse it; and thanks to their weekly meetings over many months, many among them had already attained to considerable skill in three-part singing. Every Singing Lecture concluded with a performance which added new aspirants to the singing classes. Press notices speak of sixty, ninety, or more than a hundred singers who performed on these occasions in Boston and in some smaller towns as well. Of the performance following Cotton Mather's sermon on March 5, 1722, the *Courant* reported that the singing had been performed "to the great Satisfaction of a Numerous Assembly there present". A year earlier Samuel Sewall had made note of Cotton Mather's Singing Lecture preached "in the School-House to the young Musicians" from what would seem to be a most unfortunate text,

"And no man could learn that Song" (*Revelation* 14, 3).

"House was full", says Sewall, "and the Singing extraordinarily Excellent, such as has hardly been heard before in Boston".[9] The adjective *excellent* frequently appears also in press notices of these occasions.

But in many rural parishes it was a different story. Looking back three years, Cotton Mather wrote to Thomas Hollis in 1723,

"Numbers of Elder and Angry People, bore zelous Testimonies against these wicked Innovations, and this bringing in of Popery. Their zeal transported some of them so far that they would not only use the most opprobrious terms and call the Singing of these Christians a worshipping of the Devil, but also they would run out of the Meetinghouse at the Beginning of the Exercise".[10]

Other opposers kept their seats and either refused to open their mouths in praise at all or tried to drown out the unholy din by a greater din of their own. On one Barnstable occasion the civil authority had to be called in "to detect and bear testimony against such iniquity".

Young people, on the other hand, flocked into the singing classes. Parental authority was defied. True to prophecies of their elder opposers, some of these younger ones became "airy", even "light and prophane" while they were learning the new tunes in the evenings, but they were enjoying themselves and bringing their new knowledge and their exhilaration to the Sunday "exercises". Women, who in many congregations had never been allowed to sing, now moved into the liberated zone. You have pleasanter voices than the men, the singing lecturer had told them. God means for you to use them. Deborah and Miriam sang. Why not you? How will you answer to God if you do not use this gift He has given you? Deacons were discomfited. Lining out was not what it used to be. Those who continued to lead by unction of divine grace, and never mind the *fa-sol-la* of it, sometimes found themselves drowned out. Occasionally a deacon retired in tears. Others who refused to be defeated by the younger generation replied by letting out all the voice they had. Jargon worse than ever resulted.

One such episode at South Braintree, Massachusetts, got front-page prominence in the *Courant* for August 12, 1723. The "hand of the Devil" was in it, says the bewildered reporter, who appeals to *Janus* for guidance.

"No sooner was the Psalm set, than the bawling Party made such a hideous Noise, that the Minister forbid the Deacon reading any farther, upon which they carried on their Noise without reading, whereupon the Minister solemnly charged them to forbear; but notwithstanding they persisted in their Disturbance (with unaccountable Yells) to the End of the Psalm."

The reason for this Braintree violence of opposition owed much to the attitude of the pastor, Samuel Niles, who was one of the very few ministerial opponents of the New Way. He had previously forbidden its use in his congregation, had suspended the members who practiced it, and had informed his congregation that he would not even come to the meetinghouse to preach to them unless they would promise to cease all New Way practice. They would not promise; whereupon he preached at home to his fellow-opposers, and the New Way adherents listened to a sermon read to them by the deacon. Several Church Councils endeavored to deal with this two-way stubbornness. They restored the suspended members and ordered the church to sing alternately by New and Old method, but so early as 1723 peace would not come by such a compromise. Six months later Samuel Niles' adherents seceded even from their secession, broke away and publicly declared for the Church of England, a threat they presently found it too difficult to carry out. Braintree's drama of resistance was more stubborn and sensational than most, but only in the violence of it, as any one of the many pamphlets which memorialize this warfare makes clear enough.

Thomas Symmes of Bradford, Massachusetts, had gotten to the printing house first with a Singing Lecture of 1720. He called it

"The Reasonableness of, Regular Singing, or, Singing by Note, in an Essay, to Revive the True and Ancient Mode of Singing Psalm-Tunes, according to the Pattern in Our New-England Psalm-Books, the Knowledge and Practice of which is greatly decay'd in most Congregations. Writ by a Minister of the Gospel, Perused by Several Ministers in the Town and Country; and Published with the Approbation of all who have Read it".

This cumbersome title is a true labelling of what follows. The whole New Way doctrine is here, and all from the point of view of *reasonableness*. After an elaborate introduction he announced his particular purpose as an attempt to set forth the case for "Decent, Regular Singing

> in the plainest, most easy and popular Way I can, (for 'tis for the sake of common People I write) to shew, That *Singing by or according to Note*, is to be preferred to the *Usual Way of Singing*, which may be evidenced by several *Arguments*".[11]

1. It is older. Singing by note was known and approved by the first settlers of New England. It was studied and known in "our College, for many Years after its first Founding". Else, why are there notes in our New England Psalm Book?

> "There are many Persons of Credit now Living, Children and Grand-Children of the *first Settlers* of *New-England*, who can remember, that their Ancestors sang by *Note*."[12]

The proof is that they can still do it. Why then was it changed? Because "*Singing-Schools* and *Singing-Books* being laid aside, there was no Way to learn". The change came too gradually to be noticed. Deacons added little Turns and Flourishes of their own, and in fifty or sixty years there had been a great change. It had not been intentional.

2. Regular Singing is more melodious. "Who made *your* Ear a Judge of the Controversy?" You are used to the "Common Way of Singing". Want of skill in Regular Singing makes the Usual way "seem more delightful". Meditate on Solomon's sentence, *Proverbs* 18, 13, "He that answereth a matter before he heareth it, it is folly and shame unto him".

3. Regular Singing is more rational. Singing is as truly an "Art or Science, as Arithmetic, Geometry, &c."

> "There is a Reason to be given why each *Note* in a *Tune* is placed where it is, and *why* and *where* every *Turn* of the Voice should be made. . . . God is a God of Order. In all Things God deals with us as with *Rational Creatures*."[13]

By following your own bent, you bring confusion and disorder into what God meant should be orderly. He does not like confusion.

"Singers by *Rote* have little else to guide them but their *Fancy*. Their Pretended Rules are only *imaginary*."[14]

4. Regular Singing is more agreeable to Scripture. There was a Singing-Master in I *Chronicles* 15, 22, 27,

> "And Chenaniah, Chief of the Levites, was for song: he instructed about the song, because he was skillful".

Psalms 33, 3, says "Play skillfully"; there is as much reason to sing skillfully.

Then came the best argument, born of the best reason. Regular Singing "most nearly resembles the Singing which will be the Employment of Saints and Angels in the *Heavenly World*".[15] We shall sing in heaven. We had better get ready to do it decently.

Don't be discouraged. Anyone can learn. Some "upwards of Forty Years of Age" have learned.

> "If all in this *Province*, who can never learn one *Tune* in the *Usual Way*, would industriously apply themselves to learn to Sing by *Note*, and in order to that, furnish themselves with *Singing-Books*, and go to a *Skillful Singer* for Instructions, it is tho't by a very moderate Computation, that in one Years Time, more than *Ten Thousand* Persons might learn to Sing *Psalm Tunes* with Considerable *Skill* and *Exactness;* and of the *Rising Generation*, Yearly more than a Thousand."

This would be no small result, for then all Congregations would sing alike. Suppose you were to take two or three evenings a week, from five or six to eight, "Would not this be an innocent and profitable *Recreation?*"[16] Regular Singing would "banish *Pernicious Songs and Ballads and all* such *Trash*" from young people's minds.

"All in this Province" were by no means immediately convinced, however, not even as more Singing Lectures and more pamphlets setting forth the reasons for reform carried the battle to nearly every parish in the colonies. In 1721 Thomas Walter printed his *Grounds and Rules of Music Explained*, the preface signed by fourteen ministers. Cotton Mather's *The Accomplished Singer* appeared in the same year. In 1723 Samuel Danforth asked and answered sundry helpful questions in his *Cases of Conscience Concerning the Singing of Psalms*.

Question 16 read,

> "Is it possible for Fathers of forty years old and upward to learn to sing by Rule?"[17]

The answer was that it had been known to happen.

Other publications followed in rapid sequence. As late as 1728 Nathaniel Chauncy entitled his sermon preached before a ministerial association at Hartford,

> *Regular Singing Defended, and Proved to be the Only True Way of Singing the Songs of the Lord.*

This was thirteen years after it had all started and yet defence was still necessary. Singing not by Rule is "a flat Drink", he said, as compared to that which is "lively, brisk and full of Spirit". The most sprightly sentence in this sermon probably put more than one deacon in a rage. It read,

> "As Old Men are not always wise, so Young Men are not always Fools. They are generally more free from Prejudices than elderly People; their present Age disposes them to Mirth, and it should be a very Joyful and Acceptable thing unto Elderly People to see them forward to improve their Mirth according to Scripture directions".[18]

More easily said than complied with. This was a battle of the generations, and the oldsters not only were uncompromising in their opposition, but had reasons for the faith that was in them.

"Is it equal", they said, "that the Elderly be turned out of the Old Way of Singing to gratify the Youngerly who urge on the Regulation the most?" Perhaps not, but so it was; and in the end "turned out" they were.

The most revealing array of counter-arguments appears in Thomas Symmes *Utile Dulci or a Joco-Serious Dialogue concerning Regular*

Singing which appeared in 1723. The disputants are a minister who is *pro*, and a layman who is *anti*. If the prefatory statement of the author may be believed, he began to write this gay piece after noon on one day and finished it before noon on the day following, "without one tho't of its ever being thus Exposed to the publick view". It was worth better pains, although with all its marks of haste and carelessness it has a directness the singing sermons often lack, and because it spoke the language of a "common" layman, it may have reached his ear more successfully. The light touches help, although as a whole the piece is more *serious* than *joco*, doubtless intentionally. The doubting layman is listened to respectfully, allowed to talk back, and given a man to man answer to each of his very real objections. He could hear the sound of his own voice in each of them.

> This is a new-fangled way of singing, and in a language we do not understand.
> We don't like the sound of it. The old way is more melodious.
> There are so many tunes, we shall never have done learning them.
> The New Way "Roils and Exasperates men's Spirits". It "grieves good people" and causes them to act "unmannerly".
> The next thing will be instrumental music in the meetinghouse.
> *Fa-Sol-La* are "bawdy, yea, Blasphemous names".
> Our fathers got to heaven without knowing the New Way.
> Singing Teachers just want the money.
> Learning the New Way takes too much time and keeps young people out nights.
> Young upstarts fall in with it, "loose and lewd persons".

This was quite a battery of objections to face, but Thomas Symmes was undaunted. To him the whole controversy was "Ridiculous and Groundless", but he proceeded to say something to each of his hypothetical opponent's reasons; answering grave objections gravely, conscientious ones softly, and untoward ones with more "smartness". There are a few bright moments.

We have to learn to sing. Certainly.

> "We don't come *Singing*, but *Crying* into the World."
> "Men don't Sing as *naturally*, as *Pigs Squeak*, or Children Cry."[19]

Some object that Regular Singing is too easy.

"Surely no man need go Seven years to College to know how to answer this."[20]

Some object that it is too hard.

Well, "I'll leave you to reconcile 'em, or e'n let 'em fight it out".

To the objection that some elderly people can't learn, he replies that God does not expect it of them.

That instrumental music will surely follow if regular singing is adopted wins this jibe,

"I'll give you an unanswerable argument, that may put you out of all pain about it. . . . *It's* too *Chargeable* a piece of worship ever to obtain amongst us; and you may depend upon it, that such as are not willing to be at the cost of a Bell, to call the People together on the Lord's Day, will never be so *Extravagant* as to lay out their Cash (especially, now Mony is so scarce), to buy *Organs*, and pay an *Artist* for playing on 'em".[21]

And so on down the list, making each argument ridiculous in its turn.
The most significant remark in this colloquial dialogue comes at what was probably the touchiest point in the whole controversy, namely, the pastor's right to set a tune the New Way without a *Vote* of the church members, authorizing the change.

"Here you *Blunder* most miserably, and are *ignorant* of your own *Principles*",

he said; and then quoting the Cambridge Platform as to the range of congregational power, he added, Why Vote? Sing or not, as you like, for

"*Every one* in the Congregation has as much Liberty to Sing, as the *Oldest Deacon* in the Church, and as good a Right to decide this Question".[22]

All over New England congregations proceeded to do so.

Sometimes the opposing majority walked out and formed a new congregation where they might sing as they pleased. Sometimes it was the minority that seceded. Usually both sides stayed; and when they tired of their own competitive noise in psalm time, they presently compromised though reluctantly and, later still, were pleased with the change. By 1730 the battle was over in most places. Town votes from many places show the same pattern of surrender.

Barnstable voted in December, 1726, "yt we sing half a year in ye method called ye old way, the other in ye regular. In ye Old Way Bro Bodfish to sett the Psalm". Apparently he had rough going, for the record as of July, 1727, reads, "During this half year while we sang in ye old way the singing was very broken & confused Bro Bodfish setting ye Psalm". In 1729 they called a council and voted "to sit down satisfyd by the result". Beverly, Massachusetts, voted April 16, 1730, "to keep on singing the *Old* way". On July 3, "to sing by note the New Way *once* each Lord's Day; *once* Fast Day and Thanksgiving Day". Oct. 28, 1731, "to switch to *New* Way". One Connecticut congregation voted to sing half the time one way and half the other for a year, "or as much longer as the Pastor shall think there are five more voters for one way, than the other".

In Southbury, Connecticut, in 1734,

> "Voted and agreed, that we will continue to Sing the praises of God in the public worship on the Sabbath, in the common way wherein we have hitherto gone on, Leaving everyone to their liberty of learning or not learning to Sing the Regular way, and that when persons have generally Learned to sing by Rule, yet that way of Singing shall not be introduced into the Congregation here, but upon farther agreement and in an orderly way. Voted and agreed that he who Setts the psalm shall be at his Liberty what tunes to Sing on Lecture days".[23]

The phrasing of a late vote (1747) in Stamford, Connecticut, likewise spells progress in group living.

> "Voted yt Mr. Jona. Bell or any other man a greed upon to sing or tune ye salm in his absence in times of public worship may tune it in ye old way or new which suits you best."[24]

In its own hour this long drawn out and seemingly petty contest had decided more than itself. For the thinking majority it marked a distinct terminus in the inherited ritualistic battle. The "dumb reading" controversy would still break out sporadically, but it would fail to catch the imagination or be fought with the passion or interest of the singing quarrel. There would still be singing troubles—plenty of them. Congregations would still have to weather many months of anguished discussion as to whether or not to adopt the Tate and Brady edition of the *Psalms,* and later, whether or not to permit the singing of the hymns of Isaac Watts in place of the traditional psalmody. The opposition would retire from the house rather than hear "the words of the Devil". Later still, it would be whether or not to permit a bass viol to assist the chorister, there being no bass viol mentioned in the Scriptures. To fiddle the Psalm or not to fiddle it would raise tempests and bring on earthquakes, but no new fundamental issues would be involved.

Even in "polite Boston" instrumental music was accepted slowly. In 1711 Thomas Brattle, a wealthy Boston layman, brother of William Brattle, minister in Cambridge, imported an organ and installed it in his own home. When he died two years later, he bequeathed it to Brattle Street Church, if they would accept it, but they refused. 1713 was still to early for such boldness. King's Chapel dared take the risk, because by Thomas Brattle's will provision had been made for "a sober person that can play skillfully thereon with a loud noise". Boston gradually got used to the idea. Even as late as 1800, however, a census of New England church organs would still show scarce a score. There was no Bible authority for such an innovation. In many rural parishes the "devil's fiddle" was taboo until well after the Revolution, but the New Way of singing had prepared the way and given it a fighting chance. "Catgut churches" would survive the obloquy they invited.

Singing by note also gave birth to choirs, thereby inviting a thousand strifes. Choirs would secede because they were not seated as they thought their importance warranted. Town meetings would be convened; voters would disagree and more meetings be convened in the stormy effort to decide whether the singers shall "Set in ye

seat behind the Deacons, . . . in the hindmost seats on the men's side
. . . or in the same seats on the women's side". It took thirteen years of
strain, including most of the Revolution years, for the Hingham
choristers to achieve "Liberty to set in the front Gallery where it best
suited them". The "Singing Seats", wherever finally designated, would
usually take more voting time than any other square feet in the meetinghouse, or for that matter in the whole town; and when finally
voted, not even all of the singers would be pleased.

Sometimes there would be rival choirs, each one bursting into the
hymn at the same split second, only it would be a different hymn. All
this was the singing quarrel with a difference. It was no longer a
matter of the notes and whether or not to obey them. It was a matter
of *rights* and the proper recognition of them. Those who had been
"at cost and pains to learn themselves to sing" were entitled to something and they would fight for it. The "great Mr. Locke's *natural
rights theory*" would one day bear strange crops.

All of these minor upheavals in the area of the "singing seats", and
far hence the "great stove war", would keep the meetinghouse in a
state of siege for months together. As to stoves, there would be much
to decide. Whether to have a stove at all and why. Who should sit
nearest to it and why. What of the rights of those whose assigned
seats were not so comfortably near? Worse still, what of the rights of
those in direct line of the "black drip" from the moist pipe extending
diagonally the length of the building? All this would be settled by
many meetings and more argument. The price of even remote warmth
on Sunday would be strife. Life had been simpler when the water
froze in the baptismal bowl and a huddled congregation shivered together in the wind-ridden little building on the hill. But the days of
simplicity would then be long past and no one would wish them back.
Before that time also congregations would have accepted the principle
of majority rule and would either abide by it or go elsewhere. In the
New Way contest of the 1720's majority rule was still on trial. It was
making its way slowly and under great protest, but the time was already past, when as was once reported of a far earlier day,

"In case there should any difference arise (. . . all not being able to see alike) then such as dissent from the Brethren . . ."

are duly heard and answered, but if they are not convinced, and refuse to yield,

"It is either through the *weaknesse of their judgment*, or the *stiffnesse of their will*; if the former . . . the rest lovingly inform them and patiently beare with them till things be in some sort cleered up; that they are content wholly to submit and make no further trouble, . . . but if stiffnesse of will plainly appeare, the liberty of their voyce is taken from them, till they have removed the offence".[26]

In these intra-mural contests of the 1720's men differed in both ways, but it was already far too late in the story of things American for anyone to think that differences could be settled by taking away the "liberty of their voyce" from the opposers, whatever the issue. Furthermore, when battles ceased, much that was good would cease with them, but in the 1720's that time was not yet.

Viewed in series, these several battles and others like them, which look so much alike to later times, and were so fiercely individual to those who fought them, assume a pattern which clarifies a long process of social change. They were incidents in a long panorama of unrest, single skirmishes in several major campaigns, milestones, marking trial and error in the long, slow movement toward self-determination and self-government. The rule of the people in its earlier stages is a fumbling business, and the simplest procedures are not simple at all.

The vehemence, even passion, with which this process slowly established its direction is also neither surprising nor discreditable. The fellowship of the New England saints had been born of Dissent and naturally enough the dissenting spirit persisted. That protest should occasionally concern itself with trivia as well as with fundamental issues was inevitable. A town of forty or fifty families was a small world, and there were those who from birth to death did not go so far as to the next town. Life wore upon life. Protest became a habit of mind and exercised itself with objects great and small as occasion offered. Moreover, the fact that congregations had been gathered in the detective spirit helped to keep them perpetually on the alert, ready at a hair's breadth provocation to take the offensive against their fellow-members as well as against false doctrine or unholy practice. Militancy was an attitude they all understood and for which they made no apology. Except in pastoral eyes it carried with it no sense of unworthiness. They quarreled openly and unashamed, airing their complaints in public with amazing unrestraint. If a deacon had used "irreverend speech" or punctuated his dissent with a broken bench at Town Meeting on Monday, he took his front seat as usual on the following Sunday and, at the proper minute, rose and "deaconed" out the hymn. Why not?

Viewed at long range, these village upheavals do not tell an ugly story. There was life and energy in the insurgent spirit. Belief was vital, thought was active and conviction strong. Everything that concerned the meetinghouse mattered and mattered intensely. Moreover, as the embattled saints (and sinners) lined up against one another time after time, they were deciding far more than the immediate issue before the meeting. There is hardly one of these seemingly trivial village tempests which does not in some way illuminate the long slow process of adaptation and compromise by which a transplanted institution struck roots into a new soil and began to grow and branch independently. In human terms this is seldom a quiet process. It would also take time; generations of time. It had been one thing for a long-forgotten balladist to sing,

"We hope to plant a nation, where none before hath stood";[26]

it was quite another to lay the foundations stone by stone. It was also one thing for a prayerful company just off the boat to covenant together as a "desirable company of the faithful"; it was quite another to live together amicably around the town pump. Perhaps the occasional vote to expunge from the Church Book "our late difference, as not suitable for record", shows that they were on their way.

BOOK FOUR

RULE OF THE "LORD BRETHREN"

CHAPTER ELEVEN

"The Brotherly Watch of Fellow-Members"

WHILE the long, slow lesson of majority rule was being learned in one series of situations around Meetinghouse Hill, the sense of individual rights was becoming more strongly articulate in others. As is not surprising, the most militant expression of these rights often came from the covenant members of the congregation, who by their initial vows had in a sense relinquished these rights, or at least made them secondary to group agreement. In all matters of private conduct each member had willingly at his admission made himself subject to "holy watching" by all his fellow-members.

To the founders of the early church societies, single-minded in their zeal for "holy walking", to be thus "watched" by their fellow-Christians was a privilege double-starred and urgently desired. It was also an obligation that worked both ways. Every "faithful Soul" had bound himself by his covenant vows to "watch over his neighbour's soul as his own", and in fulfilment of this brotherly purpose, to "admonish him of his sin". He might expect the same treatment in return. One need hardly ask why. Granted that one's salvation was the supreme quest—in fact, the chief reason for having been born into this world at all—granted also that one's chances of winning it might be dim to the vanishing point, any suggestions from any quarter as to what to do or what not to do in one's daily walk should be thrice welcome. How could members of a fraternity do less, one for another?

How could practical men and women be so unrealistic, is the modern counterpart of the question. If they had not known it before, one might think that an eight- or ten-week imprisonment in an over-crowded ship with their assorted fellow-passengers would have supplied more chances than anyone would need in this life to learn the obtuseness and angularity of mortal man in a communal society, whether voluntary or forced. How could they immediately afterward have written espionage and tale-bearing into the very constitution of the circle within the circle of a one-street village? Anyone who had ever had a zealous next-door neighbor in kind should have known better than to lay such an obligation on his fellow-villagers. Were the ministerial leaders who wrote the first covenants, and the first laymen who subscribed to them, blind or merely naive?

The answer is of course that they were probably neither, but that, in the first flush of their zeal to make the Scriptures their precise guide of life, they remembered the first half of the Pauline injunction, "Submitting yourselves one to another in the fear of God", and forgot the second half. The unwisdom of so literal an interpretation of the Pauline phrase apparently occurred to no one. To be "united in holy walking" was all their thought, and to this end the number of Christians who might covenant together in one society was in the beginning limited to "No more than can exercise a mutual watch". It was a crucial mistake. By it they not only defied the laws of growth but opened the door to dissension from the first day of their covenant relation forward.

Intrusion in each other's affairs was no part of their intent. Meddlesome busybodies they certainly were not. The sole thought back of this "mutual inspection" (at least in the beginning) was that the church was the household of God and that as such it must be kept untainted from within. For "scandalous persons" to be continued in the fellowship was to blaspheme God's name and defile holy things. "Disorderly walkers" were also bad apples in the dish. They must either through "brotherly censure" be "built up in Faythe and Love" or be cast out. "Holy Watchfulness" was the means to either end, and it was therefore imposed on every covenant member as a solemn duty.

Anyone might have predicted what would happen. In Monday to Saturday practice this high-thoughted purpose quickly lost itself in the specifications thereof. Concern with souls quickly became concern with visible behaviors. Watchfulness was not always "joined with tenderness". "Seasonable admonishments" were not always administered in the spirit of love, nor received in the spirit of meekness, as covenant vows had promised. Almost from the beginning jealousies, suspicions, and "secret risings of spirit" against the watching brethren gave more trouble than the offences these same vigilant brethren uncovered. How could anyone have thought it would be otherwise?

The pulpit of course had an answer, or rather a justification for the system. For the health óf the saints, the preachers maintained, two things were requisite: first *Restoratives,* that is, Sunday sermons and the sacraments, "choice diet to refresh the souls of the faithful"; and second, *Purgatives,* that is, brotherly censures to cleanse and purify the souls of the erring.[1] Censures were safeguards, not punishments; they were a means of health to the whole body of Christians. Spoken from the pulpit, this distinction may have looked clear as sunlight, but in congregational practice the line blurred. Campaigns of watchfulness often became important for themselves. They filled the docket at church meetings until the hearing of "cases" became a chief matter of business. They opened the way to unbrotherly strife and perennial mischief. Most unfortunate of all, they soon caused "pious walking" to be defined in the breach and acceptable church membership to be conceived as obedience to a code of behavior. Ministers continued to preach against pride in the heart, but laymen reported each other for sleeping in meeting and letting the sap run on Sunday. From the minute a new applicant laid his past life bare before the "scanning committee", he gave the watchers a head start toward detecting later outbreaks from the same quarter. Similarly each public confession of each erring member alerted the whole congregation for future discovery of "unholy carriage" in the same area of sin. Much mischief was thereby invited.

Nevertheless, in the beginning the scheme worked and effective protest against it was voiced slowly. In moments of extreme temptation early members may have avoided the eye of the more watchful, but if they were caught, most of them "submitted" in good Pauline fashion. There were sporadic outbursts, even early in the story, but usually these were mere rumblings. The earliest case of discipline in

Charlestown was that of Major Thomas Gould (obviously Baptist tainted), who, after being duly admonished for his "*long withdrawing* from public ordinances on Lord's Day" and finally shut out from the Lord's Supper, angrily protested that he had "no more privilege than an Indian".[2] In this phrasing of his grievance he was some distance ahead of other early and equally resentful culprits, but his recalcitrant attitude is symptomatic of what would presently be felt by many. Their long silence is easy to understand. Group control of their own affairs had been dearly won and it would be savored pridefully for a long time before even those who were hurt by it would be ready for a new battle. Individual rights could wait a little, but a cloud the size of a man's hand could have been detected in this quarter almost from the beginning.

Procedure toward making a "case" out of anyone's misstep involved first of all a report either to the pastor or to the regularly elected laymen whose business it was to "inspect ye walk of Professors"; namely, the deacons, elders, or sometimes a special committee. These representatives conferred with the pastor or the pastor with them as to whether the offence should be brought before the whole church, for right of censure was vested in the fraternity alone. If the charges were minor and if due penitence were promptly forthcoming, congregational practice sometimes omitted the public humiliation. Some congregations stipulated that charges could not be acted upon unless "proved by the mouth of Two or Three Witnesses", but this was a late amendment not generally insisted upon.

Accordingly, once the pastor and other officers had conferred, and had come to a decision as to the seriousness of the offence, the whole congregation was "stayed" on the following Sunday morning after the sermon. The offender was not even given the privacy of X, but was named by name, as by a written statement his "sinne was laid open in public". One pastor's private record of this procedure suggests what any culprit might expect to hear as the pulpit Bible was closed and the sermon booklet slipped back into the minister's pocket. This from John Swift of Acton, Massachusetts, after the hearing of "cases" had been standardized through a century of routine practice. He wrote,

"*I made a speech* to the church thus. Brethren, I doubt not but you have taken notice of the long absence of Brother Mark White, Junior, from the ordinances of God, in this place. If you request it of him to give us the reasons of his absence, some time hence, I desire you would manifest to it by an uplifted hand, whereupon there was an affirmative vote".[3]

Immediately thereafter, one of the deacons would wait on the offender, acquaint him with the verdict, and deliver a formal summons, which would read something like this,

"You are directed by ye Pastor with ye consent of ye Brethren to attend ye Church of which you are a Child, within 2 or 3 Sabbaths, to receive an Admonition for your sin of ——, according to Gospel rule".

If Brother Mark White, Jr., and his hundreds of fellow-culprits, before and after, were properly concerned over their standing with the church militant, they would appear on one of these immediately following Sunday mornings, present reasons for their wrongdoing (in writing) and also make written confession. Then by another show of hands from the brethren and "uprisings from their seats by the sisters" they would be reinstated or not, according to the blackness of their guilt, the anguish of their repentance, and the mercy of the brethren.

There was nothing gentle about the process at any point. Too much was at stake for the sparing of a culprit's feelings to be permitted. A fair example from early times and one for which a full account is preserved in the records is that of Brother Sunderland of the Second Church, Boston, in 1675. He was the clerk of the church and his offence was the rendering of a false account. He had kept back the sum of eight pounds. The discrepancy was discovered and duly reported. The church was "stayed' and he was suspended from the "Lord's Table". A week later he answered the formal summons and stood condemned before them. An abstract of the Teacher's reproof (as written by himself) runs like this:

"Brother Sunderland, I shall apply myselfe unto you.
Attend unto what I say.

I speak unto you not only as a friend, but in an Authoritative way, as a watchman whom the Lord hath set over your soul, & as one yt hath an awfull sense upon his spirit, yt he must give an account for your soul.

1. You have broke ye 8th Commandment wch requireth yt goods should be gotten honestly, [whereas] you have done yt wch is dishonest in ye sight of all men.

2. You have broke the 9th Commandment. [You have not been faithful to truth.]

3. You have broke the 10th Commandment. [You have lusted after that which is another's.]

4. You have broke the 3rd Commandment. For a man to Falsify his oath is one of the greatest violations of ye 3rd Commandment.

5. You have brought a reproach upon ye ch[ur]ch yea upon New-England. You have brought an ill report upon a good land.

6. [You joined in this sin with a wicked man who is not a ch[ur]ch member.] Your Evill is greater than his. You are an aged Professor. What a sad thing it is that now in your last days you should thus miscarry.

7. It is to be feared that ys evil doth not go alone. [What else have you done?]

8. Have you not got loose from God? [You were suspended last Sunday from communion. You can't partake with us until you] shall manifest unfeigned Repentance for these Evils.

And this is all that we have to say to you at present."

The Teacher then charged the church not to be prejudiced, and not to condemn all on account of one. "And let us pitty him that hath fallen".[4] Three months later in open congregation, Brother Sunderland acknowledged his "great evil", gave suitable evidence of contrition, and was restored to the fellowship. He was again on his way. The records of nearly every church society in New England supply dramas in kind: error, accusation, confession, penalty, restoration, and reinstatement. "Pious walking" was a crooked trail, interrupted by many turnings.

By contrast with such typical church procedure, the civil process was far more definite. Colonial life was ringed around with proscriptions, all of them duly published; penalties were clearly stated and clearly understood; culprits knew exactly what to expect. In early Massachusetts practice if one were absent from preaching on Sunday, he either paid a five shilling fine or was locked up in the market-place cage or the stocks for an appropriate number of hours. Noise or tobacco during time of divine service also carried fines or the cage. The price for swearing was not stable; one "profane oath" usually cost four shillings, but there is abundant record of less or more. Benjamin Tauter's records show one Joseph Rice paying eight shillings for three profane oaths and two profane curses (whatever the fine spun difference). Another swearer paid six shillings for two profane curses; but allowing for price fluctuation, the fact remained that one paid for what he had done and, once the fine was paid, he went free to sin again.

Sometimes there is record of discount for two sins at once. If on Sabbath morning an "ungodly sinner" *straggled* about on the Common, smoking his pipe as he *straggled,* there was chance of a bargain in fines. A Hingham culprit who once dropped off during preaching and then struck the brother who wakened him was twice guilty. He got an adjustment in the penalty. Another who helped himself to tobacco during the sermon and then closed his tobacco box with a loud click, also broke two laws at once, *noise* and *tobacco.* A three shilling fine covered both. When one remembers the harsh banging of the hinged seats, as the congregation rose and sat to pray and to sing, the judgment against the tobacco box seems almost malicious. Nevertheless, it was "noise", and two and two made four in civil law.

Not so in the church process. Even for the trio of most frequent offences: Sabbath breaking, "needlessly drinking" and "committing the sin of fornication", the church books show little that could be called routine. Within the covenant circle there was a persistent, if often inept and stumbling attempt to touch the issue underneath the rule and to discover the personal reasons and attitudes back of both the violation and the confession. Each case was considered individually, as though it were the first of its kind in the town, if not in man's erring pilgrimage through life. By this standard there was no such thing as a minor sin, nor any so grievous as unalterably to merit the penalty of being "cast out" of the fellowship. By the same token some apparently trivial error might appear mortal sin, as a "stayed" congregation watched the face of the culprit who stood condemned before them, and as the deacon took down his verbatim replies. He was always given a chance to state his own side of the case, usually in writing. He could not escape the admonishment which followed, but it would be his attitude of contrition which would determine the penalty. How "humbled" was he?

Even absence from meeting was considered a sin of the heart. Grave issues were at stake. Absence spelled both breach of covenant and indifference to one's eternal welfare. Sermons set forth the grounds for the doctrine according to Scripture, and as one listened to one more able than himself to interpret these grounds, he might better measure his chances of being among the elect. Not to take advantage of this great privilege was grave negligence indeed. Not to participate in the ordinance of the Lord's Supper was far worse. One sought admission to the fellowship in order to enjoy this most precious of all Christian privileges, and neglect was a sin proportionate to the privilege. Once inside, "enjoyment" became an obligation. Hence, while those present participated in this sacred ordinance for themselves, they looked sharply around to take note of absentees. Those whose seats were vacant were promptly reported as "Disorderly Walkers".

It is easier to laugh at these assorted Sunday rules than to understand them, particularly as the carefully considered plan of men whose practical wisdom in various other directions was often uncannily realistic. The best that can be said for the devisers of the Sunday code is that they saw the practical advantages of such strictness for the sake of other religious duties.

"Our whole religion fares according to our Sabbaths", Cotton Mather said when it came his turn to lament the current slackness. He was right. "Poor Sabbaths make poor Christians, and a strictness in our Sabbaths inspires a vigor into all our other duties",[5] he went on, and he was still right, but he was beginning at the wrong end, just as his father's generation had done. Besides, in their earnest zeal to carry out the Scripture injunction to the letter, they had been specific beyond all wisdom. Principles were obscured by minutiae and specifications invited infringement by their very definiteness. To know that "laying downe ye head upon ye Arms in a sleeping posture" during sermon time was taboo, was enough to make the urge irresistible, as the toll of those guilty of "ye carnal sin of sleepiness, (extraordinary cases excepted)" will show in almost any congregation. Similarly, the minor comfort of reaching in one's tobacco pouch pocket, turning one's back on the minister before the final blessing was pronounced, or rejoicing in the freedom of the street once it was all over (that is, until two o'clock in the afternoon)—the very thought was an invitation to trespass.

Time would take care of most of these specifications, as one by one they were reduced to absurdity or nearly so. The picture of a group of Yarmouth Christians gathered about a forty-foot well at sundown on Saturday evening, debating whether to continue digging for Ebenezer Taylor, trapped below "in the Belly of Hell", or to abandon rescue operations until Monday morning when they would be legitimate, suggests how far village literalness in such a case could go. Some were for waiting until Monday. Others said, "Let's go on with the digging". Still others, "He can't last another night. Why dig for a dead corpse on Sunday?" While his brethren in the Lord carefully balanced the arguments, Ebenezer Taylor, who had "gone down to view the breach", sat perilously on a jutting rock down in the blackness. How clearly the absurdity of the situation was apparent to him or to any of his fellow-Christians, safe in the upper air, is not recorded, but it was by such episodes through the years that the earlier rigorous specifications as to the Sabbath code were gradually relaxed.[6] New situations changed old rules. The system bent to the facts, but not soon enough to save from dishonor the best that lay beneath it.

Within the covenant circle the code had bent to the facts from the beginning, even in the matter of Sabbath violations. Almost any church book will show parallels, perhaps many of them, to the case of Benjamin Lawrence of Harvard, Massachusetts, reported by his brother in the Lord, Eliphalet Wood, who had seen him cleaning his cattle on the Sabbath day. When Benjamin Lawrence, standing accused before the church, maintained that he didn't know this necessary chore was a "Crime", his brethren believed him, and since he promised never to do it again, they restored him to their fellowship. When John Bailey, Jr., of Hanover "sinned grievously with his tongue" on one occasion, the church voted "to a man", that because he was one "in no way given to evil speaking", he must have been extremely provoked when in his passion he uttered the words which had given offence. Just the same, he had to listen to these same words, as they had been written into the accusation, and also to the solemn *Admonition* they had merited. His confession having a true ring, the church voted their acceptance. The civil code had no such flexibility. Shoot a deer on the Sabbath; pay your fine. Go a journey; sit in the cage. Law was law.

Because of this emphasis on the sinner's state of mind rather than upon the letter of his offence, any list of church "cases" and judgments over the years defies classification and sometimes logical explanation. The same sin may run the whole gamut of possibilities from acquittal without penalty to excommunication. Examined in their details, this same array of cases shows an attempt at fairness and a regard for individual rights which go far to exonerate many of the brethren from the literalness which was their besetting sin. Charity is also more frequent than harshness, and harshness itself more understandable.

Particularly the many cases of those "disguised with drink" (or "overgone") show more concern for the sinner and more patience with his stumbling attempts at reform than any harshness of rebuke for the sin itself. For a first offence reinstatement was usually immediate, if the repentance seemed genuine; for a second or third it would probably be conditional upon a good record for a month, a "quarter of a year", or longer. A usual phrase was "from winter to spring", or "from spring to winter". Since such cases were usually chronic, extensions of time were almost as regular as the summons to appear. Congregational patience seemed exhaustless, as time after time all postponed their cold lunch at the Sabba-Day House to listen yet once more to the same confessions, the same brittle promises, from the same "clump of sinners". Nearly every church book had its hardy perennials in such sort, many of them being women.

Samples of the care taken to amass evidence before conviction, even in the case of one who might well seem past likelihood of reform, survive in various church records. From the Second Church of Boston in 1685 it was Goodwife Fuller who had fallen. Six testimonies as to her dereliction, presumably in the handwriting of her accusers, are filed with the church record. They are signed by Phillipa Phillips, Hannah Clap, Elizabeth Arnold, John Jenkins, John Bushnell, and Hannah Brown, all of them her near neighbors. Said Phillipa Phillips,

"I do hereby testify that Sometime in the Last Summer observing my Neighbour Goodwife Fuller in the Street, her Speech and Gate, and her whole deportment was Such as that both mySelf and others did apprehend that wee had just Cause to Suppose her overcome with Excessive drinking, to the dishonor of herself and her profession.

Phillipa Phillips".

Hannah Clap had observed her speech and carriage "to be Such that to the best of my Apprehension, she had been drinking to a Scandalous Excess".

Elizabeth Arnold, who had often seen her in such a condition and had "faithfully told her of the same", testified that on this particular occasion she was so "scandalously disguised with Drink" that she could not "walk uprightly". John Jenkins supplied the further detail that she was "holding by the pales with her left hand, and having a Candle in her right hand under such Disorder, that I feared she was overcome with Drink".[7]

John Bushnell said that she "faltered in speech". Hannah Brown had seen her "raise the Rum Bottle", had helped her home and put her to bed "whilst she was in this Drunken Condition". On the basis of all this evidence and doubtless even more, the church likewise was forced to conclude that she had been "in Drink" and they "cast her out". She was not present to "hear the Sentence", but her watchful neighbors probably saw to it that she was informed that she had been "delivered up to Satan".

Cases which ended in this "great and dreadful ordinance of excommunication" provide one of the best indexes to what was meant by "Holy Walking", as currently defined, and also some of the best examples of that "moderation, pity, patience and long Sufferance" expended on cases of sin so "Famous and Notorious" that there was nothing else to do but to "cut off the gangren'd member", lest God's household be profaned. In some congregations there is no record that excommunication was ever used; in others it appears periodically, but always after all other means to bring a sinner to his knees had failed. Only the membership, acting as a whole, could invoke this awesome penalty; for, as was clearly understood from the beginning and so written into the Cambridge Platform, excommunication was not an "act of Power" to be vested in an office, but an "act of Judgment" to be "seated in the whole fraternity". Laymen might not be able to read or write, but they knew the difference, at least in this application, between an act of power and one of judgment. No other group right was so jealously guarded by a church society; and had the minister or the elders ever attempted to exercise it on their own authority, they would have had an immediate mutiny on their hands; possibly even worse.

Those "cast out" are a strangely assorted company. The Record Book of the First Church of Boston during its first ten years provides a fair sampling. In addition to those who took the part of Anne Hutchinson, the "gangren'd members" include:

Robert Parker (1635)

> "for scandalous oppression of his wives children in selling away their inheritance from ym, & other hard usage both of her & ym".

Judith Smith (1638)

> for her obstinate persistence in "Sundry Errors" before the Congregation and for "sundry lyes then expressed by her & persisted in".

Anne Walker (1638)

for "Sundry *Scandalls,* as of Drunkenish, Intemperate, & uncleane or wantonish behaviours, & likewise of cruelty towards her children & also of manifold lyes & still to this day [per]sisting impenitently therein".

Our brother Richard Turner (1638)

"having beene openly found drunken by the excessive drinking of strong water".

Our brother Richard Wayte

"having purloyned out of buckskyn lether brought unto him, soe much thereof as would make 3 mens gloves to ye Scandall of sundry wthout, as well as of his brethren, & also having beene by some of ye brethren dealt wth all for it, did often deny & forsweare ye same, wth out harkening to their Convincings according to ye Rule".

Philip ye wife of our Brother Robert Harding (1639)

"for speaking evill of Authority both in Church & Comon Weale; for having said in open Cort yt Mrs. Hutchinson neyther deserved ye Censure wch was putt upon her in ye Church, nor in the Comon Weale; It was p[ro]ved against her in ye Church by ye witness of o[u]r Brother Richard Truesdale & o[u]r Brother Samuel Cole yt she had also spoken ye like words of Defamation both in her shopp & other meetings, whereof not being able to give any account from Scripture, she was finally Cast out of ye Church as a Slanderer & Revyler".

Captaine John Underhill (1640)

for "Comitting Adultery . . . Revyling ye Governor . . . writing slanderous letters to England . . . and enticing some to folly or lewdness upon pr[e]tence to knock ym off from their owne Righteousnesse".

Sister Temperance Sweet [despite her name] (1640)

for giving "entertainm[en]t to disorderly Company & ministering unto ym wine & strong waters even unto Drunkenesse & yt not wth out some iniquity both in ye measure & pryce thereof".

On the same pages "our Brother Robert Keayne" got off with nothing more than "Admonishment" for

> "selling his wares at excessive Rates, to ye Dishonor of God's name, ye Offense of ye Generall Cort & ye Publique Scandall of ye Cuntry".

Our Brother John Pemberton was likewise only admonished for

> "his unbrotherly Contention with o[u]r brother John Baker, & for his unsavory Revyling speeches given to him, to ye Offence of ye Church at Newberry to whom they had beene Recomended".

On the same day John Webb received admonishment for being absent on a day of humiliation and also for taking the liberty

> "to spend part of ye day in ffeasting & sporting at Quoytes abroad, & yt in ye Company of such whereof some of ym were Scandalous".[8]

Sister Cleaves of Roxbury was publicly admonished in 1681 "for unseasonably entertaining & corrupting other folks servants and children". She had "corrupted Mr. Lamb's neger" so that "in a discontent" he had set two houses on fire "in the dead of the night".

> "Isaac Heath Senor for attempting to kill himself", Joseph Gardner for "wicked conversation", the wife of Joseph Lyon for "pilfering money from her grandfather & hiding it wth lying".[9]

Particularly disreputable cases here and elsewhere were sometimes recorded in Latin, or with a plentiful sprinkling of asterisks.

The theory back of these public admonishments is clearly stated in connection with a Roxbury case of 1686. It had concerned "certain persons convicted of a filthy lible" for which they had also been censured by the civil authority. The church

> "took note of Six, who humbled ymselves by publick confession in the church & we have cause to hope yt the full p'ceeding of discipline, will doe more good yn their sin hath done hurt".[10]

In 1686, possibly so, but the time would come when this would be a false hope.

From one church book to another it is much the same story; a list of offences as varied as man's originality in sin, and the penalty having more reference to the sinner's attitude under censure than to what he had done. In Barnstable, John Hull and his wife were "cast out" in 1641 because they had broken covenant and joined with the Yarmouth church; Barbara Hinckley because she did not "carry with A Loving humble reverence to her husband as is required, *Eph.* 5, 33"; William Carsley for "Carnall Carriages and too much Jeering"; Goody Shelley for "slandering two sisters" because they had not invited her to a church meeting; Christopher Winter of Scituate

> "partlye for marrying of one Mrs. [Jane] Cooper a woman of scandalous carriage, being vaine, light, proud, much given to scoffing. ... partly for breaking his promise not to marry without the church consent, but largely because in his final Summons before the church he seemed to cast aspersions uppon the church, & rather to justifye than to humble himselfe".[11]

In 1668 Benjamin Morgin of Beverly, in partnership with another sinner, stole two horses and several oxen and then lied to those who found him out. He obeyed the summons to appear before the church,

> "But by his Irreverend Carriage & Dumbe silence manifested himselfe to be A lamentable spectacle of a Stupifyed Sinner".[12]

He was cast out, presumably for the theft and the lie, not the stupefaction.

Social or official prominence protected no one. Mrs. Eaton, second wife of Governor Eaton of New Haven, was excommunicated for opposing infant baptism, striking her mother-in-law so that the blow hurt three days afterward, and for exceeding impertinence under censure. The mother-in-law episode had been witnessed by four Indians in the Eaton kitchen. Their sensational testimony at her trial stands at one extreme; the hair-splitting arguments of the elders as to whether the fifth commandment protected mothers-in-law as well as mothers at the other. The verdict of the elders was that mothers-in-law counted; therefore Mrs. Eaton was guilty. Several brethren spoke "weightily" to convince her, but they spoke in vain. Her impertinence under censure sealed her doom and she was "cast out". Naturally, Governor Eaton's position in the colony made hers a notorious case, but the church process could be no respecter of office.[13]

Early resistance was rare; but it occurred, usually to be withdrawn in the end. The case of John Farnam, one of the original Seven Pillars of the Second Church of Boston, lifts the curtain on one fairly complete drama of such resistance and, for its day, uncommonly bold resistance. The seat of John Farnam's trouble was obviously Baptist doctrine, although the word *Baptist* is carefully avoided in the Teacher's story of the case preserved in the record of *Censures*. John Farnam's original offences were that he "broke ye Rule of truth" by saying that Thomas Gould of Charlestown was excommunicated, criticised the church for taking this action, broke his own church covenant and became "guilty of Schism" by going to another church meeting on Sunday. He also "turned his back upon ye Table of the Lord" by having communion with excommunicated persons, and on top of all this he added "hardness of heart" by making "a sinful charge against many renownd men of God".

This was a good deal to answer for and required seven church meetings. At the first one John Farnam heard what he had done amiss, and justified himself in so doing, although he admitted that he might have gone a little beyond bounds in judging the Cambridge action, "wherein he was sorry". The church was dissatisfied with this answer and voted to wait for a better repentance. He might expect a call to another meeting. He replied that he wouldn't promise to attend.

At the next meeting another charge was added. He had misreported what the Teacher said to him. This he admitted, adding that

> "ye church must not expect that he should whine & Blubber & keep a stiew".

This was a strange reply in 1665. The church gave him more time to

> "consider of his evill that if possibly ye church might gaine his soule from the snares of sin & Satan & death".

They waited a month, but at the third meeting he had no further penitence to report. God had humbled him for his sins and he had peace of confession. To this the Teacher replied that his sin must be "be-wayled with brokenness of heart". He replied, "My heart is broken, whereupon ye Teacher replyed to him, But brother wee must see it broken by ye fruits & effects of it. You shall not see it", he answered, with great bitterness.

"Nay, sayd ye Teacher, but wee must see it, or how can we receive satisfaction, whereupon he replyed again, with great bitter-ness, *You see it, you shall never see it.*"

At this point one of the brethren spoke up, telling him that his speeches were very offensive and that the like had not been heard before. He answered, "I did not come here to be snapt & snubd & snarld at by every one", and turned his back to go away. "Brother Farnam", said the pastor, "In ye name of ye Church, in ye name of Christ whose church we are, You are required to stay & heare what further we have to say unto you". He replied, "I am not one that can stoop so low to everyone", and so "flung away". After he had gone the church decided to send two of the brethren after him so that he might hear the Admonition laid upon him. He returned long enough to say, "You may proceed to censure me if you please. I de-sire none of your patience"; and so "flung him out of the door in a very scornful manner."

At the fourth meeting he made a general confession in writing, acknowledging his fault, admitting that he had been "disorderly" on the last occasion, but denying that he had been guilty of schism, of breaking his covenant or taking communion with excommunicated persons. On these counts he was innocent. He also refused to answer the question as to why he left the congregation on the day the pastor was preaching on infant baptism. The church refused to ac-cept this statement of partial humbling. They demanded "orall & cordiall repentance". He had spoiled what repentance he offered by turning around and laughing while he confessed. This was "very offensive unto ye church".

The next two meetings got neither side anywhere. At the seventh meeting he said that if he heard any more about turning his back when the minister was speaking, "it may be he might doe ye like again". He named four conditions on which he would remain with them. These made it clear that he inclined toward the Baptists. The conditions were not acceptable. The pastor summed up his offences, and he was given one more month's grace.

On the Sunday of his excommunication he seated himself in the highest gallery and when called forth to receive his sentence said, "Speak to me here if you have anything to say to me, I can hear you well enough". After a long time he came down, but this compliance was also spoiled when in reply to the pastor's statement of willingness that he might oppose infant baptism if only he would "walk according to gospel", he laughed openly, turned about and said, "Ye place is too hot for me", and "flung himself out of the congregation". His words "caused many vaine youths to burst forth in open laughter in ye midst of a worke so awfull & dreadfull. When he was gone ye Pastor did in ye name of the Lord Jesus (the Judge of quicke & dead) deliver this Impenitent & profane offender unto Satan for ye destruction of the flesh that the spirit might be saved".

Eighteen years later he came back again, made full confession in writing, beginning,

> "God has convinced me of my great Evil, and Sin in the matters for which the church dealt with me about",

and ending,

> "This is freely acknowledged in hopes to find Acceptance by mee". John Farnam[14]

He heard the statement read aloud, owned it and was readmitted. 1683 was still too early for defiance of church authority to permit even so spirited a sinner an untroubled sleep.

Given time, most other offenders likewise were "restored" to the fellowship, for even this gravest of judgments was not final. Excommunicated members were ex-members, not non-members, and there was no unpardonable sin. Sometimes they were restored so speedily that confidence in their regeneration wavers a little. The wife of William Webb of Roxbury who "followed baking" had "bene long a grief of heart to her Godly neighbors" because "through her covetous mind", after weighing her dough, she "nimed off bitts from each

loaf". This was known to be her "constant practise", for which she
had been oft admonished by the church and rebuked by the Court.
Finally when against the testimony of four witnesses, she made "a
grosse lye in publik", she was "cast out". Nevertheless (so says the
record) "she was reconciled to ye church & lived christianly and
dyed comfortably".[15]

Even the wife of Martin Stebbins who had "offered violence to
her husband which being divulged was of such infamy" that she too
was cast out, "soone after humbled herselfe & was received in
againe".[16] Hardly a good risk, one might say. The Cambridge
church accepted the "publick acknowledgement" of fault from Eleazar Parker, who "stirred up by Strong drink" attempted to kill his wife
with a knife. Had she not been saved "by a Book in her Bosom"
(probably the Bible), a church forgiveness for all its elasticity could
not have saved even a repentant husband; the civil law would have
stepped in. In church records, however, one looks in vain for refusal
to forgive and restore a truly repentant sinner. Those who remained
outside the fellowship had either absented themselves when the
verdict was pronounced against them or remained obdurate and hard
of heart.

A delayed verdict, however, was almost standard; in part because
cases multiplied too fast and took too long for prompt action to be
forthcoming; too long also, it would seem, for the sinner's "grief"
to be maintained at top effectiveness. One wonders, for example,
what Thomas Grover of Cambridge, convicted of having been "disguised with drink" on January 12th, had been doing in the interval
before May 24th when he got a "Solemn Admonition" for his misstep, promised "Submission" and was continued in the fellowship on
that basis. A "mincing confession" could also cause delay. The culprit would merely be voted an extension of time and the case heard
again or indeed as many times as by "a handy vote" his humbling
was still adjudged deficient. It took Ephraim Hirreck of Beverly
three years to appear sufficiently contrite for his "lascivious speeches
and slanderous reflection" against authority in 1670. Similarly,
Stephen White of Waltham, exactly one hundred years later, for
something shady connected with the sale of a load of hay. In the

process of humbling a sinner progressed at his own speed, albeit with plentiful reminders.

Cases of extreme harshness are rare; not, however, when a minister was involved. Public humiliation could hardly go further or personal privacy be more cruelly invaded than in the case of Ruth Gooch, wife of a selectman of York, Maine, for her alleged indiscretions with a certain local Arthur Dimmesdale, the "infamous George Burdette", for whom several other "females" were publicly shamed. Her punishment was to stand in a white sheet before the congregation on two successive Sunday mornings, also "begging pardon on her knees" for her sin. She complied. The General Court imposed the same penalty but was content with only one day's humiliation. The fact that she was willing to carry out this double penalty before her fellow-members and neighbors argues as eloquently for the value she put upon church membership and her "soul's good estate" as it illustrates the cruel disregard of the watching brethren for an offender's private feelings.

It would seem that lying moved into first place early as the deadliest of all deadly sins. Offences often lightly treated for themselves became doubly serious when guilt was denied. John Smith and his wife of Dorchester were excommunicated in 1654 after the birth of a seven-month child convinced the "experts" that in their previous denials they "did Conceale their sin": until "God palpably charged it upon ym by that means",[17] says the record. Otherwise their fault would have involved no more than public confession and the immediate baptism of the "baseborn child". Two other young parents in Abingdon appealed their similar case to a council of three churches, when their own church had refused to believe their denial of the charge. This second verdict went against them also. Their own pastor was their accuser; their neighbors the witnesses against them. The findings of the council read in part,

"By Sundry Sworn evidences it was proved that their first Child had a full grown body Ripe for the birth & long hair & hard nails, & cry'd & fed well when it was first born tho[ug]h but five months & nine days from its parents marriage, & the Women made oath before Justice Edson & the Council before we went to the Meeting House, that they believed no Child ever attained to such ripenesse & perfections at 5 months & nine days from ye Conception".[18]

Thus cornered, the accused Wm. Hersey, Jr., confessed in a somewhat backhand fashion "he never would deny—" whereupon the Council adjourned. The young parents then had to face their own church once more, and either eat their previous words and make confession of two sins instead of one, or be cast out.

One of the most amazing "lying" cases on record for extreme triviality in the original circumstances, extreme gravity in the churchly interpretation, and never-let-go tenacity in the exercise of an authority that was slipping, is that of Rachel and Miriam Gray of Harwich, Massachusetts, in the decade of the 1760's. Rachel's original offence was embarrassingly trivial. She had pushed, or as the church record has it, "hunched" her sister Lydia Gray out of the family pew in time of divine service. Unladylike behavior for a young woman of eighteen, one might agree but, otherwise, what matter? Great matter, as it appeared. This was no affair for the Gray family to iron out in the privacy of their own home circle. It was an affair of truth, or became so one year later at a four-hour church session it precipitated.

At this inquisition it developed that Miriam Gray, another sister, had been accused by a fellow-Christian, Elizabeth Bangs, of asserting under oath that Thomas Gray, brother of Miriam and Rachel, was not in the pew when the "hunching" occurred. With this accusation Rachel concurred. If the accusation could be sustained, then Miriam Gray had perjured her soul. A four-hour session could never take care of so momentous a possibility, even though "a great Number of Evidences" were presented. A committee was appointed to investigate further and report back to the whole church. Two weeks later the church was again convened and after hearing the report voted that Elizabeth Bangs was wrong and that

"Sister Rachel Gray is not worthy a Chh. censure on ye Acct of pushing Lydia out of ye pew".

The evidence had not been sufficient to convict her.

> "Yet as Sister Rachel Gray hath charged Miriam Gray with taking a false oath, for this offence she ought to make a public Confession."[19]

This Rachel refused to do, with the sequel that the investigation continued at an accelerated pace, with the focus shifting to Miriam. The issue was one of timing. At precisely what minute had she said Tom was not in the pew? Was it before or after she took the oath? Two months later, when witnesses were heard on this point, the church voted that she had taken the oath before she said that Tom was not in the pew; therefore she had perjured her soul. Miriam would not accept this verdict. The case was deadlocked. Neither side would budge. Six months later, April 4, 1764, both sides were again hearing witnesses on the same doubtful premise, only now more doubtful. Did the lie precede or follow the oath? Debate was still inconclusive; but when the vote was taken, Miriam had lost and was called upon to give "Satisfaction". Rather than take the risk, since the evidence had gone against her, she declared before the congregation "yt she was Sorry for w^t she had s^d & asked forgiveness",[20] adding that at the time she had thought she spoke truthfully. The congregation accepted her confession and voted themselves satisfied.

But Miriam was not. Nearly a year later, June 23, 1765, the congregation was again voting, this time to give her a copy of their previous action so that in case she wished to call a council, she might "prepare her Defense". Apparently she thought better of this plan and merely stayed at home on Communion Sunday, when in order to partake she must be at peace with her fellow-members. After almost another year of this delinquency, April 8, 1766, and in spite of warnings, calls from the deacon, and other reminders, she was still absenting herself. This was four years after the original "hunching" affair. Miriam had grown up but apparently her bitterness was still active, for even at this late day she protested the treatment she had received and in reply, under date of April 5, 1767, received a communication from the church which comes very close to being a blanket apology. This paper admits that though a majority of the congregation had thought her guilty, there were those who had not thought so at the time,

> "nor do they at present, . . . & as a farther Evidence thereof this Message Shall be put on Record, hoping you will return to our Communion, as we are & ever have been in full Charity with you".[21]

But it was too late; her sense of wrong had gone too deep and she could no longer take joy in their fellowship. Had it all happened fifty years earlier, the Gray sisters would have been more tractable and the ending more conclusive. In the decade of the Stamp Act riots, "humbling" did not come so easily.

How did neighborhood life go on, one may ask, after such inquisitions as these? The answer would change with the generations. Recalcitrant John Farnams would meet either with black looks or with pitying ones. They had thrown away a precious jewel. Repentant and "restored" John Farnams would be greeted rejoicingly and bask in "holy love". As respect for church authority became less and as more of one's fellow saints exhibited more and more qualities of which St. Paul would not approve, boldness in rebellion grew more sinewy and unconfessed culprits had more company; possibly also more sympathy.

By the late 1720's and throughout the 1730's boldness increased rapidly and also the attitude toward it, so much so that there would have definitely been two sides to the case of a certain rebellious Dr. Bangs of Brewster, as early as 1733. After he had absented himself from Sunday preaching for as much as "half a year", he was "waited upon" by Deacon Foster and Joseph Mayo, who by vote of the congregation had been delegated to inquire into his reasons for this protracted absence. To their surprise and discomfiture he replied that his reasons for absence were "none of their business".

Nothing daunted, on the following Sunday the congregation voted that the father of Dr. Bangs endeavor to convince his son of "the evill of absenting himself from publick worship" and also for condemning the authority of Christ by returning such an impertinent answer. The mission of Dr. Bangs, Senior, was also unsuccessful, whereupon the church instructed Brother Judah Berry to direct Dr. Bangs to appear the following Lord's Day that the pastor might duly inform him and caution him of his evil ways. Dr. Bangs sent back word that "it was his pleasure not to comply". Again the church considered the case, and decided to wait a while before sending a formal admonition. A month later, "no good event having come to pass", they voted to send Deacon Lincoln to see whether Sinner Bangs would yet "bethink himself; before they send a publick formall Admonition to him". No repentance being vouchsafed, the Admonition was sent. It recalled in detail his continued obstinacy under reproof and his contemptuous response to "an Order sent by Authority of ye Lord Redeemer in this church".[22] The authoritative phrasing of this admonition was decidedly out of line with the spirit of the 1730's, as may be inferred from many other church procedures of the decade, likewise. It was getting too late for a man to be "ordered" to appear before his pastor to be instructed; also too late for men and women to submit to espionage, no matter by what name it was called. Dr. Bangs is only one of many, most of them still devout men, to whom "salvation" and the meetinghouse part in it on Sunday were still centrally important. They had merely ceased to regard the authority of the church "of which you are a Child" as divine and therefore ultimate.

"Discipline is an Edge-tool; use it carefully", Ebenezer Gay told a convention of ministers, met in Boston in 1744, and some of them were ready to follow him, but they should have begun at least a hundred years sooner. Some churches began to write into their revised covenants that

> "We will not be forward in chh. Meetings to show our Gifts & Parts in Speaking, nor endeavour to disgrace our Brethren by discovering their Failings, but attend an orderly Call before we Speak, doing nothing to the offence of the chh; but in all things endeavouring our own & our Brethrens Edification".[23]

They also were too late, however commendably their action shows their ability to learn. Some churches tried to rectify earlier mistakes.

As late as 1793 a young man of Lancaster, Massachusetts, who thirty years earlier had been accused of being "the father of a spurious child", had denied the charge and, proofs of his denial being lacking, had been suspended until such time as "the church should see further light and satisfaction", was "restored" by his surviving brethren. They did so, says the record, "in consideration of the sober life and conversation of our brother".[24] He had lived his whole adult life under the shadow. Who could blame him if official "restoration" would now not greatly matter?

CHAPTER TWELVE

"The Dire Sin of Korah"

Iᴛ was bound to come. Restlessness within the fellowship, whatever the cause, presently registered itself at the pulpit. Quarrels between the brethren inevitably broke over the minister's head at last. Resistance of congregational authority eventually meant questioning of pastoral prerogatives; a natural enough sequel, but it came slowly. There had been rumblings of disaffection occasionally from the very beginning, but large-scale rebellion or even open criticism of the minister was long deferred.

It is easy to see why. "Evil speaking against the minister" had carried a heavy penalty in the early years and few had dared. It cost Philip Read, a physician of Concord, Massachusetts, ten pounds in 1668 for saying that the blessing as pronounced by the Rev. Edward Bulkeley in dismissing the congregation was "no better than vane babbling". He paid his fine, stayed away from meeting, and kept on talking. When later he dared to boast that he could preach as good a sermon as Bulkeley himself, and that those who had called such a minister were "a company of blockheads who followed the plow-tail", he was fined twenty pounds additional and forced to leave town. The "blockheads" saw to that.

Back of the fine was the fear of danger to the state for reviling God's minister, and back of the unpopularity of the reviler was very genuine respect for the "noblest work on earth". Even when a minister's faults were plain to see and he was difficult to live with, the sacredness of his office prevented him from being judged as realistically as other men. The funeral orator of the much revered Charles Chauncy recalled the hasty temper from which many had suffered, and then quickly added, "Let the mention of it be wrapped up in Elijah's mantle",[1] saving thereby both his own conscience for truth and the immunity of the "eminent divine" whom God had now taken to Himself. The time would come when ministers would say of themselves, "We are men of like passions with Others",[2] but they did not say it for a long time. Meanwhile their immunities grew less and a more realistic judgment of their behaviors more outspoken.

Even after fines were abandoned for committing what John Wilson had identified as "the dire sin of Korah", biblically speaking, a hush still fell upon any company when the minister entered. Children stopped their play and stood in a long, silent line when he rode past on weekdays. On Sunday his congregation rose when he entered the meetinghouse and remained standing until he had ascended the pulpit stairs. In some towns the bell tolled in signal of respect as he crossed the Green en route, and if by miscalculation the tolling stopped before he arrived, his ministerial dignity had been affronted and a pulpit rebuke might be forthcoming. If the meetinghouse had no bell, homage was sometimes signalized by the rising up of the "principal men" of the town who bowed to him as he proceeded up the aisle. John Smalley of New Britain, Connecticut, is said to have scraped his feet at the threshold to announce that his triumphal march was at hand. Such gestures of intended respect, born of long custom, were perpetuated in many places long after a minister's aristocratic assumptions had fallen under reproach. Eighteenth century visitors from England were amazed at the homage paid the cloth, and also at a minister's power in the community; but had they been able to make comparison with still earlier attitudes, their amazement would have mounted considerably.

The minister's somewhat diminished influence and authority shortly after 1700 owed something to himself, something to his people, but more to the changed climate—social, religious, political— into which the third and fourth American generations were born. On a candid view and through no fault of his own he was not the man on whom the mantle of the John Wilsons, Thomas Shepards, and John Warhams had fallen. Instead, he was the quite natural product of three generations of provincial life. So were his people.

Typically, he was a son of the village, a farmer's boy, born to the tasks of the field and stable. Either his father's ambition or his own, possibly also the village minister's encouragement, had set a pulpit career before him, and in pursuit of this goal he had spent several years of his boyhood mornings at the parsonage in preparation for Harvard or, presently, Yale. Until the 1740's, when education as a ministerial qualification began to be successfully disparaged, not one young minister in ten was ordained or could hope to be until he had a college training behind him. To that extent at least the inherited ministerial pattern had surmounted all that warred against it in a pioneer society.

In the first quarter of the new century this education still meant the standard minimum in the "Tongues", polemical divinity, logic, Christian doctrine, moral theology, memory training, rhetoric, practice in declaiming and expounding. Jacob Eliot, a Sophomore at Harvard in 1717, listed in his *Diary* under the heading "Books which I have Bought since I came to Colledge",[3]

An hebrew Psalter
Wollebius's divinity
a Virgil
An English dictionary
Drexilius on Eternity
Henry on Prayer
The Art of Memory

It was a beginning, though only a beginning, toward the currently approved ministerial shelf. Ames' *Medulla* and *Cases of Conscience*, Mastrict's *Theoretico-practico theologia*, Turretin's *Cogitationes*, would be among his next purchases, and so on through the list.

In this same sixteenth year Jacob Eliot, like any other fledgling minister of his day, listened morning and evening while the president "expounded in ye Hall". Before and after these daily exercises he devoted the orthodox number of hours to his own prayers and private inquiry into his soul's health. In his turn he recited to his tutor, "held question", "studied chief of the day", kept "faithful fasts", heard sermons, read edifying letters, had "heavenly conversation" with visiting saints, dined or "supped" now and then with the president of the college or with some other local minister. For diversion, or at least for variety, he "went gunning", "went to Boston on my scates and returned", saw "negro Joseph hanged for killing his wife", watched "Phiny Fox's wife set up on the gallows and with a swift 39 lashes thence to ye garison for having a negro Bastard".

Other ministerial candidates in training sometimes record less sombre pleasures. When the Harvard Overseers met, the boys "feasted on the leavins" of the great banquet. They played pranks on one another and on unpopular tutors. Young Edward Taylor, late discovered poet of Westfield, tells of being involved in the nailing of Thomas Graves, Senior fellow, in his classroom and then hastily retreating to Boston lest he be suspected. Thomas Graves no doubt deserved the humiliation; at least he had "lost the love of the undergraduates by his too much severity"; so said the nailers. These culprits were only boys, most of them under nineteen, and for all its purposeful seriousness theirs was not a sombre life, although it was already a life around which the ministerial pattern was closing.

After a ministerial candidate had "passed through" his Harvard training, as one successful A.B. put it, he might, if particularly promising, remain at the college for several years as tutor, sometimes long enough to achieve an A.M. but usually only until a vacancy appeared. His candidating, invitation to settle, and election over, he signed his name in the Town Book, was ordained, probably married soon after, and then settled down to a lifetime of preaching and preparation, preparation and preaching, with his week-day mornings divided between the requisite "hard study" and the incessant intrusions of barnyard and field. As compared with his first generation forbears, he was more farmer than student, less a man of large interests than they had been, but he was still the *Big Man* of his distinctly smaller world.

Into this isolated community life he brought qualifications which few others, or perhaps no one else, possessed, and by virtue of his college training he would be called on to do some things community life does not go on without. In addition to minister, he was often physician, judge, scribe, and drafter of wills, petitions, protests to the General Court and other formal or legal papers. Particularly after the level of culture declined, more often than not he was the only one in the village who could do any of these things. The people turned to him naturally, and he responded equally naturally. In terms of six-day reality, pastor and people spoke the same language.

Many day to day entries in many ministerial diaries supply the minutiae of this shared experience; for, like their fathers before them, these men had a conscience for keeping accounts, not only of their soul's health and prosperity, but of their checkered country days, their dawn to dusk chores, their journeys, the weather and the seasonal marvels of nature. Said Moses Adams of Acton, late in life, as he recalled the minutiae of a long pastorate, with the diary of his predecessor, John Swift open before him,

> "I regret, that I did not at the beginning of my ministry, procure a larger book, and keep a more particular and extensive record. I hope my successor will profit by this hint".[4]

Fortunately, there were those who provided themselves with larger books for their personal doings as well as churchly detail. For the extra inches of candle required for the jottings therein and the "carnal enjoyment of sleep" thus sacrificed, we thank them. Their clipped entries fill in many chinks in social history quite apart from the otherwise recorded march of pulpit and town events, and in so doing build up the considerably changed picture of the "man of God", as compared with the seventeenth century model, now far in the background. Sometimes also these jottings let fall a bright shaft of light on some otherwise unknown individual, who thus unwittingly sits for his portrait. "I was married this evening", wrote unromantic bridegroom Thomas Smith of Portland, thereby keeping his life record up to date, and promptly. In fact, he wrote the same entry twice, word for word, sixteen years apart—promptness included.[5]

In these six-day entries, farm details take much space for most

country ministers, as season by season they alternated with sermon
preparation and pastoral duties of many sorts. The fifteen-year
record of Joseph Green of Salem Village from his twenty-fifth to
his fortieth year shows a pattern in which hand and brain worked
together and would seem to have contributed equally to the satisfactions of his farmer-scholar life. Seasonal chores were as inextric-
ably a part of the web of life for him as bookish interests, the
catechising of children, the ministers' meetings, the building of a
new meetinghouse. Ministers came from Boston and found him hay-
ing. Why not? Life was made of such opposite demands. Why
think them a duality? Almost any page of his journal is full of jux-
tapositions carrying with them the hint not of a divided life, but of a
more nearly complete one than the self-conscious Brook Farmers
ever achieved.

From among his spring items:

> "heard a Phebe and other birds sing.
> I was at home partly reading and partly pruning my orchard.
> I carryed home to Mr. Pierpont 2 books, and borrowed Ward on
> Matthew.
> I spoke to Mr Sam¹ Phillips to preserve for me a Cambridge Con-
> cordance.
> Our sheep sheer'd 311 lbs of wool.
> I went to Wenham & grafted 59 syons on 24 trees.
> 11 hands making wall for me.
> We stilled cider lees.
> I went a fishing to Wills Hill with my 3 boys.
> Burnt brush. Sowed turnips."

Summer:

> "Set 300 cabbages.
> Killed squirrels that devour my corn exceedingly. I have killed 13
> and they have eaten ¼ of my corn.
> It is said there are millions of them in this village.
> I at home. whited chimneys.

I at home. peas hooked.

I at home pease thrashed.

My pease fanned.

I at home. Shut up my hogs to keep them out of Mr. Hutchinson's corn.

I went to Beverly to a fast on ye account of ye drought. Before Mr. Noyes had done prayer ye rain came down at once on ye Meeting House to ye great surprize of ye assembly. God unstopped ye bottles of Heaven.

Very hot. Bugs!

Made conserved roses.

Began to mow.

I at study. The worms destroy ye fields.

I killed 3 dozen pigeons.

I killed 18 pigeons at one shot.

Killed 3 dozen pigeons, 10 dozen in all this year.

Gathered acorns."

Fall:

"Made a chimney in ye cellar.

We dined at Major Vaughans with my wife and had ye most genteel dinner & attendance I ever saw.

got in all our winter apples.

I killed a wild cat.

I went to Salem lecture. Mr. Noyes preached and we din'd with ye Judges of the Supreme Court.

We cut up and salted 7 hogs, all weighing 648 lbs.

My peas thrashed.

Finished husking.

I have laid in 9 barrels of sider.

I at study.

My wife brewed 3 barrels of beer.

Made hedges in yard.

I went to Wenham with my wife. Mr. Noyes and I wrote over ye minister's determination. Boiled syder."

Winter:

> "Salted pork. We have this year killed 756 pounds.
> Kill'd our cow Mulberry. She weighed 95 lbs. a quarter round
> and had 36 lbs of tallow; [he also cut her up and salted her].
> I went to the neighbors about wood.
> Killed a calf and gave most of it to our Salem friends.
> Two men sawing.
> Brave weather. I visited ye sick.
> My wife made 35 pounds candles.
> Cold. I wrote deeds for J. Ross. Brewed.
> Pain in my bones".[6]

Apparently he found it all a good life, for when his own oldest boy
was past what the village school could give, he wrote, "I went to
Salem Lecture, carrying son John to School intending (if God please)
to make him a schollar and minister".[7] At least one boy in Salem Village would go beyond the education Joseph Green himself had made
possible for the children of his parishoners. In an entry of March 22,
1708, he had written, "Spoke with several about building a school-
house and determined to do it". Soon afterward, he pled the cause before the town meeting, saying by his own report,

> "Neighbours, I am about building a Schoolhouse for the good
> education of our children, and have spoken to several of the neigh-
> bours who are willing to help it forward, so that I hope we shall
> quickly finish it. . . . Some replied that it was a new thing to them,
> and they desired to know where it should stand and what the design
> of it was".

The pastor was ready with the answers. Deacon Ingersoll had agreed
to give the land and the design was to teach our children "to read
and write and cipher and everything that is good".[8] Many commended
the design, he wrote, and none objected. Three days later he had men
cutting the timber; throughout the summer he reported himself as
"hurrying about ye schoolhouse". Before winter it was finished, a
teacher was hired, and the children of Salem Village had their new
chance.

From one diary to another the minister's story shows a similarly resourceful and sometimes imaginative sensing of his people's need, and also the practical ability to carry through the projects he had devised. The phrase "He taught the people manners", surviving for Timothy Pitkin of Farmington, Connecticut, suggests areas of pastoral responsibility which had been less insistent in the days of the New England patriarchs. To be a "great Hebrician" or, when worsted in Greek or Hebrew, to be able to retire to the safety zone of Arabic or Syriac, where one's opponent could not follow, was almost a closed chapter in the life of the country minister of the first half of the eighteenth century. Not so for his Boston brother, or for such a notable exception as Jonathan Edwards of Northampton, who would have been an exception in any age or geography.

The average country minister's day to day life differed little from the lives of most of his parishoners. Although typically he was the greatest traveller in the village, his journey usually took him no further than his horse could carry him in one day or at most two. Once a month he went to the county ministers' meeting, once or twice a year to an ordination or a church council called to settle some congregational quarrel. The great excursion of the year was to the Harvard or Yale commencement, at that time something of a combined learned society meeting, a professional convention, and a foregathering of American intellectuals, as well as an alumni home-coming. There were ministers who did not miss a commencement in all their postgraduate lifetimes. For most of them also there would be fairly frequent interim journeys to Boston, Hartford, New Haven, and probably further, but not until after Whitefield came, would any of them be absent longer than between Sabbaths.

Their mileage by the month and year adds up, however, to impressive totals.

> "I have rode in thirteen months past, more than three thousand miles. I have been to Boston four times",[9]

Thomas Smith of Portland wrote in 1738. Usually these were horseback journeys, although sometimes he saved a few hours by water.

"Sept. 1. I paddled myself to New Casco. . . . 11. I set sail for Boston. . . . 13. Set sail for Falmouth [Portland]. 14. Got home. I was
twenty-two hours going, twenty-nine hours there, twenty-two
coming home".[10]

Weather was no deterrent; hardship was hardly mentioned.
Whether from duty or necessity these journeys were attacked in the
holiday spirit. Every hour counted. Fairly typical items from Samuel
Deane for a certain February include

"A storm of snow; went to Presumpscot and married Adam Bar-
bour to Betty Knight. I made a whole sermon today, from 10 to
7½ in the evening. Four Baptisms. . . . Got 2 lbs. tobacco. . . .
I read one volume of the Vicar of Wakefield. I had a bad head ache,
and cured it by holding my feet in hot water".[11]

If there had been an ordination and another storm of snow the following week, he would have set out again, perhaps read another volume
en route and cured another headache. The tale of Parsons Little,
Hemenway, and others of the cloth who started from Wells, Maine,
to go to the ordination of Paul Coffin of Buxton, lost their way, spent
the night in the woods, and yet arrived at the ordination on time,
is a typical winter sports item for the fraternity. The melancholy
notation "Sat out homewards, I dined no where",[12] memorializing one
of Jacob Eliot's lone horseback journeys, is also uncomfortably typical.

When night came down, colonial travellers, wherever they stopped,
were always sure of hospitality for themselves and their horses, no
matter how late the hour. Ministerial travellers were also sure of the
best bed in the house, even though other travellers who arrived
simultaneously had to take to the straw in consequence. There is an
amusingly typical entry in the *MS*. journal of one Joseph Hull of
Providence which tells of a wretched night he and his companion
spent on a mattress, "stuffed with Confounded Stalks of Straw",
whereon he suffered "great torments" of the back and neck and entertained dreams of "hideous things", the "better bed being Provided for
ye Parson and his Deacon". At morning prayers the two straw sleepers

tittered when the minister gave thanks for "our Comfortable & profitable Rest", and then, still tittering guiltily, they had "apprehensive fears" that upon opening his eyes the minister would reprove them for their levity.[13] Both their assignment to the straw by their host and their own fears of rebuke testify to contemporary attitudes of awe and respect toward the minister. It took a long time to change them.

Usually the minister came back from these journeys with a new book, bought or borrowed, the last issue of the *New England Courant* or the *Boston News-Letter*. Occasionally he would see some English periodical and count the fact of sufficient importance to be noted in his journal, especially for the London imprints advertised therein. Joseph Green once double-starred a Boston journey with the entry,

"May 29, 1711. I was at Mr. Thomas Brattle's, heard ye organs and saw strange things in a microscope".[14]

Before many Sundays every family in Salem Village would vicariously share his amazement and his new knowledge. Perhaps once in his life a country minister would be invited to preach in Boston, possibly the Election Sermon, or one for some other special day, and if it were ordered printed, this would probably be his only publication. His experiences, as compared with those of his Boston or New Haven brethren, seldom touched the wider currents of life, even in America, and Europe was an unknown continent. His was not a mellow culture, even of the pulpit variety, and through no fault of his own the mark of his limitations was upon him.

He belonged to the village, and if he chafed under the limitation, the evidence is not preserved. Once after an absence of several days, young Ebenezer Parkman wrote in his diary, "I walked up to Mr. Edwards' Shop, to hear the News, and See my Friends".[15] It was a natural enough notation, not to be pressed too far—in fact, not to be pressed at all; it is also a window looking in on a far more provincial chapter of life than the first generation minister had known, but not for that reason is it to be written down as dull or unprofitable. America needed a provincial chapter in which to possess herself more consciously, and the isolated country town, encompassed with perils from within and without, was one of the units in which the roots of self-dependence stretched down to its surest anchorage and self-possession took on a confident reality.

Men had to be equal to what happened to them within the limits of their own small world. There is another entry in Ebenezer Parkman's *Diary* which can stand for many dramas in kind.

"This morning we perceived Mr. Haskills (Blacksmith) Shop was burnt down. It broke out abt. an hour before Day. The L[ord] Sanctify it to ym."

Ebenezer Parkman had his hands full that morning, but after he had visited a parishioner, prayed, catechised a young woman and delivered an "Exercise",

"I rode down to Mr. Haskills to Sympathize. Deac[on] Tainter was with me. But Mr. Haskill was not at home. He was in ye woods and [people] were generously getting Timber for him".[16]

In his next entry he sent "a Dollar by Deacon Tainter, in Billy's name to Mr. Haskill". Had he ridden down a day or two later, the shop would have been completed and Mr. Haskill would have been doing business as usual. It had to be so.

As fellow-farmer and neighbor in this isolated life the country minister was close enough to his people to be their unofficial spokesman and leader in community affairs; he was too close to maintain his inherited aristocratic prerogatives unchallenged. In his own department, namely, "looking out for souls", the town still granted him a free hand. He was God's man. But as the town minister he was also their man. They had "hired" him and, come peace or war, no town ever forgot that fact. Whatever authority he possessed was delegated power. Their own votes had conferred it. Besides, the town owned the property and held the purse. The relationship between town and minister was a strange blend of inherited aristocratic privilege on the one hand and democratic control on the other, and in the end democracy would win. The lower levels were pushing up. Those in control of both church and state were now American born. The experiences and hopes of the crusading Dissenters had passed into family tradition to be dimly recalled, if recalled at all, only on anniversary occasions. With the increase of population the "godly lump" in each village was proportionally smaller. Besides, every church society now carried its freight of "Halfway" members who wished the prestige of an assigned seat on Sunday, even if it were a seat they did not often occupy. Even so, they made their will vocal in town affairs.

Within the fellowship most churches had provided a committee of nine "wise, prudent, and blameless Christians", who acted as *Vigilantes* to discern the first symptoms of ministerial encroachment on congregational rights. The minister on his side was equally alert lest any of his time-honored prerogatives be lopped off. Accordingly, the situation for all its pleasant bucolic appearance on the surface was favorable for strain between pastor and people. Almost any circumstance could be manoeuvred into a test case and when it came it would be a test of authority. Who has it, minister or membership? Are we being told what to do, or are we running our own affairs? In the earlier day, when a congregation said *our*, they had meant pulpit and pew together; when they said it in the early years of the new century, they meant the pew alone. Somehow through the years the wall had gone up; the minister had come to be on one side and the congregation on the other, and in consequence he might expect rough going almost any day.

In many parishes trouble had already come long before 1700 over the matter of lifelong ministerial tenure, so carefully written into the bond in the beginning. The phrase "Provided he do live and die with us", which expressed one of the original conditions of election, had sometimes proved to be a sad boomerang. As old men grew older in the service, they held more tenaciously to the letter of their bargain, assuming that for a minister "to lay down his bones with the bones of his people" meant persistence in the discharge of his pastoral duties, the infirmities of age notwithstanding. The results had sometimes been disastrous. Feeble old men had continued to preach as long as they could totter into the pulpit, some of them resenting the appointment of a young colleague pastor, and when one was appointed against their wish, making his assistance difficult in the extreme. It was a great pity. Old men's hearts were sometimes broken when congregations insisted that a younger man take over. Graceful retirements were al-most unknown. Mindful of a beloved pastor's feelings, some congre-gations waited patiently until "God took him off", and while they waited, the cause languished. Again and again a minister's last day in the pulpit was the last day of his life, thereby fulfilling the dearest wish of his declining years. But at great cost.

During the first century pastorates of fifty or sixty years are easy to find. Pain Wingate served the Amesbury church for fifty-eight years. Justice Forward, second pastor in Belchertown, died in the fifty-ninth year of his ministry, "having followed to the grave more than 900 of his people". Anthony Stoddard, of Woodbury, Connecti-cut, son of Solomon, preached to one congregation for sixty years and was also their judge and physician. Joseph Adams of Newington, New Hampshire, uncle of John Adams, President, served his people for sixty-five years. John Barnard's presence in Marblehead "restrained every imprudent sally of youth" for fifty-five years. Habijah Weld of Attleborough, Vermont, boasted a record of fifty-five years without a single absence from the pulpit. Richard Mather did not miss a Sun-day in fifty years. Ebenezer Gay of Hingham missed only one, his last ·one on earth. He died just as he was preparing to enter his pulpit. He had ministered to his people for sixty-nine years. Not one of his original parishioners survived to mourn him; he had outlived two whole generations. Stephen Williams performed the whole service of his pastorate for sixty-six years, even after the pulpit stairs were be-yond him. When aged ninety, and no longer able to walk, he was carried across the Green and helped into the deacon's seat. Until he was ninety, Nehemiah Porter of Ashfield, Massachusetts, was the sole pastor. He had achieved a seventy-year span. He died aged one hun-dred and one, but (we are told) *not* from old age.

Such records can be matched many times; too many. The absurd but high-intentioned eulogy of Nicholas Noyes for his brother in the service, John Higginson, is unfortunately more true to the fact than to the poetic mood;

> "Young to the *Pulpit* he did get
> And Seventy-Two Years in't did sweat".[17]

Could the tenacity of these men and their determination to keep the reins in their own hands have been curbed or differently directed, the pulpit might not have lost touch with the common life in a period of convulsive change.

As younger men took over, towns grew more wary and supplied qualifying clauses as to tenure. Meanwhile new and even more insistent causes for strain developed, particularly as to salary. In the Golden Age of the earliest days, when settlements were still small and strongly unified as to their religious purposes, the initiative in the business arrangements had usually been with the minister. What "inducement to settle" could the town offer? What were his terms? When might they "fetch him up"? "How might they satisfy his desyre?" Even the phrasing of the town votes suggests a spirit of willingness to take care of him generously, as in the entry, "To build a good lettell barn for o[u]r Mr. Bradstreet".[18] The pleasant overtones are not misleading. Back of the vote was the conviction that the minister should have the best. What they gave him was not largess. It belonged to him by virtue of the great importance of his office and their own great need of him. Nearly all freemen acknowledged a responsibility toward his "honorable support". At any rate, so it was; the collector called, and they paid. Ever since the first question raised at the first session of the General Court in Charlestown in 1630—"How shall the ministers be maintained?" had been answered—"At the general charge",[19] "Rates" had been written into the very constitution of town life, with also the assumption that *Extras* might be needed. Consequently, when the minister needed more "cradle room", an ell was voted for the parsonage. If he asked for "more cow-commons of meadow", more "plowing land", "a better hovel for the creatures", he got them along with the "good lettell barn". For a full seventy-five years or more all this was taken for granted in most towns as part of the normal order.

As town officials had more experience with the collection of Rates from year to year and as times grew increasingly lean, however, town meetings grew more cautious as to financial involvement. When a new minister was called, the town named the terms and the minister had no choice but to accept them, often reluctantly. As the currency depreciated seriously in the early 1700's, the burden of Rates increased proportionately. Arrearages mounted; payments became slower. Collectors found themselves wrestling not only with unwillingness to meet current allotments but also with the "behindments", many of which could never be collected. The minister took the loss. Year by year he reminded the town of these arrearages and also asked for increases of salary which were usually promptly denied, at least on first request. As his family continued to increase, and his cost of living troubles became more insistent, he became correspondingly importunate and made not requests but demands. These were even more promptly and curtly denied. The families of his parishioners were likewise increasing and payment of their quota becoming ever more burdensome. Financial problems were acute on both sides. Laymen watched the minister's expenditures and criticised him openly for this or that purchase. He lived "too high". He had his suit tailored in Boston. His wife wore a jewel. Where did she get it?

Mutual criticism begot resentment and resentment begot more criticism. Ministers and their people alike chafed under the system. Ministers openly recognized that they had become "almesmen".

> "Cannot the collection of a minister's *Rate* be done so as to expose them less to the Odium of many of their People?"

This from Timothy Cutler in 1717. *Odium* is a strong word, but possibly not too strong for the current feeling. He also put his finger on one root of the unrest when he said,

> "Compulsion of Men to their Duty in this Point is a very Tender thing, and sometimes Disaffects Men to their Ministers so, as they never afterwards Profit by them".[20]

If anything, he understated the evil. The time to change the system was then. Instead, the unrest spread. Both sides became ill-tempered, and before the mid-twenties, when a truce was about to be declared in the "Singing Quarrel", nearly every town had a "Salary Dispute" on its hands. Ministers with the utmost un-wisdom went into print; a one-sided pamphlet warfare ensued. They hurt their cause thereby and seriously.

THE FIRST MEETINGHOUSE IN RYE, NEW HAMPSHIRE, ABOUT 1725.

According to tradition, the men of the town yoked themselves together
and drew the timber to the spot designated as the site of this meetinghouse, oxen not being available for the purpose. The steeple was not
completed until 1756. From a cut appearing in Langdon B. Parsons,
History of Rye, Concord, N.H., 1905. By courtesy of his son, Mr. John
L. Parsons. The original drawing was made from descriptions given by
Miss Abbey L. Parsons.

THE "OLD MEETINGHOUSE UNDER THE LEDGE", NORTH YARMOUTH, MAINE.

This building, which originally measured fifty-four by twenty-five feet, was lengthened in 1762 by being sawed apart and having fourteen feet added on either side of the pulpit. The twenty-eight new pews thus added sold for three hundred and thirty-eight pounds and paid the alteration bill. From a painting by George A. Allen. By courtesy of the Maine Historical Society.

In 1724 Thomas Symmes put the minister's grievance in his *Country Sermon* which he announced would be far from popular. He was right. He called it *The People's Interest*, but to an aroused auditory it looked more like his own interest, as he made sharp accusations of duty neglected. People are concerned, he said, "How they can get him the Cheapest"; they count "What they can Pinch out of his Salary, or save in their Bargaining with him, *Clear Gain*"; they treat the minister as though he were "as much beholden to them as a meer Beggar for an Alms; . . . I wonder where they learnt it! Surely not out of the *Bible*".[21]

In the following year, another minister, John Tufts, printed an anonymous pamphlet entitled

> *Anti-Ministerial Objections Considered, or the Unreasonable Pleas Made by some against their Duty to their* MINISTERS, *with Respect to their Maintenance Answered.*

Although it purported to be an answer to the question, Who are obliged to Endeavour a Reformation in this Case?, the author admitted that the question had not been asked. He made no effort to disguise the pulpit bias but made blunt accusation of the laity. Those who refuse to pay commit sacrilege, he said, whereas the minister suffers only in outward respects. The town could double the minister's salary without difficulty, and on this hypothesis he presented a scheme which on paper had a Townsend-plan plausibility.

Suppose a parish has a hundred families in it. Let the twenty poorest families be exempt from any payment at all. Let the twenty next poorest save one day's wages in thirty; the next twenty, one day in twenty-four; the next one day in eighteen; the richest one day in twelve.[22] Ergo! the whole problem is solved.

As the case now stands, he went on, a minister's allowance is not equal to that of "a Middling Tradesman" or "a Middling Liver". His people owe him more than that. It is as dishonorable to live below your station as above it. Ministers are "exposed to more and better Company" than laymen, and they must entertain these guests fittingly. "The Minister who is not given to Hospitality, is a Scandal to his office." Poor attire encourages disrespectful attitudes. When ministers are brought down on a level with the "Common People", religion declines.

"Poverty exceedingly hinders a Minister in his Studies; it perplexes and disturbs his Mind. Yea, 'twill often bolt him out of his Study, and send him to the Barn when he should be at his Book."[23]

Furthermore, his poverty discourages young scholars from taking up the ministry.

"In after Ages Men will rather bind their Sons to one Gainful, than Seven Liberal Sciences; only the lowest of the People would be made Ministers."[24]

That this pamphlet aroused bitter antagonism goes without saying. Unfortunately also, it revealed certain pulpit attitudes one could hardly call laudable. Laymen printed few pamphlets in reply to numerous ministerial ones, but they made their resentment vocal at town meetings when the minister's "Rate" was under discussion. The minister, on his side, continued to make demands, and when refused, to press them more strongly.

The system of "Country Pay" greatly increased the difficulties of this vexed situation. Cash payment had been rare from the beginning; the minister received most of his salary in commodities irregularly donated. His people gave what they could spare when they could spare it, and as the minister was also a farmer, when his own acres were in yield, he had abundance of the same kind from his people. When it was a lean season with him, he had leanness from them likewise and in the same commodities. Irregularity bred annoyance and sometimes hardship. At best the "country pay" system was uncertain, as a few pages from any minister's account book will show. In one month William Brattle of Cambridge had "37 pounds of beef, 2 turkeys, 10 fowls, 1 quarter lamb, Beef and mutton & 2 hogs (1 alive)". A large part of his winter supply of meat, to be sure, to be husbanded accordingly, but none the less showing an embarrassing discrepancy when compared with an adjacent month when he recorded *in toto* "a live Pork, 10 eggs from the Widow Palmer, sausages from Cousin Oliver, 6 oranges, Pudding (white and black), 3 oranges, a mess of

Fish". A certain month of April netted him "½ bushel Oysters, 1 cod-
fish from Mrs. Amsdell, one pound of fresh butter, and a mess of eels
from the wife of Z. Hicks".[25] Hundreds of closely written pages attest
to the continuance of like irregularities and, as it would seem, also of
hardships around the minister's table throughout a lifetime. The minister kept the record; his wife wrestled with the dietary unbalance
and all related problems. Any reasonable system of household
economy would have been difficult enough, no matter how intelli-
gently it was administered.

A hundred years later it was essentially the same story, as a few
pages from the books of Joseph Avery of Holden bear witness.[26]
Among many similar items, his 1782 record shows the following as-
sortment:

Of Deacon Hubbard, "a piece of beef; a pail of soap; a loaf of bread;
a few candles; 2 quarts of milk; a cheese and 4 pounds of butter".
Of Mr. Abbott, "a piece of beef and of pork, also a spare-rib, 3 can-
dles, some malt and a piece of bread, also two wash tubs and 30 nails
and a few hops".
"Of Lieut Hubbard, a piece of beef, a cheese and some malt.
Of Dea. Fiske, a piece of beef, Jan'y 5th.
Of Samuel Hubbard, a leg of pork and a spare-rib, Jan'y 6th.
Of Mr. Howe, a piece of pork, Jan'y 6th.
Of Mr. Cheney, a cheese and some sausages.
Of Mr. Josiah Cheney, Jr. some beans.
Of Mr. Jonathan Rice, a leg of pork.
Of Mr. Winch, a piece of fresh meat—lamb.
Of Capt. Davis, a cheese and some sauce.
Of Aaron Wheeler, a broom, soon after I came to my house.
Of Moses Smith, 2 doz. candles, some butter.
Of Mr. Dryden, ½ dozen pigeons.
Of Mrs. Benj Flagg, a cheese.
Of Mrs. Fisk, a lb of combed flax.
Of Mrs. Elisha Hubbard, some flax.
Of Mrs. Potter, some butter and a broom.
Of Mrs. Newton, a piece of veal and a calf's head.

Of Mrs. Holt, some cloth for a shirt.
Of Mrs. Mead, some butter, apples, potatoes.
Of Mrs. Heard, a loin of veal".

Ebenezer Parkman records a pastoral call which netted him "a pair of shoes for myself and a pair for my lad, a handsome cheese, a years subscription to a Boston newspaper and a valuable silk handkerchief, of fifty Dollars price, much wanted".[27] Doubtless he *wanted* them all; but even with the system understood on both sides, it must have required considerable personal dignity to carry off such a transaction successfully. Pastoral calls were for prayer and catechising and yet one went home with two pairs of shoes and a "handsome cheese". What about the next time he called? Would he have expectations? Would his parishioner be glad to see him?

The bookkeeping required for an accurate recording of all such piecemeal donations in pre-secretarial days is wearisome to contemplate. The minister made his own notebooks, often binding them in sheepskin from his own flock. He also made the ink with which he wrote. The worn backs of such homemade books as survive are as much a part of the story as the neatly written pages. Nor do they tell it all. Not only must he record what each member brought, reckoning its value in fluctuating Bills of Credit, but he must be ready at any time (on demand) to compute how much was still due him from this same individual. How balance, one may ask, "11 Rib spairs" from one townsman against a half bushel of oysters from another, or "one pig with Pettitoes" and one goose in one month against a bottle of syrup, "a leg of Pork and 4 chickens" the next? If the parish bargain called for an annual pound of butter from every cow in town and one cheese for each family from the same cow, how many cows were delinquent of their quota on the deadline for bringing in said butter and cheese? Many hours dedicated to prayer and study at the time of one's call to ministry and much candlelight went to this dull chore of computing credits and arrearages. No wonder ministers complained that they had become "almesmen". They might have resented also the necessity of being bookkeepers of their own indignities.

The pantry lists, however, were as nothing in comparison with the wood accounts. Every minister had his "Wood Book" and to the keeping of it went barren hours unending. Who had brought in a one foot cord and when? Who a four foot cord and how many more feet did he owe? How many "good Loads" all told, and how many "Ordinary Loads"? Who are behind and how many loads for each? Whose arrearages from last year are still overdue? How much walnut, oak, hickory and pine? The Town Book duplicated the totals; the minister kept track of the details. No other one item about the minister's relation to the town required so many separate motions, so much discussion, and often such hard feeling. Each succeeding year, as though by automatic accretion, the minister demanded more loads than he had received the year before. He was also likely to specify more hickory, less pine, more long loads, less short. The totals are astounding. How could he need first sixty, then seventy, eighty, ninety or often a hundred loads in one year? The one hundred and twenty "ordinary loads" achieved by David Parsons of Amherst brought an outburst from Sylvester Judd, historian, "I never found in any records a minister who consumed so much wood as Mr. Parsons",[28] he exclaimed, with apparent exasperation as well as amazement. "Out of wood. Burned a pig-stye"—a Parkman item—has numerous analogues in other ministerial diaries. As tension increased between pulpit and pew, something more than a note of petulance crept into the wood situation on both sides, and the one time "wood-frolic" that marked the end of the "bringing-in" lost its mirthful note. Instead, this date became a deadline after which delinquents would bring double. It would have been hard for any congregation toward the mid-century to believe that even "above 40 loads" *gratis* had once been thought an appropriate tribute to a beloved pastor as winter set in. For a day that laments its denuded hillsides, these *Wood* and *Bark Books* make painful reading.

Gradually the situation was eased, but even when salary increases were finally voted, there might be strings attached. Woodstock, Connecticut, voted a fifteen pound increase to Josiah Dwight, stipulating that henceforth he could find his own wood, and also issuing the crisp mandate that they would expect him to "devote himself more especially to his sacred function".[29] On fifteen pounds additional, one

wonders how. Such a decision settled nothing. Record of this same
town meeting illustrates another element in this widespread pulpit
and pew dissension. When the increase vote was taken, James Corbin,
citizen, registered his dissent, and on the grounds that the original
agreement with Josiah Dwight, minister, "having been complied
with" and "not seeing cause to exceed it" (not even after thirty-three
years) his vote was No. It was such literalness and rigidity on the one
side and the ministerial petulance on the other which made the "Salary
Dispute" a focal point of community unrest over many years. It
ruptured the peace in every town in which it occurred, and few towns
escaped. That ministers suffered financial hardship is clear enough;
but, as many of them realized, their pulpit influence and their status in
town life suffered more by the controversy into which financial
stringencies had plunged them.

   The most serious harm came to the pastoral work itself as the minister was forced more and more to seek "secular employment" in order to piece out his resources. Time had to be clipped from catechising
and instructing "the rising generation" in favor of more extensive
farming, more pupils to board and teach for pay, and whatever other
odd jobs he was ingenious enough to secure. More lamented still, there
was less and less time for reading and study after all these were at-
tended to. The item, "I have scarce been in my study all week", becomes more frequent in minister's diaries. Laymen as well as the clergy
were disquieted. Is it permissible for a minister to engage in "Secular
Employment", said the town, implying that the answer was No. Is it
fair for him to be "stak'd down for life" in one pulpit, said the minister, implying that the answer was also No. Why may he not seek a
better one if he can find it, said the minister, and this time the answer
was Yes. Is it fair for the richer members of the congregation to be
obliged to make up for the deficiencies of those who do not meet their
obligations, said the richer ones. And so the questions multiplied. One
very persistent question raised by both sides concerned taking money
from the public treasury to meet the need. Why not? Again and again
a church sent delegates to a Proprietors' meeting to see "what they
will du concerning the arrears of the ministry munny". In fact, certain desperate cases were relieved in this way, thereby throwing the

whole matter of "honorable support for the ministry" back on the very basis from which "the Lord's free People" had rebelled in the beginning. Was a state church once more ahead?

Young ministers were warned by all these troubles. Their letters of acceptance upon receiving a call show them grown realistic and on their guard as to their prospects. When Phineas Hemenway, aged twenty-eight, accepted "with a trembling soul" the pastorate of Townsend, Massachusetts, in 1736, he included an "extended coverage" provision as to the possible fluctuation of Bills of Credit;

> "to prevent future trouble or wrong on either side, which may arise upon that head, I desire and expect that the value of our province bills from time to time may be ascertained and secured, and that by a proper vote of the town".[30]

So saying, he signed himself,

> "Your Souls friend and Humble Servant"
> Phineas Hemenway.

"As to what you have Offered me for my outward Support I thankfully accept it", said John Emerson when invited to settle at Topsfield in 1728,

> "And inasmuch as it is my principle . . . That a Minister of ye Gospel should not intangle Himself in ye Affairs of this Life but give himself wholly to his Proper work and Business; I therefore cannot but hope that you will freely Minister as there shall be Occasion to my Necessity & for my Comfort. . . ."[31]

The phrase "free from the entanglements of this Life" is a frequent phrase in fifty years of acceptance letters. In so far as ministers meant increasing the budget by all manner of odd jobs, no one could blame them, but in so far as they meant separateness from the ongoing life of their time, they made a great mistake. They were growing realistic about their own prospects in their calling; they needed also to conceive the calling itself more realistically.

Andrew Tyler, in accepting Clapboard Trees in 1743, honored himself along with his calling when he labelled it

"this noble Employ; an Employment which there is not an Angel in Heaven but would clap his Wings for Joy to be engaged in".

So saying, he tried to forestall a personal deficit by

"hoping and expecting that from Time to Time you will make such Additions to what you now offer me as may serve to maintain me comfortably & handsomely so long as God in his holy & wise Providence shall continue me among you. And also that you will pass a vote that you will find me my Wood after three years from this Time, . . . And now here upon, my dear Brethren, I devote myself to the Service of God".[32]

Perhaps this is only a young man's clumsy way of phrasing it, but if words mean what they say, Andrew Tyler (self-styled) would seem considerably lower than the jubilant angels who would be so glad to change places with him.

Ordination sermons over many years reflect this two-way resentment between pastor and people. Until ministers began to change pulpits frequently in the 1740's, an ordination was still a once or twice in a lifetime event. People came in throngs from miles around. The meetinghouse galleries were once again propped against the extra weight they must bear. Spectators even sat on the beams over the congregation. "Horse-houses" were stocked with provender. A feast was prepared which would be talked about for months afterward. At the ordination of Edwin Jackson at Woburn in 1728 the town spent an amount equalling two-thirds of his annual salary in the four-day festivity: four hundred and thirty-three dinners, one hundred and seventy-eight breakfasts and suppers, thirty-two horses kept for four days, six and a half barrels of cider, twenty-five gallons of wine, four gallons of rum with sugar and lime juice to match, and pipes for all was only part of the total account. Lavishness was the keynote.

The young minister was the center of it all. On his side solemnity was the keynote.

"This was truely the Greatest Day I ever yet saw. . . . The Day of my Solemn Separation to ye Work of ye Gospel Ministry and my Ordination to ye Pastorate in Westborough",

twenty-two year old Ebenezer Parkman wrote in his *Diary* in 1724.

"I wish Every Day thro'out my Life, may bear a suitable proportion to this Day."[33]

Year by year he would measure his personal religious growth as well as his success in the ministry from this milestone. Ordination day was his day of dedication.

On both sides it was a forward-looking day and all anticipations were hopeful, had they only been allowed to remain so. Instead, the veteran preacher of the day, battle-scarred from his own woes, too often injected a sour note, sometimes a scolding one or, more unfortunate still, a superior one. God might have spoken to us directly from heaven by the mouth of his glorious angels, said Moses Dickinson, but He didn't. He chose ministers. Remember this and treat them accordingly. The pastoral office is of divine origin, said Thomas Symmes. Magnify it. Talk about it. Insist on the honors due you. Reprove those who speak against it. To the welcoming congregation he counselled—Don't expect us to be perfect, "We are *Men* and not *incarnate Angels*".[34] Nathaniel Henchman dared to label his sermon *The Divine Pastor*. "The Pastoral office is of Divine Institution", he said; "It is from Heaven and not of Men".[35]

Nearly all ordination sermons warned of trouble to come. Thomas Clap, aged only twenty-nine, warned Ephraim Little, five years his Junior, that ministers often have to deal with "Stiff and turbulent Spirits", and that the judgment of the pew was often governed by personal affection and disaffection rather than a "sincere regard toward religion and the good of souls". Nathaniel Henchman told James Varney that he might expect to be "expos'd to the Fury of Hell"; Yes, and in "a peculiar manner", said Nehemiah Walter. "There is no Order of Men more, or so much expos'd to the Fury of Hell",[36] Thomas Symmes announced almost as though it were a special qualification or even an honor. Excel they must, if only in temptation.

William Williams even introduced the salary dispute into his ordination sermon for David Hall at Sutton. To support a minister honorably "is not an Act of Charity but of Justice", he said. Edward
Holyoke touched another sensitive point when he defended a minister's right to "demand submission" from his people. His office is
dignified, he said, despite the many endeavors

> "in this Infidel Age of the World to make our character low and
> despis'd, while we are represented as such as should be treated as
> the Alms-men of the People. . . . *We demand of you that you
> honor and reverence your Pastor*".[37]

Why? Because he is the Ambassador of a Prince and should be so received.

Such injunctions on such a day would almost inevitably spoil a
good many things. The note of festivity would give place to resentment. One's sympathy goes out to the young incumbent who must
listen to these counsels in the presence of those he had come to serve
presumably "for life". It would take years for him to live down such
expectations of trouble.

The young pastor was often personally advised as well. Thomas
Foxcroft, having defined the ministry as "an Office of Authority",
albeit authority which might be "sweetened and regulated by Affection and Endearment", advised young John Lowell at Newbury in
1725 to conduct himself with "Gravity in the Pulpit and out of it".

> "All kind of *Levity* is childish; very unseemly in Parents . . . but
> more so in Ministers."[38]

"Gravity in Garb, in Mien, and in Language" were particularly specified. If he lived up to the ministerial ideal in these as in other respects,
he might deserve "to be mourned when dead". Hardly the counsel
for a young man, one might say. Less so Ebenezer Turrell's amendment to the early ministerial ideal, "Ministers should carefully avoid
giving Offence in any Thing",[39] although Samuel Cooke, whose
initiation he was honoring, was fortunately a better man than to heed
any such soft-pedalling counsels.

"And finally", said William Williams in conclusion, quoting the *Epistle to the Romans* but meaning the Sutton congregation and David Hall, their new pastor, "If it be possible, live peaceably". It was too much to hope in 1729.

Met by themselves in ministerial conclave, ministers spoke even more bluntly of their changed estate, and the wiser ones among them gave more good advice than was ever taken. "Don't fight back", said Ebenezer Gay at a convention in Boston; "show a Dove-like spirit";

"A Dove-like spirit is a requisite and eminent Qualification of a Gospel Minister".[40]

A dove is harmless, meek, gentle; a Dove has no Gall, he continued. Neither had Ebenezer Gay, but one may question whether the first generation story might not have been differently written had New England churches been captained by a race of doves.

Don't level your artillery against those who have offended you was sounder advice, but advice not often taken. Ministers in trouble with their congregations could too easily find Scripture convenient for their purpose. For a man on the verge of dismissal to face his Sunday congregation with the text, "Should such an one as I flee?" may have given the minister a dash of satisfaction, but he had ruined his cause beyond hope thereby. If dismissal had already been voted, he might in all safety choose *Hebrews* 4, 2: "The word preached did not profit them, not being mixed with faith in them that heard it". At least he had the satisfaction of the last word.

"It was not difficult", Ebenezer Parkman wrote in his *Journal*,

"for ye Congregation to perceive yt my Subject pointed at ye purposed Business before us on ye Morrow".[41]

Certainly not; he had seen to that, and in consequence the devil won still another battle.

Read backwards through the first half of the century, both the ordination counsels and the incessant pulpit and pew battles make one story. The issues underneath declared themselves more plainly with each new outbreak of trouble. The clergy were clinging to their former prerogatives of reproof, authority, and respectful obedience, unwilling to admit that they had already lost the battle to retain them. The pew was saying thus far and no farther, unaware that they had won the same battle. Town by town it had been a Hundred Years' War and invariably each new outbreak came to the same end. As far back as 1645 when Thomas Parker had "lovingly permitted" his Newbury people to run their own affairs as long as they did not run them counter to his desire, the clergy had been beaten in this contest for authority. Thomas Parker was not stupid and certainly not malicious. He had honestly believed that

> "The church is to be carried, not to carry; to obey, not to command; to be subject, not to govern".

Expediency was one of the grounds for his view. As he saw it,

> "There is more time spent in informing the church, than in determining the case. Must elders hold the hands of the common members (as the master teacheth scholars to write) and act only by them?"[42]

The sequel, as Thomas Parker discovered, was a twenty-seven year battle in Newbury and, in the end, two churches, two ministers, and a harvest of bitterness that could still be reaped in the fence corners after still another generation had come and gone. Underneath the now dusty and lifeless details of this long record of protests both congregational and pastoral, of church councils called year after year only to be adjourned and new councils called, of recommendations made and passing unheeded, of court sessions given over to the hearing of grievances, of fines imposed, of suspensions, of time out for the persuasion of both sides who in turn refused to be persuaded, the issues are plain to see. It was clearly a case of one man telling many men what they might do, and of these many men saying we will not have it so. Over and over in the long series of manoeuvres the "common members" were merely demanding a voice. Their side of the argument is clear in almost any one of the many pages of evidence which document this long Newbury procedure. The crux of the whole matter is contained in a single sentence from witnesses who testified under oath in the court proceedings of 1669, in these words,

"We testify that Mr. Parker in a public meeting said that for the time to come I am resolved nothing shall be brought into the church, but it shall be brought first to me, and if I approve of it, it shall be brought in, if I do not approve of it, it shall not be brought in".[43]

A hundred years later Americans would have a word for such procedures, with action to match. It would take even so long to transfer the reins to "common" hands.

Some ministers who read the signs of the times as to various parish procedures of the more practical sort, were inflexible when it came to changing the inherited notion as to the superiority of their calling and the privileges that superiority conferred.

"Ministerial Work is not to be *levell'd* with *Mechanic* Labours, *Merchandize*, nor other more *Liberal* Imployments neither; the Practice of *Physick*, or the Teaching of *Philosophy*, not Excepted",[44]

said Benjamin Colman as early as 1708, in a sermon preached before the General Court. Practicers of Physick and teachers of philosophy were few in that auditory, so that the qualified exception in their favor would have afforded scant comfort to the mechanics, laborers and local merchandisers present. Already, and long before 1708, these common men knew what they wanted, and year by year and case by case, as they protested one infringement after another, when occasion offered, it was the many saying bluntly,

"Ministers have no right or authority but by consent of the church".

By controlling the church body from the pulpit, Thomas Parker and others like him had thought to keep things running smoothly, and as he had said, "to make the church a pattern of punctual order". The long-continued ensuing battles showed how wrongly he had estimated the tenacity to principle of these "common members" and how blind he was to the future that even so early as 1645 was already casting its shadow before. Progress would come by trial and error, not by a pattern of "punctual order".

By the late 1730's that future had arrived. At one extreme, victory for the laity meant such a noisy and indecorous episode as that of Samuel Fiske of Salem in 1735, as he was restrained by force of muscle from entering his pulpit; in fact, dragged out of it and put under bond to civil authority. The importance of such an unfortunate affair had nothing to do with its sensationalism, except that by virtue of inflamed Salem feelings the issues underneath this "Great Ruffle" became better known to all wayfaring men within hearing distance. Representatives to the General Court even campaigned on a Fiske or No-Fiske platform while the great stir was on. Though fortunately such affairs were by no means typical, even one was too many; and other congregations than Salem had to witness the spectacle of their pastor's way to the pulpit blocked in the aisle or even on the pulpit stairs. If he were young and agile enough to make the desk safely the first time, he might know that on the next Sunday, or the one after, he too would be forcibly dragged out. Temporarily, preaching itself became less important than the power to control it. Whatever the circumstances framing these boisterous affairs, the issue was almost invariably authority; do we have it, or does he? Traditionally, a minister could not be legally dismissed unless he be delinquent in one of the stated qualifications: "able, orthodox, pious, and of good conversation", but as the "Lord brethren" gained the upper hand, it presently became possible to dismiss him for no better reason than that "we are tired of him", "he isn't smart enough", or "we can't reverence him any longer".

In vain ministers invoked their traditional "rights" as they saw them. Some of the more militant refused to call a church meeting or refused to put a vote which would have forced them to call one. Some even dared to "negative" a congregational vote after it had been legally taken. But they could not "negative" a town meeting vote. All that was left to do was to make vociferous protest. Josiah Dwight of Woodstock, Connecticut, having been voted out sixty to one, went into print declaring that it is "a mistake and a great one to think that the pastoral relation is nulled by a vote at a town meeting".[45] He spoke from conviction but he spoke in vain. He was out. So were others who refused to be dismissed. The option was not theirs.

At the opposite extreme from all such noisy and undignified procedures stood the willing recognition of congregational rights by ministers whose annals were mainly annals of peaceful relations. Perhaps the price of peace was sometimes too high. A notation in the handwriting of Moses Adams of Acton, Massachusetts, for June 14, 1739, shows such acknowledgment carried out to a pin-point degree. He wrote in his *Diary*,

> "It being lecture day, after the blessing was pronounced, I desired the church to tarry, and asked their minds concerning the remainder of the elements after communion, and they voted 'I should have 'em' ".[46]

Every member of the church had paid half a crown annually (in two instalments) to buy the requisite bread and wine, and because they had paid, they had the legal right to dispose of the leftovers. It was a right that mattered. Not only do the roots of democracy lie deep, but its first delicate tendrils may be all but invisible to the naked eye.

CHAPTER THIRTEEN

"Gales of Heavenly Wind"

Logically, one might suppose that the wholesale dismissals of the 1740's meant conclusive victory for the pew in this long battle against pulpit authority, but it was not so. The great show-down between ministers and their people, which had been building up for over twenty years, never came off. Instead, battle broke out on a new front. The issues back of the dismissals in nearly every parish in New England during the 1740's were only secondarily governmental. Primarily, they were doctrinal. All at once, or so it seemed, what a man believed became once more important, even desperately so. The "Gales of Heavenly Wind", set in motion by George Whitefield and other revival preachers, did freakish things to the landscape of "approved doctrine". In a month's time, chaos. Orthodoxy itself, as previously understood, became suspect. What we have listened to all our lives is not "Gospel truth". Our minister is unconverted. He is "blind, leading souls to Hell". We want Gospel preaching.

There were two ways to get it: the minister could be dismissed or the "aggrieved Brethren" could secede. Both methods presented difficulties, but to a determined minority in the New Light controversy, no barrier constituted a blockade. Too much was at stake. Let church councils recommend and the General Court censure; defy them. Let our own church suspend all of us at once; we can build another meetinghouse and call a minister of our own. Let the town demand that we continue our Rate to our former pastor; refuse to pay. Stick together and win. In the end the aggrieved party usually took the simpler of the two methods; they merely walked out.

Belligerency was not the main drive back of these many dismissals and separations. Nor, for all the intensity of feeling, was it mainly disaffection toward the minister. Fundamentally, upheavals came because the time was ripe for change. The ministerial pattern had become too rigid. Sermons were too stylized; doctrine as preached too negative. There was too much scolding. A new emphasis was imperative if religion were to retain its vitality in life as it was being lived. The "deadness in religion" was a stale pronouncement; the itemized list of community sins too familiar. It would take more than committees appointed by the General Court and by ministerial associations to change either.

Into this framework of long admitted "deadness" came word of the Northampton revivals of the late thirties. Ministers went to see for themselves and brought back reports to their congregations. Jonathan Edwards printed his *Faithful Narrative of the Surprizing Work of God . . . in Northampton,* so that the story could be read, as it was, and widely. Here was miracle, romance, excitement, hope. If such marvels could happen in Northampton, only a horseback journey away, why not in Longmeadow, Boston, New London, everywhere? Oldtimers recalled far-off revivals as evidence that a new outpouring might yet be possible.

At this moment George Whitefield arrived, with the record of revivals even more amazing than Northampton's immediately behind him. He could not have asked for a better prepared or more alert auditory. His phenomenal success was all but foreordained. His was a new voice and a golden one. He was young and magnetic. His powers of spontaneous eloquence had no parallel in America. His pulpit innovations, the dramatic impersonations, the moving appeals, the frightening predictions of doom if they were ignored, made the usual Sunday sermons and the decorous routine of the meetinghouse dull and unprofitable. In a month's time he had made both the familiar fare and the method of imparting it obsolete. He had also widened the distance between the old and the new until it could no longer be bridged. Moreover, by his own bold iconoclasm, his criticism of the settled ministry as unconverted and presently as "enemies to the Great Work", he gave direction to the hunger for change for which the time was well ripe and provided lay restlessness with a concrete program of action.

Henceforth almost every congregation in New England lined up in opposed factions, New Lights against Old Lights, and the pastor obliged to take sides with one or the other. In this warfare there was no neutrality. Reconciliation was seldom possible; in fact it was seldom attempted, with the result that presently every congregation became two and the unity of the town in religious matters was gone. The 1740's were a Great Divide and many things would never be the same again.

The Great Awakening cannot be disposed of as merely extravagant emotionalism. In ways not immediately discernible, and in spite of all its frenzied excesses, its "Errors, Irregularities, Mischiefs", it was a constructive, liberalizing force in mid-century life. Far more was involved than the new-style preaching, new ways of thought and action for both pulpit and pew. Its fundamental philosophy was a leaven which presently would have to be dealt with politically and socially as well as religiously. A plain man's war was coming, and a war for what he believed to be his rights as a human being. Whitefield's doctrine increased his sense of personal dignity by putting the responsibility for his salvation more squarely on his own shoulders. More important still, the New Light–Old Light controversy forced men in all ranks to take sides, make decisions, and break with the loyalties of a lifetime. It brought uncertainty into areas which had hitherto been stable, and required courage of a sort that pioneer life had not often taxed. For a covenant member to set himself and his own individual judgment in opposition to the authority he had recognized all his life as final, and to secede from the church of his baptismal vows, was an experience which had no parallel in the lives of many who took the risk. By comparison, going to meeting, musket in hand, had been far easier.

Proof of this courage and also substantial evidence as to how much religion still mattered to those who had so long been accused of "deadness in religion" survive in the individual reasons submitted in writing for each withdrawing member. This requirement was one detail of pastoral vigilance that was seldom relaxed, as New Lights withdrew from Old Lights. In order to depart in good standing, a church member must write out his reasons for becoming a "Separate". In these letters (a few of which have been preserved) one may see the plain man making up his mind on what still mattered to him more than anything else in this life, and justifying his decision not only to the pastor but also to himself.

The anguish of spirit which these letters sometimes reveal lets one into various secrets—human secrets—which have to do with more than controversial issues under the Great Awakening label. These men and women, some of whom could not sign their own names, were experiencing a conflict of loyalties such as they had never faced before, and making a decision on the deepest level of thought and feeling of which they were capable. "Heat of spirit", desire for power, belligerency, are the last motives to be fairly applied to these statements of desperate earnestness from men and women who admit their confusion, their fear to go and fear to stay. The combination of untutored eloquence and pulpit language in such statements is sometimes strangely moving.

A sheaf of MS. letters surviving from Sturbridge, Massachusetts, presents fair samples of this desperate struggle.[1] The fact that these particular letters happen to have been written (or dictated) by men and women of limited horizon, some of whom appear never to have "labored in their minds till now" is unimportant. When intellectuals wrote out their reasons for separating, they attempted to clarify their position logically, minimizing the personal in favor of the doctrinal issues involved. Their letters illuminate the New Light controversy as an intellectual movement. By comparison, the letters of the Sturbridge Separates merely lay bare the hearts (among others) of Jonathan Perry, Hannah Cory, David Morse, Jerusha Morse (who could not sign her name), John Corey, Sarah Morton, Hannah Collon, Naomy Ward, Sarah Wood, Stephen and Sarah Blanchard. Excerpts can hardly do justice to these unrehearsed answers to the pastor's reproachful questioning. Why did they break covenant and leave their brothers and sisters in Christ?

Said Jonathan Perry, April 5, 1749.

"My Resons for Seperating from you are your not walking according to the order of the Gospel as you ought to dwo and in perticular that Transaction Committed and Countenanced by maney of you on the 16th of May last which the Lord made use of to open my Eyes and to Shwo me what you ware and what your Religion was and he has showon me that you are not a Church of his according to the order of the Gospel". [He quotes *Revelation* 18, 4–5 and II *Thessalonians* 3, 6–19 in support of his accusation.]

Said Hannah Cory, April 5, 1749.

"Whereas I am desired to give my reasons for separating from you, one time as I was coming to the Lecture the words come to me in Cor. come out from amongst ym, and then these words in Amos, can two walk together Except they be agreed, so I went to the meeting house, and when I came in there was no body & as I set there these words came to me my house is a house of prayer but ye have made it a den of thieves, then sudden fear came over me so I got up and went out and walked over the burying place and I thought I had rather lie down among the Graves than go into the meeting house, but when I se Mr Rice [minister] comeing I went in but it seemd to be a dark place Ministers deacon and people lookt Strangely as if they were all going Blindfold to destruction, and tho my body was there, my soul was with the Seperates, praising God as soon as I was dismysd at the meeting house I went to Brother Nevils where my Soul was sweetly refresht, the Lord alone be praised for it was he alone who Brought me out and not any Creature. . . . yet altho I was not free of some degree of rising against some outward actions or noises of the Seperates yet this avanisht upon the sweet oneness of soul I felt toward them. . . ."

Said David Morse, April 8, 1749.

"My dear Brothers and Sisters, In answer to your Request I freely give you my Reasons why I Sepperated and also why I joyned with you at the first. I being satisfied of my own Convertion and that theare was a Church of Christ heare upon Earth, and God not have-ing shown me then the forme and fashion of the house and this was the Door I ran Into your Church In ignorance and Darkness not knowing how the Church of Christ was bu[i]lt by the fellowship of the Gospil. then by the Goodness of God I being Leid [led] by his holy word and spirit to see how the Pastor and Deacons should be Quallified and also how Church members be the members of Christs body [he quotes many N.T. verses] now my dear Brethren which of you Can Set to your Seal that God has Really founded you upon the Rock of Ages for according to the word of God this Church is Right the Reverse. . . ."

On the opposite side of the same sheet, Jerusha, presumably his wife, makes her mark after a somewhat nearer approach to *reasons*.

"My Brethren In answer to your Desire I freely Give In my Rea-sons why I Seperated, I being at a Church meeting and seeing so much want of Love and faithfullness at that time as well as at many other times notwithstanding the Covenant obligations which we had Laid ourselves under proving to me the wants of Gods Presents and notwithstanding my attending on the Publick worship in this place and ordinance of the Lords Supper—Especially the Last Sac-rament Day I was with you I still Labouring under Darkness and Drestress and Separation Comeing on and haveing an oppertunity to hear the sepperate ministers—",

she was confused. Both sides said they had the right way. She was more confused. She "laboured long in her Darkness", was afraid to come to the sacrament, and finally in her great distress went to Mr. Rice to be guided. Wisely or unwisely, he told her that he could not advise her, and that maybe the Separates were right.

"which now my Dear friends and fellow morltals, if my teacher was not founded upon a Certainty I might be evrr Larning and never able to Come to the Knowledge of the truth wharefore I taking David's Advice in the Psalm It is better to trust In the Lord than put Confidence in Teachers and by Looking to God I am more and more Confirmed In the Religion I am now In and now my friend Let us Remember this one thing to pray with and for one another for whatsoever is not of faith is sin."

her

jerusha X morse

mark

John Corey gives as his "reason" a sermon by Mr. Rice against the Separates, which was "as a Sword in my flesh and was a grate greef to me". Later as he was going along to the meetinghouse, a clap of thunder seemed to him a warning from heaven. He could go no further.

"The Lord then gave me to see the Sepperates God was my God and thay was my people—."

Said Hannah Callon, April 5, 1749.

"The reasons why I separated from you as a church was these. I was after great tryals brought to see that the Church was not right; but still at a Loss where to go; at Last I was Constrain to Cmitt the Case to God and cry to him that he would teach me my Duty, and shew me his way, and he answered me and shew me clearly that I must leave you and joyn to the Seperates; . . . from that text 2 cor 6 from the fourteenth to the End, and here I must Confess my Sin of unfaithfullness in not reminding you of what I saw amiss amongst you especially on Sabath Day noons."

hannah Callon

[The nature of the Sabbath noon dereliction is not revealed.]

Sarah Morton admitted at first she had been "a fraid of the Separate teachers because they had no larning", but then she had been led to open her Bible to *Acts* 4, 13, and finding it there written that Peter and John had been "unlearned and ignorant men", she henceforth listened with a clear conscience. As is apparent in all of these alleged "reasons", thanks to an hourglass twice turned during a lifetime of Sabbaths, these men and women knew where to find what they needed in order to support their case against a learned ministry.

Stephen Blanchard is content with his new choice. All doubt and distress have vanished. He is "conscience convinced" the Separatists are right.

> "My friends, I darst not refuse to hear thos powerful truths which ware delivered by them—because they had no more then common human learning but I must tell you that this to me rather proves that herein is the grat power of God manifest that the glory may apear of God and not of men—"

Sarah Blanchard, wife of Stephen, is the most articulate one of the group and her story one of the most detailed. In her long circumstantial account of her progress toward a "soul satisfying" decision, she does not spare herself. The utter honesty of her self-revelation is disarming. A more worldly-wise Separate would have held back much which she openly reports to her own disadvantage, but Sarah Blanchard was a realist. She tells that at first she was "resolved not to weigh things to know what was of God & what was of man"; she was going to heaven the regular way, but she slipped into several Separate meetings on week days, "more to find what I could git against them than to finde the truth", but the preaching was so powerful that she forgot why she had come and was

> "conscience convinct & sure that that was the gospel of Christ . . . it apeard plain to me that thes unlarned men ware the foolish things that God had chose to confound the wisdom of the wise . . . but notwithstanding there was a grate struggle between my concence & my pride . . . for that I was convenced that this was the truth as it is in jesus . . . yet I could not bear to be cald a Sepperate and bare the flouts & scoffs of those my Companions . . . so I went to the meeting house still".

She even talked against the Separates to get the esteem of her fellow-members and then went home to suffer privately for her duplicity. Presently there came a day when she was ready to know the truth, whichever way it led her, and the Separates won. The core of her reasoning, as of that of all in this particular group, was "godliness and the gospel was a mistry out of the reach of all human larning and natural understanding"; therefore when proclaimed by an ignorant man it seemed more genuine than when it came by way of a Harvard graduate. The learned ministry was beaten before they even attempted an answer.

These confessions do not belong to Sturbridge alone. There were hundreds of Sarah Blanchards whose bewilderment and anguish make one story. Whether they went or stayed, these covenant members faced a crisis on a plane where they were not at home. Their decisions were reached slowly, prolonging the anguish and the bewilderment. These Sturbridge Separates had waited nine years before announcing their shift of loyalty. Some of them reversed themselves, begged forgiveness and returned to their former communion. Between the lines of Naomy Ward's recantation after thirteen years of Separatism one reads a disturbing story of more confusion, more anguish of spirit. She had "gone Contrery to the Mind and Will of God"; would they take her back? She pled no redeeming fact in her tale of error for which she deserved "to have been left of God to have walked in Bitterness of my Soul in Darkness all my Days". Sarah Wood in her recantation comforted herself that at least she had not consented to "reBaptism by being dipped". Many Separates, in fact, most, had become Baptists. A long sectarian battle was ahead over what may now appear to be relatively minor matters, and it would be not only the Naomy Wards who would consider them of major importance.

Unlearned preaching had also come to stay, and for the best of all reasons; the audience was ready. Ten years earlier when George Weeks of Brewster, Massachusetts, had attempted to preach to some near-by Indians "without ever saying a word to his pastor about it", there had been consternation in the Brewster pews as well as in the pulpit. A man "with a barely common education", how dare he thrust himself into a calling intended only for "distinguishingly qualified persons"? It was "inexcusable presumption", a violation of George Weeks's "covenant ingagement" and tended to bring "absolute confusion in all our instituted church".[2] In the early 1740's such confusion had arrived. Even after revival excitement had faded, the demand for an extemporaneous preacher, who could substitute warmth of zeal for formal training, remained; and there would continue to be a place for him on the expanding frontier more than a hundred years later. Often but not always he was a man from the ranks, uneducated, a man of one book, an easy flow of words, and powerful lungs. His voice could be heard "as far as the old market" was the recommendation of Joseph Snow of Providence, a man "brought up in the business of house carpentry", and ministering for fifty years to a Separate congregation born in the Tennent revivals. Such a man would henceforth be the rival and often the successful rival of the ministerial candidate, who by virtue of his college degree had been "duly approbated for preaching".

Whig and Tory sympathies began to be apparent in the secessions of the late 1740's and early 50's. This was no longer a Holy War; it had gone far beyond the meetinghouse walls, beyond infant baptism or not, dipping or not. Party alignments, which had harried most towns since their founding days, now had more than personal elements as their *raison d'être*. The "aggrieved Brethren" had also learned how to make their "smart opposition" more than a thorn to those who did not see eye to eye with them. Secessions were one expression of a growing boldness in organized opposition. How effective and how formidable could a plain man's opposition be? He would try it and find out.

His methods may have been clumsy, but his motivation in these Separate upheavals was better than personal. He wanted to know the truth. The Connecticut layman who (according to family tradition), when doctrine as preached was not in line with his straight-edge went axe in hand to the meetinghouse, chopped out the sheep-pen pew in which he and his family had sat ever since the meetinghouse was built, and transferred it "root and branch and all in all" to his own attic, was not a vandal. He was a man of conviction, and furthermore he had the courage to declare it. Thirty years hence he would be one to erect a Liberty Pole or perchance to cut one down. The fact that this same uprooted pew became the rallying ground of other "aggrieved" members of the congregation and that presently this small group constituted the nucleus of a new church society is in itself something of a parable of growth according to life, at least for new churches of the mid-century. The Cambridge Platform had symbolized growth somewhat differently. When the hive grew uncomfortably crowded, said the 1648 brethren met in conclave, a company of unhoused bees sallied forth in peace and harmony to make honey elsewhere. They did so neither by the logic of bees nor that of the propagation of churches, as these framers of the 1648 Platform might have been surprised to discover had they returned precisely a hundred years later.

But a disordered beehive was only part of the story. The Great Awakening invites inquiry in various other directions than as the cause of "disquietude" in the instituted fellowship. In the long view its importance was chiefly doctrinal. It had truly meant what its sponsors and adherents called "Gospel Freedom", in that it was one of several successful challenges to the old orthodoxy; in fact, the most successful. Socially and politically, its effects were far reaching and on several planes of thought and action. Not all of its effects were good, either immediately or in the generations that followed, but all are part of the American story beyond the meetinghouse walls as well as within them. For the thirty years immediately preceding the Revolution, its importance, both for good and for evil, went far beyond its extravagant evangelism, its unseemly behaviors, its endless bickerings and the too sudden release from traditional restraints which occasioned most of its excesses. The upheaval itself was important, as such. In village terms it amounted to a minor civil war, family against family, neighbor against neighbor, laymen against their leaders. It meant defiance of an authority that in current thought was still representative of God Himself. Perhaps most important of all, in the longer story, it meant the facing of essential principles and the courage to translate them into action. In the words of one body of "aggrieved brethren" in one disordered congregation, as they engaged in a three-year correspondence with their pastor, several houses away, and sought admission to another church fellowship,

> "Now brethren, we lookt upon it as the natural right of every Man to enquire and judge for himself in matters of Religion & that without Check or Control from any Man. He is bound to act according to the Dictates of his own Conscience".[3]

This was in 1746. Forty-six years further on this conviction would be written into a notable American document. 1746 would have been too early to write it; experience had not yet caught up with the principle as stated, but the decisions which the Great Awakening forced put men in a state of mind favorable to inquiry as to the principles by which they wished to live. In the troubled 1740's they learned fast and thought passionately of their rights and privileges in this present world. The "wide door of libertie" which the 1630's had talked about was now opening more widely before their eyes.

BOOK FIVE

~~~~~~~~~~~~~~~~~~~~~~~~~~~~~~~

POWDER IN THE MEETINGHOUSE

CHAPTER FOURTEEN

"A People in Love with Liberty"

Lᴇss than a decade later the clergy had a new chance and took it. In the 1750's ànd 60's ministers could not have been currently chosen for the rôle they were to play. Nor could they have assumed it themselves. Unofficial leadership in time of crisis was theirs by virtue of the part they had taken in public affairs from the beginning. When crisis came again and it was time to speak out boldly and to act, parish quarrels were shifted into the background. People turned to the minister with complete naturalness and he with equal naturalness moved over into the political arena. Dismissing him was no longer the main business before the meeting. Besides, he had already been dismissed; perhaps several times. As the area of thought and action became larger than the village, it was fortunate indeed that some of the major issues now to be clarified nationally had already been faced time after time within the narrower world of the meetinghouse walls.

Partly as a smoke-screen no doubt, the opposition (for this was to be a civil war) raised the cry of politics in the pulpit. Stick to your last, they said, in effect, and they said it so often and so vehemently that some of the clergy felt obliged to answer, thus deflecting emphasis for a time from current issues. In this preliminary skirmish, and in the popular mind long afterward, the term *politics* was loosely used to cover the whole area of contemporary affairs. Hence, various ministers, who wished to speak to "our present unrest" at any point, felt called upon to justify their excursion into a realm not strictly religious. The prefatory apology to a "political" sermon became a convention.

"Obedience to the civil magistrate is a Christian duty"; then why not talk about it in a Christian assembly? This from young Jonathan Mayhew in the preface to his 1750 *Discourse concerning Unlimited Submission and Non-Resistance to the Higher Powers,* a sermon preached "by order" on the anniversary of the death of Charles I.

> "Besides, if it be said, that it is out of character for a Christian minister to meddle with such a subject, this censure will at last fall upon the holy apostles."

He cushioned this latter remark by adding, for the ears of officialdom present,

> "GOD be thanked one may, in any part of the BRITISH dominions, speak freely (if a decent regard be paid to those in authority) both of government and religion; and even give some broad hints, that he is engaged on the side of Liberty, the Bible and Common sense in opposition to Tyranny, PRIESTCRAFT and Non-sense".[1]

Jonathan Mayhew himself was speaking freely on this occasion, not least when he attacked the very "order" he was obeying in preaching this anniversary sermon. "How came this anniversary of King Charles's death to be solemnized as a day of fasting and humiliation", he asked, obviously in protest. It was instituted to soothe and flatter Charles II, and at the expense of English liberties.

> "Suppose *our* forefathers did kill their *mock* saint and martyr, a century ago, what is that to *us* now?"[2]

As for Charles himself, he was "A man black with guilt and *laden with iniquity*". As for this anniversary,

> "It is to be hoped, that it will prove a standing *memento,* that *Britons* will not be *slaves;* and a warning to all corrupt *councellors* and *ministers,* not to go too far in advising to arbitrary despotic measures".[3]

Combative vehemence such as this was Jonathan Mayhew's characteristic idiom and he could use it to turn a brush fire into a conflagration on almost any subject he touched. "Morning gun of the Revolution" or not (probably not) he was an exciting force of considerable strength in the pre-Liberty Pole era, and had he lived to bear a part in the main drama, his contribution may well have been memorable. Every crusade needs such a voice. When this 1750 sermon made him the target of hostile criticism, he welcomed it and proceeded to court further attack by calling attention to his own boldness. In a 1755 preface he announced that if his sermons contained "dangerous errors and mistakes", at least they did not "skulk in the dark". "They appear in open day-light, with all the naked boldness of truth and innocence." Oppose me or refute me as much as you like, he went on (overdoing it a little),

> "But I must now declare, once for all, that I will not be, even *religiously* scolded, nor pitied, nor wept and lamented, out of any principles which I believe upon the authority of Scripture, in the exercise of that small share of reason, which God has given me".[4]

These principles were of course not new; Americans had heard them all their lives, but Jonathan Mayhew had the good fortune to be uttering them again and with militant earnestness when men's minds were deeply stirred over far more than the politics in the pulpit issue to which he was immediately addressing himself. Chiefly, they were stirred by the threat of what looked like a large-scale French invasion now taking shape on the northern frontiers. This was more than a military threat, formidable as it promised to be through an alliance with the "barbarous nations". It was also a threat to religious freedom. Once more popery reared its head.

> "Do I behold these territories of freedom, become the prey of arbitrary power?"
> "Do I see Christianity banished for popery! the bible for the massbook! the oracles of truth, for fabulous legends!"
> "Do I see a protestant, there, stealing a look at his bible, and being taken in the fact, punished like a felon!"

First Meetinghouse in Vermont, erected in Bennington, about 1763.
From a painting owned by the Bennington Historical Museum and Art Gallery.
By courtesy of the Museum.

There could be no blight more ruinous to everything New England had cherished from the beginning,

> "all liberty, property, religion, happiness, changed, or rather trans-substantiated, into slavery, poverty, superstition, wretchedness!"[5]

Death itself would be preferable, at least in pulpit rhetoric.

In 1750 there were also vague rumors afloat that an American episcopate was in prospect and at no very considerable distance. This too would be a threat which concerned laymen as well as the clergy. If it came, the liberty to exercise congregational self-government would again be in the balance, a cause for which every church society in the colonies had staged enough bitter fights already. More ominous still, there had been of late a note of authority in Parliamentary attitudes which was arousing undercover resentment and suspicion on every level of colonial thinking. For all these reasons and possibly more, Jonathan Mayhew's "extended forecast", "By the looke of the clouds, we are to expect bad weather"[6] was no merely generalized warning. His 1750 hearers knew the precise danger zones, and if the preacher's warning were justified, the politics in the pulpit case was won.

Not all his brother ministers, however, saw eye to eye as to such use of the "sacred desk".

> "I am by no means fond of employing your sacred time in harangues upon political and military subjects",

said Samuel Davies of Virginia in a Thanksgiving sermon of 1759, after the French invasion had long been a reality,

> "and last Sunday I intended to touch upon them once for all, and then confine myself to the more important concerns of religion and eternity . . . but Providence in one week has surprised us by so many good turns that we are forced to take account of them".[7]

Considering that the "good turns" included Crown Point, Ticonderoga and Niagara, with "the sword of the Lord and of General Amherst gleaming from afar", this excursion into gratitude would seem to have needed no apology, but, as the evangelist in Samuel Davies saw it, "We are still a wicked lot", and he needed every minute of sermon-time to say so. Presently, he too would think differently. In fact, he had already preached one of the most successful recruiting sermons of the war, a sermon memorable to later times for the prophecy (tucked away in a footnote) of "that heroic Youth Col. *Washington*, whom I cannot but hope Providence has hitherto preserved in so signal a Manner, for some important Service to his Country".[8]

While this controversy over politics in the pulpit was waxing alternately hot and cold throughout the decade, Election and Artillery sermons remained unchallenged territory for ever bolder comment on public affairs. On these annual occasions the "Art of Government" and the "Art of War" continued to have their traditional hour. To a casual ear Election and Artillery preachers might seem to be saying only what their predecessors had said for a hundred years, and in a literal sense they were. In stiffly patterned fashion they still enjoined newly elected magistrates to be "nursing fathers" to the church, still proved by Scripture that civil government is a divine institution and the foundation of all social happiness, that without it "civil society must disband or prove no better than a combination of Pirates and Highwaymen", that religion is its greatest ornament and its surest guarantee of prosperity, and that liberty has foundation in law and the obedience to it. Good rulers were still taken apart, lineament by lineament, and put together in ideal proportions; the religious motives of the fathers still extolled, current sins deplored—particularly "the worse than British sin of drunkenness"—and the rising generation warned.

Artillery sermons likewise still rang the changes on traditional counsels appropriate to the day: the need for a well-trained militia; the justification of a defensive war but of no other kind; biblical examples of warlike men since the days of Moses; warnings against the army as the "school of vice". Soldiers encamped for training might expect without fail to be told: first, to put on the whole armor of God; and second, to resist temptation and behave themselves during training days. The façade of these traditional sermons remained essentially unchanged; so much so that in terms of Texts, Doctrines, Reasons, Objections and Uses, most of them could be shifted backwards or forwards fifty or seventy-five years with apparently slight need for revision.

Looked at more closely, however, they have more than flavorless repetition to offer. To listen as the 1750's and 60's listened is to feel the tensions and alarms of the time on every page. That which had once been theoretical had now become fact. Audiences took the familiar scaffolding for granted; they heard only the contemporary accents of foreboding. We are now at peace, said Samuel Cooper in 1751. New England's armies have helped to bring about this peace, but mistake not; human nature has not changed. War will come again, and soon. A new war is already in sight.

"Peace is a great blessing; peace is what we all would chuse; peace is the desire of all who *deserve* the name of Christians", said Jonathan Mayhew in 1754.

"But shall the trumpet sleep?
Shall the sword rust?
Shall our gold and silver lie cankering in our coffers?
Shall our military garments be moth eaten when such things are doing?"[9]

In the following year Samuel Davies' notable recruiting sermon began on the same note.

"An Hundred Years of Peace and Liberty in such a World as this, is a very unusual Thing; and yet our Country has been the happy Spot that has been distinguished with such a long Series of Blessings, with little or no Interruption. . . . But now the Scene is changed: now we begin to experience in our Turn the Fate of the Nations of the Earth . . . Our Continent is like to become the Seat of War; and we, for the future, . . . have no other way left but to defend our Rights and Privileges."[10]

After fighting had begun, tenseness and uncertainty are reflected even in the stereotyped commonplaces repeated from earlier years.

"None of my present Audience will question, whether the Profession of a Soldier is consistent with the character of a Christian", said Ebenezer Pemberton in 1756, and he was right; no one would question it. Nor would anyone miss the implication of present danger in his

> "*If ever* this Land stood in Need of wise and valiant Commanders, it is in the present Day".[11]

Likewise in Thomas Barnard's unflattering picture of "Our Militia", which consists chiefly

> "of Children, Apprentices, and Men of the lowest Rank".[12]

In Amos Adams's 1759 Artillery sermon it was the dread word *Invasion*.

> "Should God suffer us to be invaded, we should not have to deal only with raw undisciplined *Savages,* but with regular Battalions, expert in all the Arts of War—What Perplexity, what Amazement, what Confusion would such a powerful Invasion throw us into? We may expect in our Turn to be invaded. Some of us may see our Plains flow with human Blood."[13]

On the printed page generations afterward, this reads like florid rhetoric. It was not rhetoric in 1759.

Even after peace in the French and Indian War had come, there was no end to warnings. They now pointed to more and greater troubles ahead. "Have we not seen the Importance of well-disciplined Troops in the late War?" said Thomas Balch in 1763.

> "Nevertheless—the Time may come even in our Days . . . when those who envy our growing Greatness, may form deep Plots against us. . . . Is it not then our Wisdom even in a Time of Peace to prepare for War, and cherish a martial Spirit, that we may be in a ready Posture of Defence on the Turn of Affairs?"[14]

There is much of this from year to year. A whole generation grew up under such threats of danger from "a foreign rapacious Power", also of invasion in the "perhaps not very distant Period", and under continual reminders that a well-trained army was imperative. The "rapacious Power" was obviously France, and the threat of invasion obviously to the north and west; but the preacher's habit of presenting the *doctrine* underneath whatever he had to say made these warnings easily transferable to other areas and led to the forming of deep convictions as to the uncertainty and transiency of peace, the inevitability of war, the urgency of preparedness.

"Peace is desirable", Samuel Davies had said, but when the lusts of men "enslave the free-born mind", and when our frontiers are invaded,

"Then the Sword is, as it were, *consecrated* to God, and the Art of War becomes a part of our Religion".[15]

It had already become a part of his. Likewise for many a younger man who had grown up in this uncertain and confused time. The realities of war, almost unknown to the older generation, had quickened the minds of these younger men with a livelier sense of their privileges as Americans, and in so doing had thrown a bright new light on the whole corpus of governmental theory to which they had listened all their lives.

Reminders of the new emphasis in extant sermons, pamphlets, letters to the press, town meeting resolves, and other records of current thinking came in certain words; and these, by the frequency and the strategic position given them again and again, became in a sense epochal words. Old words, most of them: liberty, happiness, patriotism, constitutional rights; but old words which had acquired new associations and with them a new vitality of meaning. New words, some of them: slavery, tyranny, arbitrary power, non-compliance, revolution, independence—words soon to be on everyone's lips. All decades have such words; usually not recognized as such until the decade has passed and left them cold with its passing.

Of all these words *liberty* was easily chief. It was the word of the hour, and this in spite of the fact that no significant word had been more frequently invoked on public occasions since the far-off beginning. Lifetime by lifetime it had appeared in new contexts and with new connotations; and this series of fresh applications had given it continuing power.

A century earlier it had been *liberty of conscience,* as yet a doubtful blessing to some election preachers. This is the "Diana of some
men", Urian Oakes, president of Harvard, had declared in 1673,

> "and *great is the Diana of the Libertines of this Age.* . . . But re-
> member, that as long as you have liberty to walk in the Faith and
> Order of the Gospel, and may *lead quiet and peaceable lives in all
> Godliness and Honesty,* you have as much Liberty of Conscience as
> *Paul* desired under any Government. . . . Oh take heed in all
> Societies, and in all Respects of an inordinate and undue Affectation
> of Liberty. *The latter end of it will be Bondage and Slavery".*[16]

Such notions were already growing mossy as early as 1673. Election
day audiences even then were not asking what Paul desired, or even
what their own emigrating fathers had desired. It was already far
later than Urian Oakes dared to think.

By the mid-century the liberty of conscience battle had long been
acknowledged as won on most fronts. The "Right of Private Judgment" they called it now, to be extolled along with other rights, both
natural and *British.* Besides, it had recently been put to the test in the
Great Awakening upheavals and it had held. When the election
preacher came annually to his own phrasing of this familiar assumption, "Every man has a natural unalienable Right to think and act for
himself", he was speaking to those who, like the Sturbridge Separates,
had themselves invoked this right when they had separated from the
church of their baptismal vows. "This greatest Privilege Man can enjoy on this Earth" had ceased to be a word; it had become a fact. The
liberty battle had now shifted to other areas and acquired other connotations. Moreover, the bedrock assumptions underneath all applications, old and new, had become more deeply imbedded with each
new battle.

By the mid-century no American needed to be told that liberty was
a God-implanted right, and therefore not subject to surrender; a right
confirmed by Scripture, and therefore not open to doubt or even
argument; a right guaranteed to Englishmen anywhere on the globe,
and this by Magna Carta. This three-ply assurance had been basic
to all thought of government longer than anyone living could re-

member. Election preachers had long called it "our ancient heritage of liberty". "We were free born, born to Liberty",[17] they said, and no pronouncement was safer from contradiction. In the preceding generations a good many fathers had christened a good many sons *Freeborn* in testimony of this assurance. In popular thought *liberty* and *British liberty* were one and the same. All privileges stemmed from it; all protests were grounded upon it. Some eloquence in its praise was due on all anniversary occasions and always in superlatives. So Nathanael Hunn in 1747.

> "To speak of the opposite of liberty is to speak a Language unintelligible to the greater Part of the New-English people. . . . We enjoy Liberty to as great Perfection, if not greater than any People besides on this Earth. When I look over a numerous Assembly of New-English People, I can but bless GOD, and congratulate my Country, at the Sight of so many free People, who carry Liberty in their very Faces."[18]

If asked for the tangible evidence back of such easy statements, Nathanael Hunn and his brother ministers, who were wont to indulge in such flights, might have been hard pushed, but they were secure; no one was asking them for proofs. By the mid-century both the fact of British liberty and the privileges it guaranteed were past question.

Likewise, with certain qualifications, *equality* among men. "And if all men be born equally free (as I hope to prove)," Samuel Rutherford of London had said in 1644. There was no need to prove it in America in 1744. Election day audiences had heard from year to year that there is "no reason in nature why one man should be king and lord over another", but that as "concerning civil power" all men are "born alike".

> "No man cometh out of the womb with a diadem on his head, or a sceptre in his hand."[19]

Nor does the fact that a man is born into the world as a member of one kind of political society rather than another make him by nature subject to a king. Subjection political is purely accidental; Cain and

Abel might have been born under two different forms of government. In spite of occasional protests against levellism, it was still standard gospel in the 1750's and 60's that

> "There is not a Member of the Body politick to be despised; nor may one glory over another, as if he stood in no Relation to him, or had no Dependance upon him. . . . We are all, even Rulers themselves, and Ministers of the Gospel, subject to the same Laws, as the common People; and we are all Members of the same Commonwealth".[20]

Nor was this *equality* on a low level. Popular thought had changed a good deal since William Adams, in pronouncing upon the nature of man in 1685, had asserted that we are all but worms to the Lord.

> "It is indeed wonderful condescension in the infinite GOD, thus to vouchsafe His Regard to such low worms as the *best* of the children of men are. That the Great God should look upon such nothings is a great stoop",

he had said, with *Psalms* 22, 6, "But I am a worm, and no man", as his authority. Also, with *Isaiah* 40, 15, to stand upon, he had added,

> "If the nations be as the drop of a bucket and as the small dust which won't turn the Ballance, what then is a small handful of people, and what are single persons to Him?"[21]

In the 1750's no one would as yet contradict the Scriptures on such a point, nor were devout men less concerned as to how they appeared in God's eyes, but they were mightily concerned as to their own rights as individuals. In election day precept it was already an early hour in the day of the common man, although still with some condescensions. To say with the preachers that no man can say he has no need of those in a lower condition or meaner circumstances, for without their aid and service he would lose the advantage of his elevation, is still to be some leagues from the ideal of equality the pulpit thought it was asserting.

Arbitrary power, both in word and in fact, had been anathema since the first settlers had matched their protest against it by their courage in flight out of its reach. Periodically, as occasion arose, it had invited fresh anathemas on the American side. Arbitrary power is unthinkable; don't try it on us, John Wise had said in 1710.

"All Englishmen live and dye by Laws of their own making. . . . Englishmen hate an arbitrary power (politically considered) as they hate the devil. The very Name of an Arbitrary Government is ready to put an *English* Man's Blood into a Fermentation; but when it really comes, and shakes its whip over their Ears, and tells them it is their master, it makes them stark mad. They turn arbitrary too."[22]

John Wise himself had turned all but "stark mad" as he had protested the scheme of Messrs. Mather, Willard and Pemberton which would have taken away from New England societies the "liberty" of managing their own affairs, leaving them only

"Liberty to be Governed by a Hook in their Nose (like wild Cattle in a string) by the mercy and pleasure of their drivers; but as for any share in the Exercise of Government, they would have had no more than Horses in the Royal Stables, . . . I shall enter a caution against taking down the sides of the City or opening the Walls of our Zion to let in this Trojan horse".[23]

John Wise was a second generation minister, the son of an indented servant and the first American boy to be admitted to Harvard College from that humble rank. His vehemence in 1710 may have owed something (perhaps much) to his own fine and imprisonment during the Andros régime, when he had led his own Ipswich townsmen in a rebellion against the collection of a penny tax. Arraigned, he had claimed his rights as an Englishman under Magna Carta and had lost. Seven years later he had set forth his political convictions in a pamphlet which for clarity and trenchancy of argument surpassed anything of its kind yet published in America. Most notably he had made civil and religious liberty identical. Man's right to govern himself was not permissive; it was inherent. Why? Because in a state of "Natural

Being", man is not depraved; he is noble; standing at the upper end of nature,

> "a Freeborn Subject under the Crown of Heaven and owing Homage to none but God Himself".[24]

He had also spoken out firmly for democracy as the form most likely to "Promote the happiness of all and the good of every man in all his Rights, Life, Liberty, Estate, Honour &c. without injury or abuse done to any".[25] From an aristocracy to a monarchy it was only two steps, and thence but one to a tyranny.

If ideas were effective according to their priority in time, John Wise might have been America's "natural rights" schoolmaster, but it was not so. Men were not yet ready for what he had to say; but fortunately he had left his 1710 and 1717 ideas on natural rights as the foundation of all government in print, for 1772 to discover and use in a fresh application long after "the great Mr. Locke" had made these same fundamental principles current coin for more than a generation.

John Locke (like John Wise) was of course the transmitter of these ideas, not their originator. He had died in 1704 and at that date was unknown in America. By 1720, although he was still unknown to the general, his *Two Treatises on Government*[26] had become the classic textbook on government at Harvard and Yale. That was enough. With his "natural rights" theory accepted and taught as living political gospel to all young ministers in training, he could ask no surer guarantee that soon afterward his ideas would get to the ears of the American citizenry, wherever they lived. It mattered little that few except the clergy could have called their teacher by name, or that few of them paid him honor for the ideas they so freely borrowed and proclaimed. Not one of them through a thirty- or forty-year period would have faced an election day audience without reiterating in some form this "law of God written in men's hearts with a pen of iron and the point of a sword". In consequence, "natural rights" became the most potent slogan of the mid-century, and only slightly less familiar to the rank and file than the Calvinistic Five Points had been to their fathers and grandfathers.

In Locke's "state of nature" all men are free and equal. They have no common superior on earth. Their rights are not bestowed; they are a natural possession. They also have obligations to other men. By what he called the "law of nature" or reason, no man has a right to rob another man of "life, liberty, and property", and by this same law any man has a right to punish whosoever so transgresses. It is only because this right of individual punishment sometimes leads to confusion and disorder among men that government is necessary at all. Furthermore, when a man surrenders certain of his own natural rights in order to erect a common authority with his fellows, he has in effect given up nothing. His own agreement and consent make this common authority his own. Every American voter in church or town meeting already knew this and had practiced it. John Locke's "natural rights" case and also his case for "government by consent" had been won before he spoke a word. In fact, both lessons were learned before they were ever taught. Even before Locke's birth in 1632, consent of the governed had been a foundation stone in New England town and church life. Every voter who raised his hand or put his corn and beans in the ballot box did so with the full confidence that he was running his own affairs. Locke's contribution was to give these familiar ideas a fresh emphasis and a philosophical basis. By the pith and cogency of his arguments he had consolidated the political thought of Thomas Hooker, Roger Williams, John Wise and other previous champions of the individual rights of man, and he had done so at a time of peculiar ripeness. By 1750 these assurances were the very A B C's of political theory for Americans. Everyone knew that, by virtue of his "natural rights", *liberty* was his just and inalienable heritage. Men were just beginning to realize that it had to be kept as well as won.

Read backward through the 1750's and 60's, the superlative eulogies of British liberty, Magna Carta, British government, and the privileges it guaranteed, often suggest defensive thinking at just this point. It is apparent that the roots of unrest and suspicion already lay deep, although the superlatives still came. No minister omitted them in any election sermon or on any other public occasion for which the subject of government was appropriate. Mention of them was in part a convention, but not altogether.

From Samuel Phillips in 1750 (Election Sermon)

"We have very great Reason, *Sirs*, to give Thanks to *Almighty GOD*, that our civil Liberties, as granted by the *Royal Charter*, are still continued to us".[27]

From William Welsteed, 1751 (Election Sermon), beginning,

"No Nation can be more happy than ours, where the Balance is steadily maintain'd between them, i.e. the Sovereign's just Dominion, and the People's true Liberty".[28]

From John Cotton, 1753 (Election Sermon), as his concluding hope,

"That our *PRIVILEDGES*, *civil* and *sacred*, may be continued; that we may never come to know the Worth of them by the Want of them".[29]

From Gad Hitchcock, 1756 (Artillery Sermon).

"We have Liberty to follow the Light of our own Consciences. [We may not always have it] in the great Uncertainty of human Affairs".[30]

From James Cogswell, 1757 (Sermon to Israel Putnam's company),

"When our Liberty is invaded and struck at, 'tis sufficient Reason for our making War for the Defence or Recovery of it, . . . To live is to be free,—Therefore when our Liberty is attacked, . . . 'tis Time to rouze, and defend our undoubted and invaluable Privileges, We fight for our Liberties, our Religion, our Lives".[31]

From James Lockwood, 1759 (Election Sermon, Connecticut),

"We—are called to Freedom and Liberty. Liberty! May we never know its worth and inestimable Value by being strip't and depriv'd of it".[32]

And in the same sermon, these words:

"When King Charles the first attempted to introduce Arbitrary Government, it blew up a Civil War, which ended in the Loss of his Head; and when his Son King James the Second, took large strides toward arbitrary Rule, the Nation, jealous of their Liberties, invited over the Prince of Orange".[33]

There is much of this and from many sources. A note of uncertainty had crept into the familiar equation of *Liberty* and the *British guarantee* of it. Was it a guarantee and would liberty continue? The vicissitudes of the war with France and the fear of popery, if she should be victorious, account for some of the tension, but hardly for all. Men were uneasy and alert for new alarms.

In the late 50's several circumstances on the home front seemed to present new threats. Two of these which localized in Connecticut had repercussions throughout New England. If men had not been uneasy over the issues involved, they might not have thought twice about either of them. One was what amounted to an *Affair of the Oath* at Yale College by order of President Thomas Clap, a rigid Calvinist. Mindful lest young and tender ministerial candidates be corrupted by New Light doctrine, he had demanded in 1757 that all professors, fellows and officers of the college declare publicly their acceptance of the Westminister Catechism and the Saybrook Confession. An outburst of indignation followed; the whole colony was shaken. Liberty of conscience and right of private judgment had been invaded. Laymen as well as ministers went to press and a spate of pamphlets, pro and con, resulted. They kept on coming until 1763 when the General Assembly was petitioned to examine the state of the college. But President Clap was obdurate and held out until his retirement in 1766.

More important, because it raised a new issue, was the Wallingford tempest which began in 1758 and was also long-drawn-out. It concerned the calling of a twenty-three year old minister, James Dana, by a majority of the church members. The Consociation of Churches to which the Wallingford body belonged objected on the grounds of young Dana's supposed unorthodoxy. The church defied the Consociation and went ahead with his ordination. Consternation followed. The Wallingford case became the talk of the hour, both within and without church circles. The issue of group liberty challenged by the interference of outside authority was not new. The significance of this mazy Wallingford quarrel lay in the fact that it threw a strong light on the importance of a written constitution as a safeguard of the people's rights or, in current phrase, "a barrier against autocracy". If the right of interference in the matter of pastoral qualifications had been written into the Saybrook Platform (Connecticut's constitution for churchly practice) then such interference was legal; but if not expressly stated therein, then it was tyranny. As New England laymen followed the windings of this case, *liberty* acquired an important new association with constitutional rights which would be remembered long after James Dana and the uproar his ordination had caused were forgotten.

For those to whom these Connecticut upheavals were too remote, there was dynamite closer at hand; namely, taxation for ministerial support. Ever since the many congregational separations of the 1740's, there had been increased restiveness over the compulsory Rate to the "standing order" minister. Protest was everywhere. The increase of Baptist and Universalist congregations, and of the number of residents acknowledging no congregational affiliation, had set men's tempers on edge over the injustice of compulsory taxation. A tax eruption was long overdue in the 1760's. It might have occurred almost anywhere, had conditions been sensational enough to enlist spontaneous protest. Instead, trouble continued to be sporadic until Parliament forced the taxation issue on quite different grounds.

With unrest fomenting over this very real grievance, and a sense of rights infringed beginning to find articulate expression from the citizenry, no election preacher was ever more wrong than Thomas Barnard, who in this sensitive and over-charged atmosphere asserted in 1763,

> "Now commences the Aera of our quiet Enjoyment of those Liberties, which our Fathers purchased with the Toil of their whole Lives, their Treasure, their Blood. Safe from the Enemy of the wilderness, safe from the griping Hand of arbitrary Sway and cruel Superstition; Here shall be the late founded Seat of Peace and Freedom". [34]

Instead came the Stamp Act, bringing with it a "Cloud of Difficulty". "God only knows when or how it will end", Edward Bowen wrote in his journal on November 6, 1765.[35] This was six days after the Act became effective in the colonies. Business had been suspended. Flags had flown at half mast. Muffled bells had tolled the death of liberty. Stamp officers had been threatened; some of them had resigned; others had fled. The new meaning of liberty had been disclosed, as though by official proclamation. This record is written in protests of town meetings, in resolutions of committees, letters to the press, and in many sermons. No excerpts from any of these can quite clarify this new meaning or even state it. Newness was as much a difference of tone as a difference of connotation, and it was inseparable from the occasion which had made it a reality in men's consciousness.

The protest of Lexington, Massachusetts, voiced on October 21st, ten days before the Act went into effect, suggests this tone which the ensuing months were to deepen throughout British America. This document, together with various others, still exists in the handwriting of Jonas Clarke, minister in Lexington; and by comparison with his extant sermons, it would seem to owe more to him than mere penmanship. It called itself *Instructions* and was addressed to William Reed, "the present Representative". It begins,

> "Sir,— We have always looked upon men, as a Set of Beings Naturally free:—And it is a Truth, which ye History of Ages, and the Common Experience of Mankind have fully confirmed, that a People Can Never be divested of those invaluable Rights & Liberties which are necessary to ye Happiness of Individuals, to the well-being of Communities or to a well-regulated State; but by their own Negligence, Imprudence, Timidity or Rashness. They are seldom lost, but when foolishly forfeited or tamely resigned".

The Act itself was named and asserted as

> "imposed directly in opposition to an essential Right or Priviledge of Free and Natural Subjects of Great Britain, who look Upon it as their Darling and Constitutional Right, Never to be Taxed but by their own Consent, in Person, or by their Representatives".[36]

This is a strong protest, full of pulpit phrases which now lost any doctrinaire flavor they might have had; a new situation had given liberty a new application. Henceforth consociation battles were dwarfed. The line from religious to civil infringements had been crossed without anyone knowing there had been a line.

On May 29th, two months after Parliament had approved the action, Andrew Eliot preached the Massachusetts Election Sermon before Governor Bernard. He faced a hard situation, for the spotlight was squarely on him. Perhaps wisely, he decided to keep within the white lines of Election Day propriety, but without compromising his own forthright opinions. Perhaps never before had he faced a more attentive audience or a more critical one. He spoke quietly, addressing himself to the reason, not to the emotions of his audience, and communicating more by implication than by direct statement. This was the very day of Patrick Henry's impassioned speech before the Virginia House of Burgesses, and had the two speeches been broadcast to a listening America on that day, the contrast between them might have been more apparent than real. Andrew Eliot was no phrasemaker and permitted himself no flights of oratory, but he had his power.

He began disarmingly, and in traditional fashion, with the children of Israel and the government under which they lived.

> "Each tribe was under its own proper and distinct government, and order'd it's affairs by it's own princes, heads of families, elders and courts."[37]

At the same time there was a union of the tribes. The whole congregation had a right to meet together, either personally, or by their representatives, to consult the common good and the prosperity of the whole. Brethren, "You have here the model of a happy state".[38] But why say this to an inflamed and unhappy America? Was he merely taking a safe course? Rather too safe for a "Patriot" at such a time.

> "In GREAT BRITAIN",

he even dared to continue,

> "there is a happy mixture of monarchy, aristocracy, and democracy. This is perhaps the most perfect form of civil government. It is the glory of Britons and the envy of foreigners".[39]

He was on thin ice, but he immediately moved to a firmer footing.

"In free governments [that is, as distinguished from absolute mon-
archies] people are apt to feel much quicker. To touch their liberties is to touch the apple of their eye; every attempt alarms them.
. . . Rulers ought to know very well—where power ends and
liberty begins."[40]

At this point every "patriot" present began to feel that the preacher
was on his side. "I am very sensible", he continued,

"it is difficult to . . . determine where submission ends and resistance
may lawfully take place, so as not to leave room for men of bad
minds unreasonably to oppose government, and to destroy the
peace of society. Most certainly people ought to bear much, before
they engage in any attempts against those who are in authority".[41]

At the same time

"Submission [to tyrannous rulers] is so far from being a duty, that it
is a crime. It is an offence against the state of which we are members, and whose happiness we ought to prefer to our chief joy; It
is an offence against mankind; . . . an offence against God".[42]

He spoke directly of the present crisis,

"when all orders of men are so generally alarmed . . . and apprehend their most valuable privileges in danger. I am far from im-
peaching the justice of the British Parliament".[43]

There is some mistake back of all this.

"If any acts have pass'd that seem hard on the colonies, we ought
to suppose, they are not owing to any design framed against them,
but to mistakes and misrepresentations. To you, our honoured
rulers, it belongs to rectify such mistakes.
Our fathers dearly bought the privileges we enjoy . . . they thought
the rights of Englishmen would follow them wherever they sat
down, and be transmitted to their posterity; and we hope their
posterity have done nothing to forfeit them."[44]

"We highly value our connection with Great-Britain, there is perhaps not a man to be found among us, who would wish to be independent [of] our mother-country, we should regret the most distant thought of such an event; we should regret that there is anything to create the least suspicion of want of tenderness on their part, or of duty on our's. We hope there is no ground for either. We trust our King and his Parliament will yet hear us and confirm our liberties and immunities to us."[45]

Darker clouds than this have hung over us.

"Nothing is so like to make our case desperate as to conclude it so."[46]

Having so said, he concluded the sermon safely on "our internal vices", our luxury, our extravagance, our intemperance, more dangerous all of them than any "external impositions". These stereotyped warnings, however, would not figure in the conversation at the election dinner which followed, nor in shop and field on the next day. This is not a great sermon in any dimension, nor one from which schoolbook histories would care to quote, but it had hit a good many important nails squarely on the head and at a strategic moment. After the official election preacher had dared to speak out so clearly, others could do so with impunity, as many did throughout the bleak months which followed. Extant sermons for this period admit the universal gloom, but have little to offer as to the way out. Men were stunned.

When news of repeal reached America on May 6, 1766, nearly a year later, timidity on all sides was forgotten. Long stifled emotions were released. Resentment, indignation, fear, the anguish of divided loyalties gave way to sudden rejoicing such as comes only once in a given crisis. Ironically, it was the rejoicing of the false Armistice Day, (or the real one) in the innocent assumption that henceforth all would be well. "Intoxicated with gladness" was Samuel Stillman's phrase, in his sermon *Good News from a Far Country*, preached on May 17, 1766, and so indeed they were. Sermon response to repeal both reflected and shaped popular thought. If we had not asked for release, said Charles Chauncy in one of the many Thanksgiving sermons, we should have been stupid.

"And such an union in spirit was never before seen in the Colonies. Nor was there ever such universal joy as upon the news of our deliverance. . . . No man appeared without a smile in his countenance."[47]

This was universal joy over rights restored, he carefully pointed out, rights that our forefathers had earned in "subduing and defending the American lands". "We had always thought ourselves a part of one whole, members of the same collective body. What affected the people of England affected us". No wonder the fervor in our breasts was cooled.

"The colonies were never before in a state of such discontent, anxiety and perplexing sollicitude",

but God brought it about that "A SPIRIT was raised in all the Colonies nobly to assert their freedom as men". May He continue to us "all our enjoyments both civil and religious . . . as long as the sun and moon shall endure".[48]

Nathaniel Appleton, also speaking immediately upon news of repeal, willingly granted God's hand in the passing of the Act, but had it been continued, "We should not have been the free people that once we were". God's hand was also in

"the universal uneasiness and clamour in all the colonies upon the first tidings of it, all as one man rising up in opposition to it; such a union as was never before seen in all the colonies".[49]

Now that our mourning is turned into dancing, may we remain "in the quiet possession of all our constitutional rights from age to age". Demonstration of "civil joy" is fitting. And as this religious exercise will be followed with public rejoicings, . . . let me exhort you to conduct them with "decency and decorum".

"Don't insult anyone at home by your triumph (for I know of none among ourselves) who have appeared zealous promoters of the act which is now abolished."[50]

Break up your diversions in good season, and return every one quietly to his place of abode. Have respect to the civil magistrate. Submit yourselves to every ordinance of man—"that is, to every constitutional ordinance . . . not repugnant to the superior law of God and nature".[51]

One of the most stirring expressions of this universal rejoicing to be preserved was Jonathan Mayhew's *The Snare Broken*, preached from the text, "Our soul is escaped as a bird". The text chosen is better than the sermon; but, since by his own admission he was attempting to give "a general sense of the colonies respecting the whole affair", his sermon becomes something of a news broadcast of the popular response and as such has special value. In its printed form it was addressed to William Pitt, as were other sermons of the hour.

"We have never known so quick and general a transition from the depth of sorrow to the height of joy, as on this occasion, nor indeed so great and universal a flow of either, on any other occasion whatever.

But never have we known a season of such universal consternation and anxiety among peoples of all ranks and ages, in these colonies, . . .[52]

But the greater part, as I conceive, were firmly united in a consistent, however imprudent or desperate a plan, to run all risques, to tempt all hazards, to go all lengths, if things were driven to extremity, rather than submit, preferring death itself to what they esteemed so wretched and inglorious a servitude.[53]

It can answer no valuable end, for us to harbour grudges or secret resentment on account of redressed and past grievances; May God give us wisdom to behave ourselves with humility and moderation on the happy success of our late remonstrances and struggles.[54]

But let none suspect [however] that I mean to dissuade people from taking a just concern for their own rights, or legal, constitutional privileges.

History affords no example of any nation, country, or people long free, who did not take some care of themselves; and endeavour to guard and secure their own liberties.

These colonies are better than ever apprised of their own weight and consequence, when united in a legal opposition. . . . It is to be hoped we will never abuse . . . any influence we may have when united."[55]

Although his final injunction is to "bury in oblivion what is past" and to begin anew "from this joyful and glorious aera of restored and confirmed liberty", it is more likely that his audience would remember such a question as, What do you think "of British subjects making war upon British subjects on this continent"? Or answer in the negative his injunction not to let the King suffer in their eyes for what has happened. "I have not the least suspicion of any disaffection in you to his Majesty",[56] he added, and also let us pay our respect to the British Parliament. It is likely that the final effect of this sermon had more to do with increasing the "just sense of liberty" which had prevailed during the dark preceding months, stimulating their imaginations as to the possibilities of union in a common cause, and implanting a fear that maybe all infringements of that liberty were not yet over. History had been made in this time of storm, and some things would never be the same again. The privileges of subjects under a just government had ceased to be theoretical.

When it became apparent that this "civil joy" was but for a moment, caution disappeared. The words *tyranny* and *revolution* began to appear in pulpit and press. Ministers became realistic and spoke directly, although always with chapter and verse as a smoke screen. "In Hamaan we see the tyrant in real life", Richard Salter announced, as he began his Election Sermon in 1768, and no one before him needed to be told that he did not mean Hamaan.

"But the vengeance of heaven soon awoke. Thus he dropped into oblivion, like other tyrants, unregretted and his memory rots."

But this is not a hopeful sermon as to immediate release from "tyranny";

"The dangers and calamities we are threatened with can scarce be painted in too horrible and gloomy colors.
We were ready to bless ourselves when the stamp act was repealed, in the pleasing prospect of future tranquility and peace; and the lasting enjoyment of our distinguishing privileges".[57]

We were mistaken. The "present dark and cloudy day—portends the most insupportable and fatal calamities. We are filled with anxious solicitude".

In these sermons after 1765, John Locke's name came to mind afresh, and his most timely contribution to American political thinking became apparent. His equating of "natural rights" with justice as opposed to tyranny, and his sanction of revolution as a justifiable way of securing these rights in case they were jeopardized by any form of oppression, was precisely the gospel for this dark hour. Writing for Englishmen, Locke had thought to present an apologia for a revolution already accomplished; for Americans, he helped to inspire one not yet born.

Perhaps logically, in view of the general gloom, the word *happiness*, always a favorite word in political sermons from the beginning, ran *liberty* a close second in the pulpit protests, and in the resolutions of outraged town meetings during the last years of the decade. It continued to do so until it took its place as the third member of Locke's familiar trio, "Life, liberty and property".

"That God made Mankind free (as being essential to their Happiness)" are (typically) among the first words of a protest from the towns of Litchfield County, Connecticut, in 1766.[58] "The communication of happiness being the end of creation", said Daniel Shute in beginning his Election sermon of 1768, and his final word, sixty-two pages farther on, matched it;

"In fine, to secure his own, and to promote the *happiness* of others, is the part of every one in this great asembly . . . *To this end* were we *born, and for this cause* came we *into the world*".[59]

In between the beginning and the end of the sermon, the word *happiness* occurs on nearly every page, sometimes four or five times. Man, he made clear, in the very nature of things,

"is invested with certain rights and privileges, . . . so adapted to his nature that the enjoyment of them is the source of his happiness in this world, and without which existence here would not be desireable".[60]

These rights are inalienable; man cannot give them away, nor is it fitting that anyone should deprive him of them. Civil government exists to secure them. These truisms and also the phrases in which they were expressed are repeated many times in many other sermons. These same phrases would sound very familiar, read out from every pulpit in the land, by order of the Continental Congress, less than a decade farther on, and in their familiarity would be their power.

In the pulpit and out of it, the most discredited word was *non-resistance*. To a man the clergy repudiated the notion, calling it "the former doctrine of passive obedience and non-resistance". It was now "thoroughly dis-relished", had been "fully exploded", was at this day "generally given up as indefensible", and "voted unreasonable and absurd". In fact, it was "so big with absurdity, that one would think no one of common understanding could embrace it". Put into practice, a "doctrine so inconsistent with prudence, reason and revelation" could lead only to "fatal convulsions in a state". It was as "fabulous and chimerical as transubstantiation". As for Americans, they were through with it. "It came not down from above." Hence, *non-resistance* was an obsolete principle, and whoever might have dared to speak a word in its praise did but invoke the air. He might also invite a blow.

In its place came *non-compliance*, the boldest of all new words, although new only in its application. As early as 1718 Samuel Sewall records a sentence which had so impressed him in a sermon of Josiah Dwight that he had copied it into his *Diary*. Dwight had said,

"When the Authority over us require that which is unlawfull of us, we must be Non-Compliers and Dissenters".[61]

Such action with reference to ecclesiastical authority needed no justification even in Sewall's day. In fact, Josiah Dwight might have taken it straight from John Calvin, had he so desired, and almost in the same words. Later still, in its political connotation, preachers quoted it from John Locke. In the Liberty Pole era it was no longer an idea at all, but a concrete plan of action, for which resourceful ones among the clergy invented practical ways and means and supplied a setting.

One of the most practical and constructive directions of this inventiveness concerned the encouragement of home industry. Let us prove to ourselves and to Britain, said the Sunday preacher, that we can feed and clothe ourselves and let us begin immediately. There will be a Spinning Bee at the parsonage tomorrow. The idea pleased, and in a very short time the parsonage Spinning Bee had become an institution in many parishes, providing not only cloth for current needs, and giving Non-importation one more chance to succeed, but also adding another social activity and a pleasant one to community life in a worried time. Some ministers wisely organized the women into competitive groups, thereby increasing the excitement by a dash of sportsmanship. Of far more importance, these busy all-day occasions developed a spirit of unity and self-confidence, the results of which it would be hard to measure. In between the lines of Ezra Stiles' brief entries recording these occasions in his parish one may read good news concerning tolerance, no matter which method of baptism one might advocate.

For April 26, 1769, Liberty Day, or the anniversary of the King's signature to the repeal of the Stamp Act, he wrote,

"Spinning Match at my House, *thirty-seven Wheels;* the Women bro't their flax—& spun *ninety-four* fifteen knotted skeins; about five skeins & half to the pound of 16 ounces. They made us a present of the whole. The Spinners were two Quakers, six Baptists, twenty-nine of my own society. There were beside fourteen Reelers &c. In the evening & next day, Eighteen 14-knotted skeins sent in to us by several that spun at home the same day. Upon sorting & reducing of it, the whole amounts to One hundred & eleven fifteen-knotted Skeins.—In the course of the day, the Spinners were visited I judge by six hundred Spectators".[62]

For May 30, 1770, he wrote,

"This day a voluntary Bee or Spinning Match at my house. Begun by Break o' Day, & in fornoon early were sixty-four Spinning Wheels going. Afternoon seventy wheels going at the same Time for part of the Time. Ninety-two daughters of Liberty spun and reeled, respiting and assisting one another. Many brought their flax, especially of my Society. . . . The spinners were of all Denominations, Chh: Quakers, Bapt. & Cong. &c. They spun One hundred & seventy Skeins".[63]

For May 31st,

"This day from a cursory Reckoning found *One hundred and thirty Spinners* in my Congregation".[64]

The Spinning Matches went right on, and not in Ezra Stiles' parish only. His own three-word verdict of one dated May 21, 1772, as "innocent, cheerful, decent", is a modest understatement. Far more had been accomplished than "Skeins" on these parsonage occasions.

As the decade of the 1760's closed, sermons struck an ominous note, presaging a crisis ahead. There was little rhetoric. No one was saying, as in safer times, "Liberty, darling liberty, where art thou now?" Instead, 1769 sermons sound the note of alarm in realistic prose.

"Mutual confidence and affection between Great Britain and these Colonies, I speak it with grief, seems to be in some measure lost",

said Jason Haven on the Election occasion in Massachusetts.

"People indeed generally apprehend some of their most important civil rights and privileges to be in great danger.—How far these apprehensions are just, is not my province to determine.
The Ministers of religion will unite their endeavors, to investigate and declare, the moral cause of our troubles."[65]

It was a pledge and they kept it. They did far more. Eliphalet Williams, speaking on the Connecticut election occasion in 1769, first reminded his audience of the civil liberty they had hitherto enjoyed. They had lived under an "equitable, benign, gentle" government up to this time. It had been a happiness so to be governed. Then addressing not only the newly elected magistrates, but the whole assembly, whether quietly or with full voice no one knows, he said, "Ye are, as *yet freemen*".[66] He would have been a poor preacher if he had not known how to make these words electric. It would be easy to find a more dramatic battle cry in many sermons; but, at this particular 1769 date, this one would do very well as a northern counterpart of the "Give me liberty or give me death" rallying call. A people who had been told, ever since they could remember, that they were "A People in Love with Liberty" would know what to do next.

CHAPTER FIFTEEN

"*Pulpit Drums*"

By 1770 the spade work was all done. The Doctrine was as familiar as a copybook lesson and needed no further clarification. The Application was now at hand. Henceforth as crisis followed crisis, events themselves would determine what the Uses of the Doctrine would be in a given case, and sometimes determine them as speedily as over night or from sunrise to sunset. After the "Boston Massacre" of March 5th, almost any town, large or small, might be called as witness to an Application already accomplished.

On Monday morning, March 19th, precisely two weeks after word of the first bloodshed had gone forth, the citizens of Abington, Massachusetts, met in the meetinghouse and took action in sixteen separate items of which the first two were as follows:

"1stly, That all nations of men, who dwell upon the face of the whole earth, and each individual of them, are naturally free, and while in a state of nature have a right to do themselves justice when their natural rights are invaded.

2ndly, Voted, as the opinion of this town, that mankind while in their natural state, always had and now have a right to enter into compact and form societies, and erect such kind of government as the majority of them shall judge most for the public good".[1]

So far as Abington was concerned, the Revolution was already accomplished; only the fighting remained.

Month by month over the next five years, towns kept on acting, each in turn writing its own Declaration of Independence. As though by common agreement they spoke with one voice and often in the same words: "unalienable Rights", "Life, Liberty and Property", "public Happiness", "free Consent of the governed", "Right of Compact", "our native Freedom"—words long familiar in press and pulpit, all of them, and because long familiar, more powerful than any new slogans could possibly have been.

The Mendon Resolves of 1773 were nineteen in number, beginning,

1. "Resolved, That all men have naturally an Equal Right to Life, Liberty and Property.
2. Resolved, That all just and lawful Government must necessarily originate in the free Consent of the People.
3. Resolved, that the Good, Safety and Happiness of the People is the great end of Civil Government, and must be considered as the only rational object in all Original Compacts and Political Institutions. . . .
6. Resolved that a Right to Liberty and Property (which is one of the Natural Means of Self Preservation) is absolutely UN-ALIENABLE, and can never, *lawfully*, be given up by ourselves or taken from us by others".

The end of this document, like various others of its sort, reads,

"Voted that the foregoing Resolves be entered in the Town Book that our Children, in years to come, may know the sentiments of their Fathers in Regard to our Invaluable RIGHTS and LIBERTIES".[2]

John Winthrop, Thomas Hooker, Nathaniel Ward, John Wise and the others, who in the earlier days had held a far futurity in their eye, might have envisaged self-determination somewhat differently, but they would not have been surprised at the fact. From Dissent to Independence had been a long and not always a direct path, but it had been a path to a predictable, not to say inevitable goal. That goal was now just ahead.

For the American story it is significant that these *Resolves* and the many other documents similar in purpose and content were stated as group convictions and registered by votes taken at a town meeting. Of the details at Abington, Mendon, Litchfield, Lexington, or wherever else such formal action was taken, no record: who moved, who spoke, who dissented, what was the final toll of corn and beans, Yeas and Nays. Town clerks were a tight-lipped sort, and that they owed something more to posterity than a bare statement they could not have been expected to know. Nor are such details important. What is significant is that in towns whose total population did not require more than three figures, as well as in the larger centers, men met together day after day, held debate, argued, voted, rescinded their action and voted again, until a clear majority decision had been reached. It is also significant that such majority agreement concerned first, not concrete action, not the shouldering of arms or the voting of sums for home defence, but rather the registering of convictions as to the principles on which such concrete action might justly and rightly be based.

Behind these many *Resolves, Recommendations, Protests,* the later *Instructions* to committees and delegates to conventions, both as to the principles themselves and the phrases by which they were expressed, lay whole lifetimes of tutelage in the ways of government. Behind them also for each New England town lay something more or less than a hundred years of experimentation and discovery (sometimes reluctant discovery) as to what constituted the "public good" in the affairs of that town and of every church society in it, large or small. How to find that "center of gravity", the good of the whole, had been a long and troubled process. Behind these town votes of the 1770's lay also five turbulent years with their Liberty Pole demonstrations, their mutual suspicions, fears, debates, and occasional outbreaks of violence, their unrest and confusion. The most critical chapters were still ahead, but by 1770 the root system of representative government was already strongly developed. The basic principles were well understood. It was now time to test their strength and durability.

Under stress of perilous events town and parish were again one as in the earliest days. The meetinghouse once more became the center of community life to a degree more nearly complete than any of the voting generation would well remember. Once again it was the town arsenal, with "Powder and Balls" under lock and key in the "Garrett" or, more conveniently still, just under the pulpit. The Rev. John Adams of Durham, New Hampshire, preached Sunday after Sunday with the town's supply of powder directly under his feet. So did other "warm Patriots" among the clergy, and doubtless found their eloquence and the effects of it greatly improved thereby. The meetinghouse was also the recruiting center, the place of rendezvous for troops, the point of departure when it came time to go. Later, as messengers brought back news from the front, it became the broadcasting station, whenever the bell or beat of the drum called the inhabitants together for announcement.

As great events broke in, the line between the godly and ungodly, those who had Lord's Supper privileges and those who had not, was temporarily-obscured or even erased. Men were now lined up according to the cause—"the American cause", as Gad Hitchcock presently called it. He had hit upon a fortunate phrase. Most of the "standing Order" clergy were "staunch Patriots". Many Baptists were not, at least not in the beginning; after the Declaration of Independence many of them moved over into the "Patriot" camp. Church of England ministers were sharply divided. As tension increased before 1775 and more emphatically thereafter, congregations watched for "signs". Did the minister pray for the king? If so, the "Patriots" in the congregation promptly sat down. Later still, they stalked angrily out of the meetinghouse.

"I learn that the people are very ready to misrepresent my words, even in prayer", venerable Stephen Williams of Longmeadow wrote in his diary the Sunday after the battle of Lexington and Concord. His misstep had been to pray for the king, as usual. On the following day he added,

> "I perceive the people are out of humor with me for things I have said and done. My own conscience don't upbraid me for what they pretend to be uneasy at".

The uneasiness continued. A month later he wrote,

> "I perceive a coldness among my own people towards me because they apprehend I don't think with them as to the present times and

measures. I heartily desire their welfare and happiness. My conscience is void of offense".[3]

His sixty-year record with them was as clear as his conscience, but the one word *king* was all that they heard.

Samuel Parker of Trinity Church, Boston, forestalled trouble by calling the proprietors together and securing their consent to omit prayers for the king for the duration, on the ground that

> "It would be more to the interest and cause of Episcopacy and the least evil of the two, to omit a part of the liturgy than to shut up the church".[4]

Other cautious ministers who had occasion to use the word *king* in their scriptural analogues for the day took care to locate it by precise text and to explain that it had no British associations. Some went so far as to proclaim as dogma that the only reason there had been a king in Israel was that God "in His anger" had given them one.

The number of ministers branded as Tory sympathizers throughout the whole of this inflamed decade is after all few, particularly in view of the flimsiness of the evidence which might lead to a conviction against them. Eleazer Wheelock of Hanover, New Hampshire, failed to observe a 1775 Thanksgiving day on the proper date "in concert with the other colonies", according to Proclamation. He was obliged to travel a hundred and fifty miles to answer for his "gross neglect", and when in his attempt to defend himself he called the principle on which the Proclamation was based, of "the very essence of popery", his accusers were sure that he was a traitor. Ebenezer Morse of Shrewsbury had prayed too fervently for the "king, queen, and royal family, the lords spiritual and temporal" and, in consequence, was obliged to "surrender his arms, ammunition, and warlike implements of all sorts", and not to cross the boundary line of the second parish without a permit from the Committee of Correspondence. Willard Hall of Westford, Massachusetts, was dismissed after a forty-eight-year pastorate and still later voted "enemical and dangerous to the State". He had pled that he was too old to change his principles and could not be disloyal to his king. He died soon after this second accusation. There were three counts against Jacob Bailey of Pownal-borough, Maine: he had prayed for the king, preached a seditious sermon, and failed to read the Declaration of Independence to his congregation on the first Sunday after the messenger reached him. For safety's sake he went into hiding and remained there for months. Samuel Dana of Groton preached against resistance the month before the battle of Lexington and Concord. His house was fired upon and he was not allowed to enter his pulpit on the following Sunday. The conduct of David Parsons of Amherst (he of the record wood consumption) was voted "not friendly to the common cause". He was dismissed. The full list of those accused would not be long, but it is doubtless long enough to include some who were unjustly suspected. That it was to the advantage of the minister to be on the popular side, since he was employed by the town, is of course obvious, but evidence of self-interest as the motive for his patriotic attitude would be hard to find. Moreover, few of them said anything in the 1770's that they had not already said many times before in their own pulpits and on other occasions.

Naturally, after March 5, 1770, loyalties acquired a sharper edge. The "Boston Massacre" was a dividing line. The time for halfway measures was past. Public feeling sanctioned plain speaking and ministers spoke out. On Sunday, six days after this first act of "violence", John Lathrop of the Old North in Boston took as his text, "The voice of thy brother's blood cryeth unto me from the ground". He began his sermon without benefit of apology or even of Scripture explication. Instead, he spoke directly.

> "We should be criminal to let such an awful affair pass over without taking notice of it in a religious manner. The unparalleled barbarity . . . will never be forgot. The now lisping child will rehearse the tragical story to his attentive offspring, when revolving years have covered his head with silver locks."[5]

From this let the whole world learn

> "the infinite impropriety of quartering troops in a well-regulated city. . . . It is time for that magistrate to resign, who cannot depend

on the assistance of his *neighbours* and *fellow citizens* in the administration of justice! And that Government which rejecting the foundation of the *law,* would establish itself by the *sword*—the sooner it falls to the ground the better, that in its stead another might be established, more agreeable to the nature of man, and consistent with the great ends of society".[6]

Neither John Lathrop's congregation nor any other in New England needed to be told what those "great ends" were, but as he repeated yet once more the familiar aphorism that the goal of government is the *happiness* of all who live under it, his congregation may well have thought they were listening for the first time to a fresh new pronouncement. He spoke under stress of great emotion and, as he said, "while innocent blood was still fresh in view", and "dying groans" still in the ears of those who had been present, but he spoke with a sense of pulpit responsibility from which few would have dissented. Henceforth "civil and religious", "liberty and religion", had equal rights on Sunday. Why? Because "liberty and religion" are worth contending for.

In the preface to the published sermon he said that "some few among us were displeased with the notice the ministers of this town thought themselves bound in duty to take of the late murders". Nevertheless, on second thought he will print the sermon, and here it is. Previously John Lathrop and other "Patriots" among the clergy had been the people's tutors as to the privileges of "Life, liberty, and Property". They now became the encouragers of their boldness in making these privileges a reality. "Incendiary", said the opposition, but if so, all election preachers had been incendiaries ever since Harvard students first studied John Locke and substituted the right of revolution for the previous gospel of non-resistance. The only difference was that now they were raising their voices and calling names. They continued to do so.

"A number of the troops, with other sons of Belial"; (John Lathrop, 1770)

"Wicked rulers, such as Nero, and others of later date"; (Gad Hitchcock, 1774)

"It would be highly criminal [a frequent word] not to feel a due resentment against such tyrannical monsters"; (Samuel West, 1776) "Unjust and impious claims of Britons, worms of the dust, like ourselves". (Samuel Cooke, 1777)

Sermons throughout the decade are plentifully sprinkled with such lively epithets, which no doubt evoked a lively response, but after all the inflammable phrases are culled from these sermons, the preachments themselves appear conservative rather than otherwise. The "thunder and lightning" which John Adams attributed to the clergy during these war years was vehemence of conviction, doubtless also vehemence of manner, rather than radical thinking. These men were not radical thinkers, nor were they original thinkers. Moreover, they were saying nothing that they and their predecessors had not said for well over two generations on similar public occasions as well as more frequently in their own pulpits. Patiently, studiously, through the years they had built up, layer by layer, a concept of government, its obligations and privileges, until fundamentals were past question. In so doing they had also made government and its ways important in their people's thought. The 1770's would have been no time for all this. Men were in no mood to be instructed. They could be reminded of what they already knew and their emotions could be aroused in its support, but they could not be put to school. The power of the familiar in a time of crisis has seldom been more amply demonstrated than in the patriotism, "which burst forth like a flame", with the pulpit phrases worn smooth by several lifetimes of preaching as its watchwords.

In general ministerial counsels took two main directions during the five years between the Boston Massacre and the Lexington and Concord fight. First, let us be prepared to defend ourselves; and second, let us be united. In both of these directions the tone of these pulpit counsels suggests that men still needed to be convinced that a war was coming, and to be assured that, when it came, Americans had a fair chance of success. Ministers were in no sense trying to hold an excited populace in check, nor were they trying to inflame it. Instead, they were facing an ominous situation realistically and saying, let us get ready. At the outset they were also combatting not only lack of confidence but also apathy, particularly as to military preparedness. This suggestion is strongest in the Artillery Sermons, where of course one would expect to find it.

"In the matter of soldiership", said Samuel Stillman in 1770, we have "degenerated in a great degree from the noble spirit of our ancestors". They thought the character of a *good soldier* was "not repugnant to that of a *real Christian*". We act as though it were. "Brave men have lived in *New-England*; brave men no doubt still live", but if so, why is it that of the more than two thousand men who are able to bear arms in Boston, many are excused from duty except in cases of alarm, and others "chuse rather to pay their fines than appear in the field".[7] This will not do.

Eli Forbes in the following year announced in the preface to his printed sermon that he was not using the separate words *British* and *American*, but rather considering the military character in general and with the intent of reviving the true martial spirit which "is sunk in this province much too low for the present day. You see, Gentlemen, the dignity and importance of the character you sustain". This military spirit is "truly honorable". It is also very ancient; in fact, " 'tis almost as old as the creation, and as important as life and liberty, as public peace and happiness".[8]

War is not new, said Simeon Howard two years later on the same occasion. Cain began it and it will be with us to the end. If no one had ever infringed on the rights of anyone else our history books would shrink to very small size indeed. In an atmosphere grown decidedly more tense by 1773, such a statement would not be so mild as it looks in print. This sermon has ominous undertones along with its almost conversational simplicity and directness. What does a man do in private life when his personal liberty is threatened, the preacher asked. Why, if he is a good Christian, he first tries gentleness. He reasons with his enemy, tries to persuade him to desist, and if this brings no results and an opportunity should offer, he "gets out of his way". It is just the same with nations: first, gentleness, reasoning, persuasion, remonstrance; and then, because experience has shown that these methods usually do not work, and because a man's nature forbids "tame submission", then *self-defence by force of arms*. Self-defence is not inconsistent with Christian principles. Not at all. We may even bear "good-will towards them that attack us, wish them well and pray God to befriend them". Furthermore, hearken to this: "An innocent people threatened with war are not always obliged to receive the first attack".[9] That might prove fatal. What then should they do? Be united, have a government that is free and easy, get weapons and learn the use of them. Trust not in a standing army. That is a precarious means of security. Rather a well-trained militia:

"An army composed of men of property, who have been all their days inured to labor, will generally equal the best veteran troops, in point of strength of body and firmness of mind, and when fighting in defence of their religion, their estates, their liberty, and families, will have stronger motives to exert themselves, and may, if they have been properly disciplined, be not much inferior to them [a standing army] in the skill of arms".[10]

Simeon Howard's boldest remark followed his statement that he would not undertake to "decypher the *signs of the times*", and then, in direct contradiction of this statement, he announced so that no one could possibly mistake his meaning, that from the course of human affairs,

"we have the utmost reason to expect that the time will come, when we must either submit to *slavery*, or defend our liberties by our own sword. And this perhaps may be the case sooner than some imagine".[11]

He did not scruple to name Britain by name nor to assert that, as things now stand, it will soon "be no longer proper for us to confide in her power, for the protection of our liberty". He complimented British America, "particularly the northern part of it", as the "nursery of heroes" and prophesied that, together with neighboring colonies, they would make up a "formidable people". Right on the heels of this encouraging prophecy, he dared to inflame popular feeling by recalling "the insulted walls of our State-House" and the once "crimsoned *stones of the street*", which still cry out against a standing army quartered among us in time of peace. Having so said, he proceeded to the conventional ending for an artillery sermon, the Scriptural qualifications of a good soldier and the never-ending warfare imposed upon us all by the "dominion of sin". This is not the part his hearers would remember. This sermon deserves mention also for a ten-word statement, soon to be recast memorably—*"God has given man liberty to pursue his own happiness"*.

Still another year later, with public feeling even more inflamed, John Lathrop, who meanwhile had become one of the "warmest" of patriot preachers, sprinkled his sermon plentifully with the words *unavoidable war, tyrants, slaves, Friends of Freedom, Life, Liberty, and Property*. In one breath he asserted flatly,

> "America never saw a day so alarming as the present. . . . Where it will end, God only knows",

and in the next,

> "We *never* will rebel against the Sovereign of the British dominions. However provoked,—however oppressed,—however threatened with Slavery and wretchedness, we will never be excited to any other resistance than what the impartial world shall Judge *absolutely* necessary to our own defence".[12]

He spoke in superlatives of America's affection to the parent state, of the "purest joy we have had in each other's happiness for more than a hundred years", and then the next moment drew a picture of Boston harbor shut up, our trade ruined, the city filled with troops, and a system of government devised "too degrading and oppressive for British subjects quietly to bear".

> "Hard is our fate, when to escape the character of rebels, we must be degraded into that of slaves."[13]

He did not plead for a united America; he predicated it as a *fait accompli*, adding that should the Prime Minister determine to

> "LAY THE AMERICANS AT HIS FEET . . . the struggle will be obstinate. . . . AMERICANS, who have been used to blood from their infancy, would spill their best blood, rather than submit to

be hewers of wood, or drawers of water, for any ministry or nation in the world."[14]

These were still bold statements in 1774 and would have brought a "vast assemblage" of worried Americans to their feet anywhere, in spite of the rumblings of Loyalist dissent which would have been articulate in any such audience of that year. Looking back at himself twenty-five years later, John Lathrop said, "When our liberties were invaded by the British government, I was not bashful";[15] and he surely was not. His oratory was in the Patrick Henry tradition though without the poetry, and yet for the most part, like most of his brother preachers, he addressed himself to the minds and consciences, not the emotions of his hearers. They were all aiming at reasoned conclusions, not at inflamed and hasty action. They were also looking ahead to far consequences:

> "*Life* and *death* in a political sense are now set before us; . . . the fate of America for many generations depends on the virtue of her sons and daughters at the *present* day".[16]
> "Future generations are really more deeply interested in our conduct in this matter than we ourselves".[17]

Such pronouncements in some form can be found in nearly every sermon. Negro slavery was denounced by some ministers and so vehemently that many slaveholders in Massachusetts and Connecticut released their slaves. The equality of men was asserted more boldly:

> "The meanest slave hath a soul as good by nature as your's, and possibly by grace it is better. A dark complection may cover a fair and beautiful mind".[18]

Such was Andrew Eliot's way of putting it, as "the good of the whole" continued to take on a wider application. It was no longer the liberty of America only, but "the liberty of the world" and of all men, high and low, black and white.

> "Our danger is not visionary, but real. Our contention is not about trifles, but about liberty and property; and not ours only, but those of posterity, to the latest generations",[19]

said Gad Hitchcock in 1774, and by that time every other "patriot" among the clergy was saying it also. Somewhere in every election or other special sermon, men heard that since our children and their children after them are not here to act their part, we must act for them. Speaking on a Thanksgiving occasion late in the year Samuel Williams voiced this expectation of new hope for all men, when he said,

"We seem to be on the eve of some great and unusual events: Events, which it is not improbable, may form a new era, and give a new turn to human affairs. The state of both countries is critical and dangerous to the last degree. . . . The cause of *America* seems to be much the better cause. It is not the cause of a mob, of a party, or a faction, that *America* seems to plead.—Nor is it the cause of independency that we have in view. It is the cause of *Self Defence*, of *Public Faith*, and of the *Liberties of Mankind*, that America is engaged in".[20]

This conviction was voiced ever more strongly and the areas of human liberty widened throughout the decade. In 1780 the pulpit was still voicing it. "If America preserves her freedom", said Simeon Howard in 1780,

"she will be an asylum for the oppressed and persecuted of every country; her example and success will encourage the friends, and rouse a spirit of liberty thro' other nations. . . . Our contest is not meerly for our own families, friends, and posterity; but for the rights of humanity, for the civil and religious privileges of mankind".[21]

As events sloped toward the 1775 crisis, sermon precept shaped itself to more immediate urgencies; ministers became news commentators and their sermons recruiting pleas. By the month of April, 1775, the tone had changed perceptibly. Speaking to the Minute Men at Menotomy, two weeks before the Lexington engagement, Samuel Cooke no doubt invited a vociferous response by the announcement,

"Lord North, according to his insulting boast, has not yet laid America at his feet".[22]

This remark has many parallels. Immediately after the battle, sermons reflect the popular indignation which they also helped to arouse to yet higher pitch. Fervid expressions abound: "Stand up for your rights; Defend our lives and fortunes; Resist tyranny; Ward off from our necks the galling yoke; Save our country; Beat our ploughshares into swords and our pruning hooks into spears; unparalleled barbarity, total slavery, shackles and chains, tyrannical monsters". "Our forefathers" grew to giant size; "this amazing continent" grew more amazing; the "claims of our posterity" still more urgent, the hope of all men nearer fulfilment. Yet the traditional sermon mold remained unbroken.

Less than a month after the Lexington and Concord battle Joseph Perry began his Connecticut election sermon with Nehemiah and his wall, the most hackneyed and threadbare Old Testament analogy in the whole election day category. One would think no election preacher would have dared to announce it yet once more. In this sermon the analogy between Nehemiah and America made the Explication; Britain's "absolute despotism", "cruel tyranny" and the "total slavery of all America", the Doctrine; the Concord fight, the Boston blockade, and the imminent danger of civil war, the Improvement; and the "what ought we to do now", the Application. Every essential of the sermon pattern was unchanged, but every word was instinct with new life. Even the time-worn list of qualities essential in a ruler became new as they were now applied to the kind of man we need to conduct our public affairs in an emergency so grave that "heaven only knows whether there will ever be another election held in America". Practical consequences were in his mind and he talked sense. Forgetting Nehemiah, he spoke realistically,

"Union, in every proper method, is a thing of absolute importance. . . . If we crumble into parties among ourselves, we can't expect to stand". There is none of the "God will direct the bullet" sort of logic, or our cause is so just that "if human efforts should fail, a host of angels will be sent to support it". Joseph Perry was no alarmist. He merely started with the facts and calmly said, "The thickest cloud we ever saw now impends our nation".[23]

The most telling phrase in his sermon came unconsciously, or so it would seem. Instead of the usual phrase, "Respectable Hearers", or something equally stiff,

"Brethren, and Fellow-Citizens",

he said, as he appealed for unity and outlined an immediate program by which to combat the many artifices designed to divide the colonies. Before such a form of address came naturally from the desk, much water had flowed under many bridges. Aristocratic ministerial prerogatives were being surrendered without a struggle. "I shall now put an end to this discourse", he announced in conclusion, "in the addresses usual on such occasions". The sermon mold had not even cracked, but it held an elixir strangely new.

Although naturally enough ministers resented the charge that they were "incendiaries", in a true sense it was deserved. To talk about the "inestimable privileges of Life, Liberty and Property", the "inalienable rights" of British subjects, the birthright of freedom, and a man's natural, God-implanted right to "pursue his own happiness", to an election day audience in satisfied times was one thing; it was quite another to speak the same words with raised voices at a time of general alarm, adding such phrases as "Tyranny, the great red Dragon", "chains and slavery", and "absolute despotism" to the list. Even such a favorite election day text as "Their governor shall proceed from the midst of them", with the annotation, as of July 19, 1775, "Yea— we may possibly live to see our governor proceed from the midst of us", might fairly enough be called incendiary, no matter how carefully reasoned a discourse it motivated, or how sincerely the preacher urged "coolness of temper" and "unshaken firmness of mind".

Presently they ceased to urge either. "Our Independence was of the Lord", said William Gordon in a spirited sermon, preached before the House of Representatives on July 4, 1777. The King was our enemy. He was also the "veryest coward that human nature can know". We are not fighting against the *name* of a king, but the *tyranny*.

"Now is the golden opportunity for banishing tyranny as well as royalty out of the American states, and sending them back to Europe from whence they were imported."[24]

"He that does not mean to bear a part in the public burdens of the day, but to escape wholly unhurt in person or in property is no patriot."[25]

He who profiteers in such a time of calamity is "a most odious character". You can all help in some way; by your prayers, your money, your bravery. Even the timid may help by "concealing their fears"; the poor by determining that though poor they will be free, "and that if they cannot have riches, they will not wear chains".

In the same year Samuel Cooke had an even better chance to enroll among the "Pulpit Drums", "Liberty-mad Men", seditious agents stirring up the people and dishonoring the cloth, except that he was already enrolled in the cause which he called "this our glorious struggle for liberty and life".

"We have been called of God, to take up arms and to separate from Britain FOREVER",[26]

he said, and the fact that he was speaking on the anniversary of the Lexington battle makes one wish for a recording of this speech and the response to it. Without the overtones of the moment, all rallying cries sound like platitudes to later generations.

Sometimes ministers were unable to control what their fiery zeal had set in motion. Samuel Eaton of Harpswell, Maine, made so spirited an address in town meeting in 1775 that those present, led by the chairman, hunted out the town Tories immediately afterward and had buried Vincent Woodside as far as his neck before they could be halted. Even at that point he had not yet renounced British rule. Other Tories were handcuffed and the "king's masts spoiled" before calmer heads took over. Ministers would have been a strange breed if they had not been pleased with their powers, however they might disapprove the breaking of windows by law-abiding citizens, in order "to prove their true joy".

On the election occasion in 1776, a little more than a month before the Declaration, Samuel West asked his audience questions for which all men knew the answers. Obviously, he was sure of his ground.

When may a people claim a right of forming themselves into a body politic? When they are oppressed by the parent state; that is, if they are strong enough to defend their rights.
What kind of government is best? Certainly not unlimited monarchy or aristocracy, both of which too easily degenerate into tyranny.
Who are the proper judges to determine, when rulers are guilty of tyranny and oppression? I answer, "the publick. . . . It is true the publick may be imposed on by a misrepresentation of facts, . . . but it is always willing to be rightly informed, and when it has proper matter of conviction laid before it, it's judgment is always right".[27]

He spoke scathingly of the present situation; not only are we living amid all the "horrors of a civil war", but impressing Americans into service "without any distinction of Whig or Tory" is a scandal to human nature.

[He who favors Britain in this case] "has arrived to the highest stage of wickedness, that human nature is capable of, and deserves a much worse name, than I at present care to give him".[28]

He has forfeited his right to human society and had better go live with the beasts of the wilderness. Savages are too good for him. Those who pretend that it is against their conscience to take up arms in defence of their country have left "the plain road of common sense".
Andrew Lee, in the same year (1776), would deprive such persons of the chance. "Indifference, at this day, is at best the badge of stupidity", he said in his preface to one of the strongest sermons of the year.[29] Of those "timorous persons" (and there are always plenty of them in every country) who had "rather be slaves themselves, and entail slavery on posterity, than enter the glorious contest against the demands of slavery and despotism"—they are to be pitied. They should not be solicited, or even permitted to enlist themselves as defenders of liberty. They would only betray it.

"There are enough in this land who are less afraid of death than slavery; and such are the men who are to be employed in its defence."

Of certain soldiers who had left the ranks "because their pay was not at the rate of twenty-eight days to the month,—to their eternal disgrace be it spoken—for the *pitiful* sum of *twenty shillings*, they would sell their country".

There is much of the need for unity, as in many other sermons of 1776, along with many evidences of the precise opposite.

> "We must never forget that we are now a united continent, and can have but one interest, of which everything is destructive that tends to create uneasiness, or divide us among ourselves. . . . Nothing can be so fatal to us as division; that would be certain ruin.
>
> This is the most IMPORTANT CRISIS for America that has ever been, or perhaps ever will be—On the part we now *act* DEPENDS the freedom or slavery of this land, probably to the end of time.— It will be greater cruelty to yield posterity as the property of haughty tyrants, than to have butchered them with our own hands, as soon as they were born."[30]

The direct participation of many ministers as elected leaders of volunteer companies, as chaplains or soldiers in the ranks, is a familiar story, sometimes a dramatic one. In many notable examples these personal contributions have long since passed into town and church history, no doubt embellished with many retellings through the years. Each town cherishes its own story. As messengers brought back the news of Lexington and Concord to remote places, the minister and the men of his congregation together began their march, gathering recruits as they went. David Avery of Gageboro, Massachusetts, called his people together, preached a farewell sermon to those unable to go and, as the elected captain of the able-bodied men of his parish, led the march to Bunker Hill, stopping only to preach on Sunday en route. He served until 1780, lost an eye when a musket ball went through his head, and lived to be a hundred. John Porter of Brockton, sixteen days after Lexington, stopped in the midst of the Thursday lecture, dismissed the meeting and reported for duty. Jonathan French of Andover went home after his Sunday sermon to get his surgical case and musket, and was off. David Grosvenor of Grafton had taken his musket to meeting with him; he went directly from the pulpit to join the march to Cambridge. Thomas Allen of Pittsfield, Chairman of the Committee of Correspondence, marched to Bennington with a company largely recruited from his own parish; Stephen Willard of Beverly left with two companies; Stephen Farrar with ninety-seven of his Ipswich, New Hampshire, parishioners. But the record is as long as the list of New England towns.

Appealed to for help by the recruiting officer at Brunswick, Maine, Samuel Eaton said, "Come back at sundown". For the afternoon sermon he took as his text, "Cursed be he that keepeth back his sword from blood", and an hour after service the forty men who heard the sermon were on their way. Timothy Walker, interrupted in the midst of his morning sermon by a messenger who reported Burgoyne on march to Albany, is said to have announced, "My hearers, all of you who are willing to go, had better leave at once", whereupon, as Concord, Vermont, tells the story, every man in the meetinghouse arose and left to join Stark's brigade at Bennington. Town by town it was the same story, with only minor local changes. There was no delay, no fanfare. When it came time to go, men went and at once. One would like to believe that Napthali Daggett, President of Yale, as tradition has it, saddled his old black mare, took his fowling piece, and was off. Why not? To William Pynchon the appearance of ministers with "carnal weapons and accoutrements", submitting to examination by colonels of the minute men, "appeared very droll to many". It was not droll to them.

Nicholas Cresswell, a British traveller, who found himself "in the enemy's country and forbidden to depart", wrote in his *Journal* in November, 1776, from Virginia,

"Volunteer Companies are collecting in every County on the Continent and in a few months the rascals will be stronger than ever. Even the parsons, some of them, have turned out as Volunteers and Pulpit Drums or Thunder, whichever you please to call it, summoning all to arms in this cursed babble. D—— them all".[31]

As recruiting officers ministers were a natural choice. Particularly those who had been revival preachers knew how to individualize the doctrine until each hearer felt the whole weight of the war resting on

his shoulders. Committees of Safety, of Correspondence, and Provincial Congresses counted on the clergy and appealed to them directly for help. In the matter of recruiting, however, many of them
did not wait to be asked. Israel Litchfield's account, under date of
January 11, 1775, is probably a fair picture of what happened on an
enlistment occasion—which, typically, was also something of a religious exercise, whoever had taken the initiative in calling for volunteers. This Scituate boy of twenty writes of his own enlistment,

"We went to the Training field by the rev. Mr. Barns's meeting
house the Lower, middle and upper Companys of the militia of
this town met there under arms in order to Enlist minute-men after
we were Embodied and marched Some the three Companyes were
Marchd into the meeting house for to hear a Lector [Lecture]. The
Rev. Mr. Barnes went to prayr then there was Sang the two first
Stanzas of the 144th psalm after which the Revr. Mr. Grosvenor
Preachd a Sermon his text Second of Chronicles 17th 18th Ready
prepared for the war It was generally Concluded that he talk'd very
well after the Sermon Mr Grosvenor made a Short prayer after
which they Sang two Stanzas in the 101st psalm Then we were
marched out of the meeting house and Embodied again and then
they beat up for Men to Enlist as minute men there was aboute 66
men Enlisted and I was one amongst them that Enlisted we marchd
into the meeting house and adjurned from there to Lanlord Fosters
there we Chose three officers . . . and adjurned till next Wednes-
day to the Same place".[32]

When news of Lexington and Concord had come, he and his company, "Compleat in Arms", set out with four days' provisions. On
April 23rd he reported that most of the company went to meeting
under arms. This picture also is probably typical.

"Our Company Sat in the westerly part of the Body of the Seets the
Royal Americans Sat in the Easterly part of the Body of Seets. I
never Saw Such a Sight in the meeting upon a Sabbath Day. I suppose that there was Near 150 men under arms."[33]

He reports two more Sundays en route, one May 11th, when preaching to "New Enlisted Soldiers at meeting under Arms", the minister

"Shed tears him Self and many of his hearers",

and the second occasion, May 21st, when messengers arrived just as the Sunday service was beginning, "their horses all of a sweat", and reported ships at Hingham, "Landing Regulars as thick as grass-hoppers", whereupon

"the people all Rush'd out of the meeting-house to hear the news, thus being allarm'd we all went home and got our guns".[34]

Ministers who were too old to join the ranks found ways to serve at home. Many gave up all or a large portion of their salaries to buy powder for the town. A "cask of powder" became a standard ministerial gift. James Lyons of Machias, Maine, refused his entire salary for three years. He also voiced the wish of his people through letters, petitions, remonstrances, as occasion offered. Most originally of all, he distilled salt from sea water and supplied the whole section below Machiasport for the duration of the war. "Parson Lyons Salt Factory" was a symbol of piety and patriotism in action which had many parallels in practical service of many varieties and on many levels. The contrast between the endless salary disputes, the incessant demands for wood and more wood, the lawsuits over ministers' "just Arrears", their public scoldings of their people, the bad feeling of the preceding forty years, and now the voluntary relinquishment for the duration of even the little their diminished congregations could supply, is sharp and eloquent. Almost any Town Book will show amounts as small as twenty pounds paid the minister annually for the eight years of the war and contributions by him of more than half that amount to the town's need. "I gave up the whole of my last year's salary to the parish, and accepted £76 for this year",[35] Thomas Smith of Portland wrote in his 1776 *Journal*. From town to town only the totals and the proportions differ.

Ministers on the home front also performed much unspectacular service which cannot be evaluated, as it was not a matter of permanent record. We know of Samuel Cooper who was much in counsel with

John and Samuel Adams, of Charles Chauncy's correspondence with Benjamin Franklin, and of various other recorded services. We know also the names of ministers who served as official delegates to state and federal conventions, or on Committees of Correspondence and Safety —and it is an impressive list—but we do not know of ex officio service in kind performed on many home fronts far from the firing line. A sentence from Ebenezer Parkman's *Diary* for 1765, supplies one such hint. "They sat in one of my Rooms to do it",[36] he wrote, meaning the drafting by a local committee of instructions for the town delegate to a convention. The minister's "parlour" was the most natural committee-room in town and his unofficial share in the deliberations an important page in a story that can never be written.

Meanwhile, as in all wars, life went on, and in the parish world battles were still called on trivial issues, as before. Shall the singers face the minister when they sing, how many basses and how many tenors may sit in a seat, shall we ask the choir to omit the repeats "until the last time going over"? "Shall we have electrical points or Wiers put on the steeple?"

But this was not all. Occasionally there is a bright hint that large events far away dwarfed petty issues at home. In 1774 the members of the divided Chebacco churches met in conference at the center schoolhouse and decided "to bury forever all former differences between them and to acknowledge the other a sister church in charity and fellowship". In order to bring this about and to effect "a visible political union" between them, they drew up a "written instrument". Their reasoning is significant. A written covenant had made each of them an individual church; a visible political union could be brought about only by another written instrument. The covenant idea had laid deep foundations, political as well as fraternal.

Four years earlier the Old Brick Church in Boston had been asked to tarry after the blessing to consider the question, "Will the ch. allow the Baptists to meet in the ch. until their ch. is built"?[37] The vote was unanimously, Yes. Each congregation was enjoined, "Mark your money on the outside so that the deacons can the more readily separate it". Thus did liberality in one area of life gain by inches in other areas, but it was a long, slow story. William Pynchon wrote in his *Diary* on August 31, 1777:

> "At Mr. Barnard's meeting. After service in the morning, he, from the pulpit, invited all of other communions in other of the neighbouring churches to tarry and partake with the communicants of this church, which was new to me".[38]

Men of William Pynchon's stamp could contribute generously to the collection taken "for the Industrious, suffering poor of Boston", when a Sunday appeal was made, more easily than they could cross a denominational line on communion day. As they would presently discover, *newness* was only beginning. Many lines would be crossed. Many walls would come down.

The clergy had a share in making all of this possible. Throughout a decade of impassioned preaching, Sunday after Sunday, they had shot many a bolt against enemies not met on any battlefield of the war. They had not only helped to awaken men to their responsibilities as "freeborn Americans" (a word of pulpit coinage), aroused them to bold action in times of particular crisis, encouraged and steadied them in dark hours; they also helped to slope men's thought toward national unity and how to achieve it, toward greater tolerance, toward a larger view of human brotherhood and its obligations. As hopes of peace began to grow brighter, many things had been settled beyond need of further argument. The pulpit contribution of these years had been vital in other ways than the *patriotic*, a word the clergy had helped to rescue from disrepute. That *patriotism* (by name) is not specifically recommended and enjoined in the Bible was no longer very important.

As to the crisis itself, perhaps their best contribution had been to make the common feeling articulate. As the "freeborn Americans" listened to enlistment sermons on their way to the front, to fast sermons in dark hours, and Thanksgiving sermons at times of victory, they met themselves face to face and heard themselves speaking. In a very true sense, these obscure men of the cloth—John Lathrop, Samuel West, Chauncy Whittelsey, William Gordon, Daniel Shute, Phillips Payson, Noah Welles, Samuel Webster, Jonas Clark, Andrew Eliot, Charles Chauncy, Samuel Cooper, Gad Hitchcock, Izariah Wetmore,

Joseph Perry, John Tucker, Samuel Cooke, Jason Haven, Simeon Howard, Judah Champion, Samuel Stillman, Jonathan Mayhew, Moses Parsons, Samuel Langdon, Ebenezer Bridge, Joseph Lyman, and an easy score of others,[39]—were the *Voice of America* at a time which needed such forthright spokesmen. Unknowns, all of them, except in local Halls of Fame, they deserve a better memorial than anyone has ever given them. It could best be made out of their own words.

CHAPTER SIXTEEN

"*A Nation in the Gristle*"

Aᴠᴛᴇʀ the surrender of Cornwallis the world of the average American grew larger. For the men who had been under arms, particularly so. Until they had enlisted, many of them had never been beyond the borders of the colony in which they were born. They returned, and consciously, to a corner of the United States. Like all other soldiers in all other wars before or since, they also returned to discover that the life they had known no longer existed. The Revolution, like all other wars, was a great solvent, breaking up what had been and causing the constituents of society to take new combinations. If they reappeared at all, they reappeared in new forms. What had been was now no more. In the smallest and most remote village unit it was a strangely different world. While life in the ranks and at home had been beset with external confusions, profound changes had gone silently on underneath, until all at once, no one knew exactly how or why, the whole of life beat to a new rhythm.

In the village world around Meetinghouse Hill, religious interests henceforth and very distinctly took second place. The disruption of parish life for the six years of the war had made such a sequel inevitable. The record from Stratford, Connecticut, that "everybody went", while not entirely typical or even literally true, fitted at least partially many another small community as well. Inevitably, not all came back. The unity of parish life was henceforth broken. Many ministers had died in service; others returned too much broken in health to resume their pulpit duties, and recruits were not immediately available to take their places. Some meetinghouses had been closed for as long as four or five years. Preaching at best had been irregular. Weeks had often passed without a sermon, and in consequence Sunday had become a different kind of day–far different. At points of particular crisis, patriotism had sometimes demanded that spinningwheels run or that lead be melted into bullets seven days in the week; and when consciences had once been quieted by such a sense of urgency, they could presently be similarly quieted for private reasons. Secular interests had crept in by a wide door, until by the earlier Sunday standards nearly the whole village would have been locked up in the cage on Monday morning. Both in the spirit and the letter of the earlier days Sunday keeping was distinctly a thing of the past.

Nor was this all. The changed Sunday was but symptomatic of other and deeper changes. These had come slowly and were apprehended slowly. It was not until returning ministers sought to resume the long interrupted regimen of life around Meetinghouse Hill that they and their people became aware that literal resumption was impossible. The 1780's were a new day and there would be no going back.

It was not only (in Timothy Hilliard's phrase) that "Oppression" and now its sequel, "Independence", had "taken men's minds off religion", but rather that the singleness of earlier American life was gone. Religion was still a major directing force in men's lives, but there were now other major directing forces as well, and other prime concerns, each battling for his time and thought. Life had fanned out in many directions and there was no longer any central unity. The strands could never be brought together again. During the fighting years a shift of center had been taking place in the common life, and by 1780 it had come to pass. The state not the church was now in sharp focus. Moreover, independence had left decisions at every man's door, and decisions that would brook no postponement. Men began to realize that, though "We aimed at nothing more than a constitutional connection with Britain", now by God's providence, it would seem that "a confederate republic" is in sight. We shall soon be called "to assume an independent rank among the nations". Before hostilities ceased, this sense of immediacy pressed hard.

"Town meeting upon the constitution", William Pynchon wrote in his diary for May 18, 1780, and three days later,

> "Mr. Prince, after service, warned the town meeting from the pulpit, and all were desired to attend on affairs of the last importance, viz; of the new constitution".

On the following day he reported,

> "The town meeting was full, and the whole day was spent upon the Constitution; many objections and several amendments were made".[1]

It would take many whole days in many town meetings large and small before the basic principles of representative government, as already practiced in town and church life, could be written into state and federal constitutions agreeable to a newly dignified citizenry.

"Shall we approve a constitution for the State to be drawn up and ratified by our representative?" was the question before one town meeting. "No", was the immediate reply,

> "No set of men can ratify a Constitution for us before we know what it is".[2]

That was the spirit, as town after town in a now hopefully independent America sat down to day-long meetings to consider their best chances of "life, liberty, and the pursuit of happiness" in this present world.

It was a difficult chapter in the American experience. In fact, with the cessation of the fighting in 1781, Americans, wherever they lived, were plunged into something resembling a cold war and a long one. Unity had been precarious enough during the war years; also loyalty, for this had been a civil war. In consequence there had been constant changing of sides, infiltrations, fifth-column activities. Pleas to enlisted companies for patriotism and loyalty had been made continually, for neither could be assumed. Nor could they be assumed now. Ministers, town officers, members of committees, delegates to constitutional conventions, were again duly "investigated" for subversive opinions and Tory loyalties. Many towns took action against the return of Tories, often in harsh terms. "Traitors to their country", said Amesbury, Massachusetts, in 1783, and then registered by vote "the opinion of this town that they ought never to be suffered to return but be excluded from having lot or portion among us".[3]

"Secret enemies" continued to be more hurtful than those who had openly joined the opposing ranks. Worse still, "the less judicious part of mankind are new emboldened to find fault with, and oppose all government",[4] said Moses Mather, and the more judicious among his election day hearers knew that he spoke truth.

During the fighting years such opposition, secret or otherwise, and shifting loyalties had been born in part of fear, local hysteria, self-interest. The confusions of the cold war went deeper and were largely ideological. Moreover, there were deep rifts in the ranks of the winners. What civil and religious leaders called "the spirit of party" was everywhere. "Anarchy and confusion working in the land", they said; and, in terms of easy majority votes, they were right.

"Shall we have a new government for the states?" Amesbury asked of its voters in 1780. "Yea", said twenty-one of those present. "Nay", said the other nineteen. On Article 3, guaranteeing protection under the law for "every denomination of Christians demeaning themselves peaceably and as good subjects of the Commonwealth", the score was thirteen yeas and fourteen nays. Brookfield, Massachusetts, had an easier time, voting one hundred and forty-three yeas in favor of the new state constitution in 1780 and only eleven against it. No such record can be called typical. There was no uniformity, nor were disagreement and disharmony necessarily born of disloyalty or even obstinacy. Men were deeply stirred. They were asking probing questions, realistic questions, and questions for which no immediate and certain answers were forthcoming. They had been told many times in press and pulpit that the strength of the "confederate republic" they were planning fitted the conditions and the people of America. Why? Because

"Here merit is more generally distinguished. Every individual considers himself, and is regarded by the community, as a person of some significance".[5]

They proceeded to vote on the several provisions of these new constitutions with this flattering verdict consciously in mind. Disagreement was not unhealthful. It merely meant more time; more town meetings. Men were also weary. There was much poverty. Money "is scarcer than it used to be, or than it ever was since our Remembrance", was the plaint everywhere.

"I hear wood is 52 dollars a cord in Boston, and flour at £50 per hundred, i.e. a barrel is more than my whole salary.—A man asked 74 dollars for a bushel of wheat meal.—Green peas sold at Boston at 20 dollars a peck. Lamb at 20 dollars a quarter. Board 60 dollars a week.—We are in a sad toss: people are moving out. Never did I feel more anxiety."[6]

No wonder. There had been years of this, and whatever the inflation record, some other town could better it.

"Tempestuous times", said Zabdiel Adams in 1782, even though

"We are now in sight of the promised land. To encourage us to persevere, let us anticipate the rising glory of America.
Behold her seas whitened with commerce; her capitals filled with inhabitants, and resounding with the din of industry.
See her rising to independence and glory. Contemplate the respectable figure that she will one day make among the nations of the earth.
Figure to yourselves that this your native country will ere long become the permanent seat of Liberty, the retreat of philosophers; the asylum of the oppressed, the umpire of contending nations."[7]

For a long minute every minister on every such public occasion permitted himself a similar flight.

Except for the fact that "God helped us" and we must not forget to thank Him, events of the war were pushed into the background. Preaching the Lexington anniversary sermon in the following year, Zabdiel Adams was only momentarily dashed when he could find no precise parallel to the battle in the Bible, "that copious Book", but he quickly substituted his own review of that "barbarous deed", and went on to the far future. It was now a case of eyes front for them all, as with one voice the clergy ushered in the millennium. Briefly, they seemed to forget even the American deadlies. Instead, there was praise for the high motives from which America had acted. In rebellion she had contended not from ambition or any desire for domination, but for "the common rights of man". She now desired, said Henry Cummings in 1783, to cultivate the friendship of all nations, "even of Britain", to whom "Americans (with few exceptions) heartily wish prosperity and happiness in common with other nations". As he entertained his fancy with future scenes, he saw America playing a world rôle,

> "extending her friendly arms for the support and protection of other states and nations against the attacks of restless encroaching ambition; and (while none dare to distrust or affront her) offering a refuge and asylum, in her bosom, to the injured and oppressed of the human race in all quarters of the globe".

He envisioned (as they all did) "wealth and opulence flowing in upon her" from her own inexhaustible resources and from her free trade with all nations. There would also be distinction in science and the arts, "sublime intellectual accomplishments above Greece and Rome, in their zenith of glory".[8] "Agreeable prospects", he called them, but whether America shall ever realize this, her own zenith, "depends much upon the wisdom and virtue of the present generation". Upon their action hangs the fate of "unborn millions". Suppose we of the present never see all this.

> We are a Free People under the sun.
> We lay foundations for a far future.
> What other nation in all history has ever had such a chance?

From sermon to sermon it is the same prediction, the same hope, the same recognition of America's unique opportunity, and always the reminder that the virtues and vices of nations are "the great hinges on which the fates of nations turn". Such sentiments were more a response to men's thought than an invention of the preacher. Briefly, American enthusiasm for the future, destined to be one of our hardiest national traits, had an almost unqualifiedly hopeful expression. All this is a far cry indeed from Increase Mather's one-time proclamation that according to the "judgment of very learned men, in the glorious times promised to the church on Earth, America will be Hell". For the extravagance of their easy superlatives these spokesmen of the early 1780's are forgivable. There is only one first time, and for reasons logical and otherwise the year 1783 became a pinnacle of vision. For a brief moment (and a moment only) the depleted present was forgotten as the far horizons of America's greatness became visible to prophetic eyes. Notwithstanding their florid predictions, these ministerial prophets kept their feet on the ground, balancing their extravagance by practical counsels. Nearly every sermon has the same array, often in the same words.

Beware of a mounting public debt.

Beware of increasing dependents on government.

Beware, above all, of a quick demobilization. It would be exceedingly unsafe for a people to "lay by their arms and neglect all military matters". (Henry Cummings, 1783)

Beware a standing army. Let our protection be a well-trained militia of the youth of the land. Let this militia be annually exercised, in peace as well as in war.

Beware too short a term for "our chief man in the government". Annual elections would be too frequent. He would "hardly be warm in his office" in a single year; a succession of years will be better, but let it always be a rotation, never a monopoly in office. (Zabdiel Adams, 1782)

Beware ignorance. "An ignorant people will never live long under a free government." (Zabdiel Adams, 1782)

Beware sloth. Till the land. "It is not God's ordinary method to rain down bread for the food of man." (William Symmes, 1785)

Never forget that wars still come. "They should be studied as a science, and prosecuted by the rules of art." (Zabdiel Adams, 1782)

The Constitution is wisely not *finished*. An orderly way is left open to make amendments as such are necessary. (Moses Hemenway, 1784)

"We should leave nothing to human nature that can be provided for by law or the constitution." (Samuel Stillman, 1779)

One of the most notable versions of this ministerial prophecy, and also one of the most realistic in similarly practical counsels, came in a sermon of Ezra Stiles, preached in Hartford, before Governor Jonathan Trumbull on the 1783 election occasion. He called it *The United States Elevated to Glory and Honour*. In its printed form running to ninety-nine pages in the first edition and to a hundred and seventy-two in the second, this sermon must have been an exhausting performance for the preacher as well as for his audience, but for those whose endurance was adequate, it might also have been a memorable preview of glories to come.

Why shouldn't America be great, he asked. We have everything out of which greatness may come; and then indulging his flair for computation, he proceeded to answer his own question in one direction after another.

"It is probable that within a century from our independence the sun will shine on fifty million inhabitants in the United States. This will be a great, a very great nation, nearly equal to half Europe."[9]

The census figure in 1880 was 50,155,783 persons, but had Ezra Stiles known how close he came to this total, he would have claimed no credit for his accuracy. The prospect was Noah's before it was his own, and he would give credit where credit belonged. For him the Bible had all the answers. Whether Noah's flood had covered the whole earth or only the biblical geography of it, whether the pillar of salt that had once been Lot's disobedient wife was still standing seven miles out of Hebron, whether the American Indians "beyond a doubt" were "Canaanites of the expulsion of Joshua", were questions that troubled his thought; but he was at home in his own day in spite of them and he would also have been almost at home in the age of B-36's and the A bomb.

In part because of his prodigious learning and perhaps in part because of something better, he saw the panorama of recorded human experience in such perspective that he once declared that "the History of the World may be contained completely in one Quarto volume, especially of such a small World as this".[10]

Ezra Stiles might not have been the one to write such a pre-Wellsian version of world history, but surely his ability to detach himself from the moment served him well when he turned his prophetic lens on the American future.

His remarks on government (given much space in this sermon) show knowledge and critical acumen. We have the enviable chance to decide what kind of government we want. It will not be a monarchy. It should not be an unsystematic democracy. That would be as detestable as an absolute monarchy.

"A well-ordered DEMOCRATICAL ARISTOCRACY, standing upon the annual elections of the people, and revocable at pleasure, is the polity which combines the UNITED STATES, and from the nature of man, and the comparison of ages, I believe it will approve itself the most equitable, liberal and perfect."[11]

He found no one of the existing state models desirable. The constitutions of Maryland and New York are superior to those of Georgia, Pennsylvania, Jersey and the Carolinas, in that the two houses are not of "one order only". Massachusetts has "shadows of royalty". Connecticut and Rhode Island have realized the best policy as to a legislature. We can learn from these various experiments. The General Congress lays a foundation for "permanent union in the American Republic", which may convince the world that America has invented the most nearly perfect government on earth.

Although in his patriotic memory an army of twenty thousand men had sprung "into spontaneous existence" after April 19, 1775, he atones for this fiction by counselling "for all our increasing millions" universal military training in peace and war.

"This will defend us against ourselves, and against surrounding states. Let this be known in Europe, in every future age, and we shall never again be invaded from the other side of the Atlantic."[12]

The speed with which "that well-built, noble ship the *Raleigh*" was "finished from the keel and equipt for sea in a few months" was to him proof "to posterity and the world, that a powerful navy may be originated, built and equipped for service in a much shorter period than was before imagined".[13]

Like his brother prophets he saw the arts and sciences flourishing here, but, linguist that he was, he predicted also that

[The English] "will probably become the vernacular Tongue of more numerous millions, than ever yet spoke one language on Earth", (except the Chinese).[14]

Its "rough sonorous diction may here take its athenian polish, and receive its attic urbanity", for it will be "unmutilated by any foreign dialects of foreign conquests". At home in Arabic, Syriac, Persian, Coptic, Chaldee, Ezra Stiles might have been only slightly confounded by *The American Thesaurus of Slang* or Eric Partridge's *Dictionary of the Underworld*. Such fallow areas would have excited and delighted him and, given the chance, he would probably have gone to work at once on additions to both volumes.

Like his brother prophets, he foresaw America's "communication with all nations in *commerce, manners,* and *science,* beyond anything heretofore known to the world, . . . and this fermentation and communion of nations will doubtless produce something very new, singular, and glorious". Unlike most of his brethren, he saw all religious sects living here "in friendly cohabitation", proving

"that men may be good members of civil society, and yet differ in religion".
"Religion may here receive its last, most liberal, and impartial examination",[15]

he dared to predict. Do not think all this is strange, he said more than once.

"We live in an age of wonders: we have lived an age in a few years; we have seen more wonders accomplished in *eight* years, than are usually unfolded in a century."[16]

Perhaps the most arresting paragraph in all this amazing array of erudition, good sense, and shrewd insight comes as part of his florid apostrophe to England, beginning,

"Oh England! how did I once love thee! how did I once glory in thee!"

One may smile at his floridity, but to read a little further down the page is also to be startled at the closeness with which what he indeed called *prophecy* hit the truth of the 1940's.

"And if perchance in some future period danger should have arisen to thee from european states, how have I flewn on the wings of prophecy, with the numerous hardy hosts of thine American sons, inheriting thine antient principles of *liberty* and *valor*, to rescue and reinthrone the hoary venerable head of the most glorious empire on earth? But now farewell—a long farewell to all this greatness! And yet even now methinks, in such an exigency, I could leap the Atlantic, not into thy bosom, but to rescue an aged parent from destruction; and then return on the wings of triumph, to this asylum of the world, and rest in the bosom of liberty."[17]

This is John Cotton's "chickens of the same feather, and yolke" in a new version; but after all, not so very different. It is possible to imagine John Cotton and Ezra Stiles talking together across the hundred and fifty years which separated them, of the roomy land of America and its future promise. They were both men of vision as to the practical things of the world and if Ezra Stiles had discreetly omitted the word *democracy*, this might have been an amicable conversation. On the ninety-eighth page of this all but interminable sermon, "our ancestors" are invited to

"look down from the high abodes of paradise into this assembly" . . .

where

"methinks they might catch a sensation of joy at beholding the reign, the trumph of LIBERTY on earth!"[18]

Obviously, this is not a great sermon, but for all its dusty erudition and prosaic literalness, it documents a high moment of the American experience and suggests at many points that the modern age was already knocking at the outer gate.

Dark days came and swiftly. It would be hard to find in all the files of American sermon history a stretch of more unmitigated gloom than the period 1784–1787. Over and over one reads that all is not well, and perhaps cannot be.

Our infant republic has suffered a severe shock.

All government tends to despotism.

Every species of human government contains the seeds of dissolution, which will some time or other work its ruin.

Tyrants are the same on the banks of the Nile or along the Potomac.

Let us not flatter ourselves with such prophecies of our astonishing future progress and glory as have grown so fashionable. We have had enough of the Lockes and Newtons to come, the philosophers and divines greater than have ever yet lived; of towering spires and spacious domes, of populous towns and cities rising thick through an empire greater than the world has ever seen.

True enough,

We are the most highly favored people on earth as to our natural resources.

Under our constitution we have more power in our hands than any other people under the sun,

but

Security in happiness is not the lot of humanity.

We have lost our heads. We are given over to luxury and extravagance.

We have grown lawless.

We have not repaid our heroes as they deserve.

We are not even paying the interest on our national debt.

God has ten thousand arrows in his quiver for such a people.

These are young men speaking; but on election day, all preachers became old men. Their warnings, however justified, have a tired sound. Their assumption that prosperity equals wickedness and that the only way to go forward is to go backward was not the gospel for a new nation learning its first hard lessons and making its first sad mistakes. The 1783 visions of America's future greatness within herself and an enlarging place among the nations had been tonic to an exhausted generation. These warnings and accusations left men spiritless.

The year 1787 marked the nadir in this aftermath of disillusionment. "Impenetrable gloom", said the preachers, but they did not keep on saying it, since fortunately they still had George Washington on whom to pin hopeful Scripture analogies. He became the American Nehemiah, *par excellence*, and his much worked-at-wall whatever needed most urgently to be done at the moment. Gradually they regained their equilibrium, and their people with them, perhaps justifying Thomas Jefferson's verdict that it is part of the American character to consider nothing as desperate. At any rate, the sermon emphasis changed, and if (from the pulpit side) the future might never look so rosy again, a more realistic view brought a new kind of hope and a more solid basis for it.

In one of the most hopeful speeches of the dark year, 1787, young Joel Barlow, about to embark on his long diplomatic career abroad, unintentionally no doubt (for he does not mention them) defined the rôle the clergy had played in the crucial years just behind and the rôle many of them would continue to play in those immediately ahead. Having first recognized "our present alarming crisis", perhaps the most alarming that America ever saw, and the causes for it,

> "We have contended with the most powerful nation and subdued the bravest and best appointed armies; but now we have to contend with *ourselves*. . . . It is not for glory, it is for existence that we contend",

he voiced his confidence that an equitable government might still be achieved, if the first great urgent step were taken; namely, "to convince the people of the importance of the present situation"; for as he saw it (and it was a young man's faith) "the majority of a great people, on a subject which they understand, will never act wrong".[19] Certainly no group of men had done more to "convince the people" throughout the entire war period than these men of the pulpit. They continued to do so with flat-footed literalness and hard-hitting blows, which usually became them better than their poetic flights.

Election sermons and those designed for other special days during

these difficult years generally show less conventionality, more directness than at any time previously, except during the war years. We
have nothing to complain of in this favored country, said James Freeman on a Thanksgiving occasion in 1796. We have the fertile soil, the
favorable climate, the abundance of natural resources, the means of
obtaining private happiness and obtaining it easily. Why these bickerings, this dissatisfaction, this "spirit of party" among us?

> "If we find any one poor, diseased, or wretched, it is not because
> he is an inhabitant of the United States, but because he is an in-
> habitant of the world."

Liberty is abused; certainly. It always will be abused in a free government.

> "The excesses of the people in a free government resemble a river
> which overflows its banks, and which may sweep away a hay stack
> or a sheaf of corn."

Some think we are too free; others that we are already losing our freedom. We have a good constitution, and the conclusion would seem
to be that "if the citizens of the United States are not destined for
permanent freedom, freedom is not then intended for the human
race".[20] Other men in other pulpits and on other special days repeated
this assurance and meant it. Hope and confidence were gradually restored.

While the last miles toward this Promised Land of the new "Confederate Republic" were being slowly and painfully accomplished, the
meetinghouse story was quietly slipping into a new chapter. Tom
Paine had been right when he asserted

> "the exceeding probability that a revolution in the system of gov-
> ernment would be followed by a revolution in the system of re-
> ligion".[21]

During his five years in America he had done much to encourage the
first revolution and later in his *Age of Reason* he would do much to
encourage the second. As he himself had said, however, this second
revolution would come slowly, in spite of the hospitable climate of

changing opinion. His own name carried authority in the 1780's and 90's, and his dedication of this inflammable book to *My Fellow-Citizens of the United States* helped to create a welcome for it, at least initially, although few could go all the way with him in his unorthodox opinions. Nevertheless, the book had a fairly wide reading by those capable of understanding it, although its immediate effect was more to encourage a spirit of skeptical inquiry and greater intellectual independence than to overthrow fundamental beliefs. Such bold statements as "My own mind is my own church", flattered the self-confidence of those who had so recently trusted their own judgment in the matter of civil rebellion. His emphasis on reason as the path to his conclusions flattered it still further. To a degree *free thinking* became stylish. The militant opposition of the clergy who labelled the book and everything in it "subversive" merely increased his audience, while his definition of *learning* as knowledge of the things that science and philosophy teach rather than "skill in the Tongues" blunted the edge of ministerial attack by those who dared to face him openly in press or pulpit. Others feared to touch such heresies, even to attack them. "Too shocking to be repeated", said John Lathrop, who had "thundered and lightened" so effectually during the fighting years. The same men cannot often carry the banners of two generations. Freer thinking must usually wait for a new generation.

In more concrete ways the second revolution was already an accomplished fact before the election of George Washington. Town and church would henceforth go their separate ways. A line would now be visibly drawn between *civil* and *religious*, *church* and *state*, *secular* and *sacred*. This was a cleavage which would cut to the very foundations of town life as it had been lived in New England since the beginning. Had it come by fiat, or had it been forced before the time was ripe, such a change would have been cataclysmic. Instead, like most fundamental social changes, it had come softly and while the spotlight had been turned elsewhere. By the mid-eighties all that remained was to recognize what had happened and to deal with the consequences.

In the outward look of town life, this meant two changes: no more compulsory "Rates" from every resident for ministerial support; no more town meetings called to order from the deacon's seat. Voters would no longer file out of the Sunday pews to deposit their ballots in the box on the long table underneath the pulpit. The meetinghouse would become a sanctuary and the town would find another place for the transaction of business. The whole structure of community life would be different. A century earlier such a division would have been unthinkable. As the Preface to *The Book of the General Lawes and Libertyes concerning the Inhabitants of the Massachusetts* had put it in 1648, church and state were planted and have grown together "like two twinnes", whereby though neither is in control, each "do help and strengthen other". How far this 1648 statement had been true to fact is a story subject to many qualifications. That church and state had remained together (at least nominally) long enough for their mutual debt to be written into more than their separate histories would seem to be true enough, but now even in name the twinship was ended. No arguments would be necessary. While it was still possible for the Baptist minister's cow to be seized to pay the "Standing Order" minister's "Rate", in the same precinct, or for the collector to remove a load of hay from a stubborn parishioner's barn for the same purpose, it was still too early to enact a Bill of Rights. That time had now come.

Some "Standing Order" men had seen it coming far enough in advance to go on record as opposed to a compulsory tax. They were the wise ones; however, some of them, it must be admitted, became wise only after attempts at compulsion had failed. Jeremy Belknap of Dover, New Hampshire, having first tried to collect his salary by force, read a letter to his congregation in April, 1786, protesting the injustice of the very method which had failed for him. Compulsion tended, he said,

> "to promote discord, hatred, and envy, instead of peace and goodwill, and to involve a minister in distress and perplexity, if he has any feeling".[22]

Other ministers, who had first tried "distress and perplexity", also right-about-faced in time, withdrew their claims and declared themselves in favor of voluntary support. Unwise ones continued to make even more urgent demands, to their own great hurt. Richard Pierce of Acushnet declared that his congregation owed him sixteen hundred pounds or sixteen years' salary. Of course he never got it. His successor, Samuel West, laid a claim for arrears as well as for other church expenses, but seeing that his "just arrears" were a lost cause, he reversed himself in time to survive. His new faith was expressed somewhat gaily, we are told, by the inscription above the collection box,

"Those who debate to pay by rate
 To end dispute may contribute".[23]

Gaily or not, *contribute* was now the word; the word "Rate" was obsolete years before the Bill of Rights provision in 1792,

"And no person of any one particular religious sect or denomination shall ever be compelled to pay towards the teacher or teachers of another persuasion, sect, or denomination".

The Massachusetts Act relating to Parishes and Religious Freedom, making this exemption official for Massachusetts, was not passed until 1834 when the long bitterness "Rates" had caused had almost been forgotten.

Some towns which for reasons of their own wished to deal out their own mercy in this connection, *sans* a national Bill of Rights, continued to require statements from residents to whom immunity was granted. Among such extant statements, various letters to selectmen suggest that differences of belief were the grounds of this exemption.

"Sir, for particular reasons I wish not to be taxed to Mr. Merrill again until I think different",

wrote one independent New Hampshire worshipper as late as 1812. And another,

"This may certify that I differ from Rev. Nathaniel Merrill's religion, and therefore refuse to pay him any ministerial tax and shall not".

Later when the same Mr. Merrill was in favor of "erecting a stove" in the meetinghouse and a town vote had permitted him to do so, one objector wrote,

> "I have attended church these fifty years; I have fought the British seven years; I have slept in a tent on the frozen ground with nothing but a blanket to cover me; I have trod the snow path with bleeding feet nearly naked,—and if Mr. Merrill needs a fire, let him go to the place where they keep one the year round".[34]

Master John Wilson would have been surprised indeed; the day of "revering one's minister" had suffered strange amendment.

"Turning the town out of doors" likewise was a change that came naturally along with town growth and the division into precincts, although the acknowledgment of change came long after the fact. The separate place of meeting was logical enough. If the minister's rate is no longer a town affair, why shouldn't the church take care of its building likewise? Then if the building belongs to us, said the church, why should the town meet here? When public feeling was not yet ripe for the complete separation, there was trouble, even violence. Portsmouth, New Hampshire, had protested "Damage done to the Pews, Seats and other Parts of the House" in 1762, as a result of boisterous Town meetings, "warm Debates and Contentions—, very unsuitable to such a Place". To put an end to all this the church voted that,

> "hereafter no public town meeting for transacting the civil affairs and Business of the Town be permitted to be kept and held in the Meeting House".[25]

This vote was backed by a lock put on the door. Nothing daunted, however, the town met, elected a moderator on the steps, took a vote to break down the door, and it was so ordered. Business was transacted as usual. Other churches which took similar action too early in the new chapter of events likewise met town defiance. In the 1780's such defiance would have been ridiculous. There was nothing to fight about.

In the post-Revolution era many towns also modified the "forever" of the action of their forefathers, selling or leasing land originally set aside for the ministry. Some towns had already done so long before. Portsmouth, New Hampshire, for one, as early as 1705, had permitted the "ministerial field" part of the original "Glebe Land" set aside "forever" as the minister's only, to be divided into house lots and so used for a period of nine hundred and ninety-nine years from that date. Presumably therefore, in the year 2704 the residents then living upon these house lots will "quietly and peaceably surrender up the premises to the church wardens of the said parish". We shall see.

Ministers also crossed forbidden lines and broke precedents belonging to the days when they had been "revered". In Dunbarton, New Hampshire, during the inflamed discussions of 1812, Walter Harris, twenty-three years minister in the town, was challenged when he attempted to cast his vote in town meeting. Hitherto he had accepted the denial of this privilege as part of his traditional *status quo*. Not so on this particular day. Drawing himself up to his impressive height from his position on the pulpit stairs, and perhaps raising a little higher than usual the remarkable voice for which he was locally famous, he said (as Dunbarton wishes to remember it),

"I have fought the battles of my country; my only brother fell by my side, and who is he who says I shan't vote?"[26]

So saying, he deposited his vote in the ballot box and walked majestically out before an awestruck town meeting. It was as easy as that when one dared.

But it took time; a long time. Courage to think one's own sermon thoughts took longest of all. Presently, however, the younger generation of ministers professed the spirit of free inquiry for which their immediate predecessors had been all but pilloried, and then dismissed.

When one John White succeeded Thomas Thacher of Clapboard Trees in 1814, he wrote in his letter of acceptance,

"as to the sentiments on religious subjects that I have expressed in public and in private, they are what I now conceive to be agreeable to the Scriptures. . . . Still, I would have it understood, that no pledge is given on my part to maintain any system of doctrine, farther than it shall appear at any time to be supported by the oracles of God. And if, in the course of my inquiries after truth, a change take place in my opinions concerning the import of sacred writings, I shall feel myself at liberty to communicate them without reserve".[27]

It was indeed a new day. New also in what constituted a "faithful ministry". Joseph Estabrook, who had been a sixteen-year-old-boy at the Lexington-Concord fight, put a *P.S.* to his letter of acceptance to Athol, Massachusetts, in 1787, which read, "I shall expect to be indulged with three or four Sabbaths yearly to visit my friends".[28] First and second generation ministers who had not taken a vacation which included a Sunday in a sixty- or seventy-year pastorate, would have thought young Joseph unconsecrated to the "greatest work on earth", and therefore unworthy "to lay down his bones with the bones of his people". Nevertheless, Joseph Estabrook stayed with them for forty-three years.

One by one the old molds were broken, usually by the courage of one man. Thought went its new way. "Knowledge has induced the laity to think and act for themselves", said one discouraged election preacher in the dark year, 1787, as though such independence were a calamity. At any rate, it was a fact. As the church body broke up into sects at an accelerated pace, small differences made chasms which men could not cross. Belief crystallized anew with each subdivision. "Sound doctrine" became many doctrines, for each of which *soundness* was militantly claimed.

To the advocates of the old uniformity, such diversity was the end of all. To the new generation whose answer it was, freedom to choose meant new life, new zest, and in many ways a new vision. The day of uniformity in belief and the power to compel it was past. Men still sought to find God, and if we may believe their own private words, they found Him on each of these new paths. More and more they enlarged their own part in their own salvation. God grew more kind as men grew more responsible. The modern age came in. Wise ones among religious leaders knew that institutions have to change

in order to remain the same; unwise ones resisted change and sometimes resisted too long.

Whether religion has been a creative element in the American experience is not a question for dogmatic answers or literal answers.
Here and there through the years the meetinghouse story supplies
hints toward an answer but only hints. The area of search must go far
beyond the history of pulpit and pew, of sermons, of covenants and
codes of conduct by which very earnest and very practical men and
women sought to "Square their Lives by the Rule of the Gospel".
That the meetinghouse way of life, as these earnest and practical men
and women charted it, did not become the American way does not
write either futility or finality on the ideas and purposes for which
it stood. Whatever the full significance of this early way of life may
be in our lengthening national record, that significance escapes easy
statement. Perhaps it has something to do with the fact that in the
beginning the meetinghouse way was not accidental, but deliberate,
that it was deeply rooted in the conditions of the earliest American
experience and that it also profoundly affected and partially shaped
that experience. It may also have something to do with the fact that
in the beginning *liberty* and the *rights of man* had a religious context
from which something impalpable remains. Certainly the significance
of the meetinghouse story has little to do with blue laws, outmoded
customs, and such external trivia as can be dramatized at a three hun-
dredth anniversary. It is the story of convictions and purposes, of
a protest plus an experience of living, of intangibles such as are not
often sowed and reaped in one generation or in many generations.
Moreover, as the seeds of its earlier plantings and reapings have been
widely blown, they have sometimes yielded unpredictable fruit.

Time after time the meetinghouse records are its own best com-
mentary. Let an entry on the Town Book of Westford, Massachusetts, speak in parable.

March 5, 1770 [the day of the Boston Massacre]
"Voted that the Committee appointed to underpin the New meetinghouse shall take as many of the stones now under the old meetinghouse as they think proper."[29]

The committee acted; the old stones were selected; the new foundation was laid. On May 10 the town voted "to have one hundred spick poles" prepared for the raising. On June 20 the people assembled. The new structure was raised on the "Good, Handsome stones" of former days. The meetinghouse story went on.

Chapter I

1. First printed, London, 1630. Reprinted, London, 1634; Boston, 1686. Included in *Old South Leaflets*, No. 53. For a brief discussion of this sermon, see Edwin D. Mead, "John Cotton's Farewell Sermon to Winthrop's Company at Southampton", *Proc. Mass. Hist. Soc.*, 3rd ser., XLI (1907), 101-115.

2. The opening line of "Kit Carson's Ride", *The Poetical Works of Joaquin Miller*, New York, 1923, p. 149.

3. *God's Promise*, 1630 ed., p. 5.

4. *The Winthrop Papers*, Boston, 1931, II, 294.

5. *God's Promise*, p. 8.

6. *Ibid.*, p. 9.

7. In a letter to Bishop Williams, Jan. 31, 1624. *New Eng. Hist. and Geneal. Register*, XXVIII (1874), 137-138.

8. *God's Promise*, p. 17.

9. *Ibid.*, p. 8.

10. *Ibid.*, p. 18.

11. Alexander Young, *Chronicles of the First Planters of the Colony of Massachusetts Bay*, Boston, 1846, pp. 438-444.

12. "Autobiography," *Pub. Col. Soc. of Mass.*, XXVII (1932), 345-400, p. 375. Shepard's reasons are also included in Young's *Chronicles*, pp. 529–530.

13. *A Description of New-England*, London, 1616, Boston ed., 1865, pp. 55-56.

14. *Colonial Tracts*, Rochester, 1898, II, No. 3, p. 36.

15. *God's Promise*, p. 20.

Chapter II

1. *New-England's Plantation, with the Sea-Journal and Other Writings*, London, 1630. Reprinted, The Essex Book and Print Club, Salem, 1908, p. 83.

2. "Bradford Letter Book," *Coll. Mass. Hist. Soc.*, 1st ser. (1810), III, 67–68. The order of these events is not clearly established. Charles Gott's letter puts the ordination of pastor and teacher on July 20, immediately following their election. Nathaniel Morton puts the taking of the convenant and the ordaining of Skelton and Higginson on Aug. 6. *New England's*

Memorial (ed. John Davis), Boston, 1826, pp. 145–147. According to usual later practice, the taking of the covenant preceded the election of pastor, teacher and church officers. Morton's statement is probably the more trustworthy of the two.

3. The covenant as renewed in 1636, sometimes called the first covenant, has nine specifications, some of which would seem quite clearly to have reference to the stormy days of Roger Williams' pastorate immediately preceding. For the text of this covenant, see Sidney Perley, *The History of Salem*, Salem, 1924, I, 162-164.

4. "Bradford Letter Book," pp. 67–68. Sidney Perley also prints this letter, I, 155-156.

5. From the *Church Records*, Vol. I, by courtesy of the Massachusetts Historical Society. Winthrop's *Journal* for August 27, 1630, tells of the election of church officers.

6. Quoted by Donald G. Trayser, *Barnstable, Three Centuries of a Cape Cod Town*, Hyannis, 1939, p. 5. John Lothrop's *Diary* is lost, but a copy made by Ezra Stiles is preserved with the Stiles papers in the Yale University Library. It is bound in a volume of Winthrop's *History of New England*.

7. Quoted by Lucius R. Paige, *History of Cambridge, Massachusetts*, Boston, 1877, p. 251 footnote, from a MS which he says he has in his hand.

8. Roxbury Church Records, as included in *A Report of the Record Commissioners*, 1881, p. 171.

9. Arbella Sermon, *Winthrop Papers*, II, 294.

10. From *A True and Short Declaration, both of the Gathering and Joyning Together of Certaine Persons; and also of the Lamentable Breach and Division which fell amongst them*. No place or date given but probably printed in London, 1583. As quoted by Henry Martyn Dexter, *Congregationalism of the Last Three Hundred Years, As Seen in Its Literature*, Boston, 1880, p. 67.

11. From John Davenport's *Profession of Faith* at the time of the New Haven gathering, 1639. The phrasing of John Cotton and others is almost identical.

12. "Letter Book of Samuel Sewall", *Coll. Mass. Hist. Soc.* 6th ser., II (1888), 194. Entry of Jan. 15, 1724. He signed himself "Your Loving Unkle".

13. *Magnalia Christi Americana*, Boston, 1702, Hartford, 1820, I, Bk. III, 357.

Chapter III

1. In his "Defense of the Negative Vote", June 4, 1643, *Winthrop Papers*, IV, 383.

2. "Letter to Lord Say and Seal", 1636. Printed as No. 3 in the Appendix to Thomas Hutchinson's *History of the Colony and Province of Massachusetts Bay* (ed. Clarence Shaw Mayo), Cambridge, 1936, I, 415. The Ainsworth statement reads, "So then for *popular government,* we hold it not, we approve it not, for if the multitude govern, then who shalbe governed?" See Perry Miller, "Thomas Hooker and the Democracy of Early Connecticut", for a discussion of early notions of democracy, including Cotton's; *New England Quarterly,* IV (1931), 663-712. The Ainsworth statement is quoted on p. 671.

3. *A Memorial Volume,* transcribed from the Church Records, Bk. I (ed. Don Gleason Hill), *Dedham Records,* Dedham, 1888, Vol. II. John Allin's account of the founding is included, pp. 1-21.

4. *Ibid.,* p. 1.

5. *Ibid.,* p. 6.

6. *Ibid.,* p. 13.

7. *Ibid.,* pp. 14-15.

8. "The Indian Grammar Begun, or an Essay to Bring the Indian Language into Rules", Cambridge, 1666. *Old South Leaflets,* No. 52, p. 5.

Chapter IV

1. *Ratio Discipliniae Nov-Anglorum,* Boston, 1726, p. 5.

2. His grandfather Richard Mather had expressed the same idea in precisely the same words. It was the orthodox view.

3. Case No. XXVI in *Thirty Important Cases Resolved with Evidence of Scripture and Reason,* Boston, 1699, pp. 64-66. This phrasing follows very closely that of the *Confession of Faith* adopted by the Second Boston Synod, Boston, 1680. No. VI in Ch. XXII, Boston ed., 1757, p. 38.

4. *Ratio Discipliniae,* p. 65.

5. Longmeadow Records, Apr. 26, 1714. Quoted in *Proceedings at the Centennial of the Incorporation of the Town of Longmeadow,* Oct. 17, 1883, with numerous Historical Appendices and a Town Genealogy, Longmeadow, 1884, p. 150.

6. Charles A. Place finds evidence that 19 meetinghouses had been "built as first structures before 1641" and before 1651, "nearly 60". *American Church Architecture,* 2 vols., typescript, American Antiquarian Society. These figures are subject to dispute. For an exhaustive and authoritative recent treatment of early New England meetinghouse architecture, see John Frederick Kelly, *Early Connecticut Meetinghouses,* 2 vols., New York, 1948.

7. Town Records, quoted by Frances M. Caulkins, *History of New London,* New London, 1852, p. 109.

8. Town Records, August 27, 1675. Quoted by George W. Perkins, *Historical Sketches of Meriden*, West Meriden, 1849, p. 28.

9. Town Records, May 21, 1729. Quoted by Elliott C. Cogswell, *History of Nottingham, Deerfield and Northwood*, Manchester, 1878, pp. 90-91.

10. *Diary of Samuel Sewall*, 1674-1729. 3 vols., *Coll. Mass. Hist. Soc.*, 5th ser., V-VII (1878-1882). Entry of Feb. 6, 1686/7, *Diary* I, 167. Another infant son, written down as having heard his first sermon, aged seven days, did not live to hear another.

11. Minister at Marlborough, 1665-1698. He kept this *Diary* in Latin. *Proc. Mass. Hist. Soc.*, 2nd ser., IV (1887-1889), 300.

12. Town Records, quoted by Ellen D. Larned, *History of Windham County, Connecticut*, Worcester, 1874, p. 54.

13. Nearly every town can show a similar entry, usually prefatory to the appointment of a dog-beater. A Braintree vote in 1715 authorized the selectmen to draw up a by-law "for the prevention of Dogs coming into the Meeting-houses, in the time of Publick Worship"; other towns similarly.

14. *Dedham Records*, Dedham, 1899, V, 14-15.

15. May 16, 1661. Quoted by Joshua Coffin, *A Sketch of the History of Newbury, Newburyport, and West Newbury*, Boston, 1845, p. 64.

16. Town Records, Feb. 1743/44. Quoted by Daniel F. Seccomb, *History of the Town of Amherst*, Concord, N. H., 1883, p. 235.

17. Town Records, quoted by Nahum Mitchell, *History of the Early Settlement of Bridgewater*, Boston, 1840, p. 62.

18. *Memoirs of Captain Roger Clap*, Boston, 1731, pp. 7-8.

19. *Ibid.*, p. 8.

Chapter V

1. *Magnalia*, I, Bk. III, Intro., p. 211.

2. His subject was "The Danger of Desertion," *Jer.* 14, 9: "We are called by thy name; leave us not". London, 1641, p. 20. For a discussion of this sermon, see Edwin D. Mead, "Thomas Hooker's Farewell Sermon in England", *Proc. Mass. Hist. Soc.*, XLVI (1913), pp. 253-274. Excerpts from the sermon are included in this article.

3. Benjamin Trumbull, *A Complete History of Connecticut, Civil and Ecclesiastical*, 2 vols., Hartford, 1797, I, 55.

4. Quoted by Walter Eliot Thwing, *History of the First Church in Roxbury, Massachusetts*, Boston, 1908, p. 29.

5. Challenged by Richard LeBaron Bowen, *Early Rehoboth*, Rehoboth, 1946, II, 25-38. This recent book devotes a whole chapter to "The Name Rehoboth", with the conclusion that there is no documentation for the previous ascription of the name to Newman.

6. *Coll. Conn. Hist. Soc.*, I (1860), 20.

7. For an appraisal of this sermon in its time and place, see Perry Miller, "Thomas Hooker and the Democracy of Early Connecticut", *New England Quarterly*, IV (1931), 663-712.

8. *Magnalia*, I, 316.

9. In a letter to Governor Winthrop, Dec. 22, 1639. "Winthrop Papers", *Coll. Mass. Hist. Soc.*, 4th ser., VII (1865), 26-27. For an account of Ward, see J. W. Dean, *A Memoir of the Rev. Nathaniel Ward*, Albany, 1868; for a brief recent account, see Samuel Eliot Morison, *Builders of the Bay Colony*, Boston, 1930, pp. 217-243.

10. This code of laws is reproduced in facsimile, *A Bibliographical Sketch of the Laws of the Massachusetts Colony from 1630 to 1686* (ed. William H. Whitmore), Boston, 1890. For No. 80, see p. 50.

11. *Ibid.*, p. 53.

12. *Ibid.*, p. 33.

13. In a letter dated Dec. 8, 1645. *New Eng. Hist. and Geneal. Register*, XX (1866), 211-212. An extract from this letter is included in the Appendix to Dean's *Memoir*, p. 201.

14. Quoted by Jeremiah Chaplin, *Life of Henry Dunster*, Boston, 1872, p. 7.

15. In his separate accounts of them, *Magnalia*, I, Bk. III.

16. *Ibid.*, pp. 474-532, a reprint of his earlier account under the title, *The Triumphs of the Reformed Religion in America: The Life and Death of the Renown'd Mr. John Eliot*, London, 1691. For a brief modern account, see Samuel Eliot Morison, *Builders of the Bay Colony*, pp. 289-319.

17. "Autobiography," *Pub. Col. Soc. of Mass.*, XXVII (1932), 393, 394.

18. Under the heading "Touching My Self", *Magnalia*, I, 408.

19. *Ibid.*, p. 456.

20. *Ibid.*, p. 393.

21. He resigned from the presidency, Oct. 24, 1654, after fourteen years. For entries concerning this case, see *Records of the Governor and Company of the Massachusetts Bay in New-England* (ed. Nathaniel B. Shurtleff, Boston, 1854, III, 352; IV, 196-197.

22. With apologies to Perry Miller, whose book bearing this title illuminates the whole panorama of colonial thought in a variety of ways. *The New England Mind: The Seventeenth Century*, New York, 1939. For pertinent details concerning many of these men, see also Clifford K. Shipton, "The New England Clergy of the 'Glacial Age' ", *Pub. Col. Soc. of Mass.*, XXXII (1933), 24-54.

Chapter VI

1. *A History of New England*, London, 1654, p. 177. Reprinted as "Johnson's Wonder-Working Providence" in *Original Narratives of Early*

American History (ed. J. Franklin Jameson), New York, 1910, p. 214.

2. "To the Reader", p. II.

3. J. Shepard, *Two Sermons preached at Lynn*, Boston, 1711, pp. 9, 57.

4. *The Plain Doctrine*, Boston, 1659, 6th sermon, p. 59.

5. *An Exhortation to a Condemned Malefactor*, Boston, 1686, No. 2, in an imprint containing Cotton Mather's *The Call of the Gospel*, preached "to a condemned malefactor" in the same year, pp. 66, 69, 72, 75, 86, 94.

6. *The Doleful State of the Damned*, Boston, 1710, pp. 32, 33-34.

7. *Wisdom in the Latter End*, Boston, 1726, pp. 35, 36, 37.

8. *Sinners Minded of a Future Judgment*, Boston, 1733, pp. 27-28, 29.

9. These specimen titles are taken, with several exceptions, from the sermon list of Benjamin Wadsworth. For a well-informed and judicious recent treatment of both the subject matter and the form of early colonial sermons, see Babette May Levy, *Preaching in the First Half Century of New England History*, Hartford, 1945.

10. Entries from the journals of Joseph Green of Salem Village and Thomas Smith of Portland.

11. *The Sin and Danger of Self-Love Described*, in a Sermon Preached at Plymouth, in New-England, Dec. 9, 1621, London, 1622; 1785 ed., pp. 4, 17, 19, 20, 25-26.

12. From his "Farewell Letter to the Pilgrims", *Old South Leaflets*, No. 142, p. 11.

13. *God's Promise*, p. 19.

14. Jonathan Mitchel, *Nehemiah on the Wall in Troublesom Times*, Cambridge, 1671, p. 12.

15. *A Sermon* (Massachusetts Election), 1762, p. 21.

16. For a chronological presentation of the Massachusetts sermons, with numerous quotations, see Lindsay Swift, "The Massachusetts Election Sermons", *Pub. Col. Soc. of Mass.*, I (1892-1894), 388-451. For a short title list, see Robert W. G. Vail, "A Check List of New England Election Sermons", reprinted from *Proc. Am. Antiq. Soc.*, Oct. 1935.

17. Quoted from the church record by Deloraine Pendre Corey, *The History of Malden, Massachusetts*, Malden, 1899, pp. 119-120. In 1656 Joseph Hills was "presented by the Grand Jury for marrying of himself, contrary to the Law of the Collony". He lived to marry again in 1664.

18. Pp. 42, 37.

19. Preached May, 1671; 1678 ed., p. 16.

20. Cambridge, 1677, p. 8.

21. *Magnalia*, I, Bk. III, p. 219.

22. Cambridge, 1670, p. 33.

23. Joseph Belcher, *The Singular Happiness of Such Heads or Rulers As are able to Chuse out their Peoples Way*, Election Sermon, 1701, p. 37.

24. John Danforth's *Sermon on the Earthquake,* 1727, p. 10.

25. Arbella Sermon, *Winthrop Papers,* II, 283.

26. From the "Epistle Dedicatory" of Robert Cushman's Plymouth sermon, 1621. This Epistle is dated Dec. 12, three days after the sermon was preached.

27. Samuel Stone's catechism answer to the question, "What is creation?" This catechism of 1684 was reprinted by the Acorn Club in 1899. William Adams' sermon (Massachusetts Election, 1685) *God's Eye on the Contrite.*

28. *A Firm and Immoveable Courage to Obey God,* New London, 1741, pp. 18-19.

29. *Against Fashions, A Parent's Advice to his Children,* manuscript owned by Massachusetts Historical Society. Dated March 20, 1728, and signed "Your affectionate Father, George Weeks". Later he became a missionary to the Indians.

30. Entry of Mar. 19, 1690, *Diary,* I, 342.

31. "An Answer to Some Tales of Conscience Respecting the Country", 1722, p. 6.

32. In his Preface to "A Survey of the Summe of Church Discipline, 1648". *Old South Leaflets,* No. 55, p. 11.

33. In Cotton Mather's account of John Eliot, "His Way of Preaching", *Magnalia,* I, Bk. III, p. 495.

34. *The Real Christian, or a treatise of effectual Calling,* Boston, 1742, "To the Reader", p. XXXI.

35. "The Saint's Jewel", in *Two Sermons,* London, 1655, pp. 213, 215.

36. "The Soules Invitation Unto Christ" (2nd sermon in *Two Sermons*), p. 234.

37. *The Sound Beleever,* Boston, 1736 ed., pp. 65, 93.

38. *The Plain Doctrine of the Justification of a Sinner,* Sermon 3, p. 28.

39. *Ibid.,* Sermon 4, p. 37.

40. Sermon 6, p. 54.

41. *Ibid.,* p. 55.

42. *Ibid.,* p. 53.

43. *Ibid.,* Sermon 8, p. 75.

44. *A Fast of God's Chusing,* Boston, 1674, pp. 1, 23.

45. *New England's True Interest,* Boston, 1670, p. 28.

46. *Magnalia,* I, Bk. III, p. 469.

47. P. 17.

48. *Three Valuable Pieces, Viz. Select Cases Resolved; First Principles of the Oracles of God,* Boston, 1747, preface "To the Christian Reader".

49. 1785 ed., p. 3.

50. Entry of Oct. 22, 1676, *Diary,* I, 44.

51. *Ibid.,* entry of Dec. 13, 1685, I, 112. When on a later occasion, Oct. 24,

1686, there was another swooning, "which makes much disturbance", Mr. Willard, apparently a more composed preacher, "breaks not off preaching".

52. Entry of Feb. 25, 1727. *Diary*, owned by the American Antiquarian Society.

Chapter VII

1. Thomas Lechford, "Plain Dealing; or, Newes from New-England", London, 1642. *Coll. Mass. Hist. Soc.*, 3rd Ser., III (1833), 106. This was a "broyle" between two individuals.

2. Detailed history of the parish would seem to qualify this peaceful record somewhat.

3. *Watertown Records* (3rd Bk.), Watertown, 1838, II, 54.

4. *Ibid.*, p. 72.

5. *Ibid.*, pp. 73-75.

6. *Ibid.*, p. 106.

7. Coffin's *Sketch of the History of Newbury*, p. 185.

8. May 19, 1729. Quoted by George Sheldon, *History of Deerfield*, Deerfield, 1895, p. 457.

9. Quoted by Henry S. Nourse, *History of the Town of Harvard, Massachusetts*, Harvard, 1894, p. 203.

10. Quoted by Samuel Orcutt, *The History of the Old Town of Derby, Connecticut*, Springfield, 1880, pp. 79-80.

11. Quoted by Eleanor D. Larned, *History of Windham County, Connecticut*, Worcester, 1874, I, 52-53.

12. Quoted by Adin Ballou, *History of the Town of Milford, Worcester County, Massachusetts*, Boston, 1882, and the procedure summarized, pp. 49-50.

13. Quoted, C. C. Lord, *Life and Times in Hopkinton*, Concord, N.H., 1890, p. 74.

14. Phrasing from Groton, as quoted by Caleb Burton, *History of the Town of Groton*, Boston, 1848, pp. 141-142.

15. Quoted by William Howard Wilcoxson, *History of Stratford, Connecticut*, 1939, p. 163.

16. Matthew Plaint's letter is quoted, Coffin's *Sketch of the History of Newbury*, pp. 381-382.

17. Included by Edwin R. Hodgman, *History of the Town of Westford*, Lowell, 1883, pp. 77, 78.

Chapter VIII

1. "Beverly First Church Records," *Essex Institute Hist. Coll.*, XXXV (1899), No. 3, p. 178. Beverly had first petitioned to be separate in 1649. Their petition was granted in 1668.

2. Quoted by Alonzo H. Quint, "Memorial Address," *The First Parish in Dover*, 1884, p. 25.

3. Petition of 1753. Quoted by Edward Clarence Plummer, *The History of Bath*, 1936, p. 83.

4. Petition of May 13, 1703. Quoted by Ellen D. Larned, *History of Windham County, Connecticut*, 1874, 2 vols., I, 120.

5. Quoted by Sylvester Judd, *History of Hadley*, pp. 87-88.

6. Petition of March, 1704. Quoted by Charles J. Fox, *History of the Old Township of Dunstable*, Nashua, 1846, p. 78.

7. Petition of Nov. 29, 1705. Quoted by Henry S. Nourse, *The Early Records of Lancaster, Massachusetts*, Lancaster, 1884, pp. 155-156.

8. Petition of 1725. Quoted by Lemuel Shattuck, *History of the Town of Concord*, Boston, 1835, pp. 255-256.

9. Quoted by Sherberne Mathews, *Manual of Westfield Congregational Church*, formerly known as the First Church of Killingly, Connecticut, Boston, 1905, p. 5.

Chapter IX

1. Paige's *History of Cambridge*, pp. 262-263.

2. Quoted by George Merrill, *History of Amesbury*, Haverhill, 1880, p. 90.

3. Quoted, Orcutt's *History of the Old Town of Derby, Connecticut*, Springfield, Mass., 1880, p. 117.

4. Action of March 4, 1754. Lucius R. Paige, *History of Hardwick, Massachusetts*, Boston, 1883, pp. 182-183.

5. *Braintree Records* (ed. Samuel A. Bates), Randolph, Mass., pp. 36, 49.

6. This entry is not dated; *c*. 1715.

7. Action of Apr. 10, 1738. Quoted by John Montague Smith, *History of Sunderland*, Greenfield, 1899, pp. 53-54.

Chapter X

1. Thomas Ravenscroft, *The Whole Book of Psalms, with the Hymnes Evangelicall, and Songs Spiritual*, London, 1618; John Playford, *The Whole Book of Psalms*, London, 1677. For a discussion of music in early America, see Henry Wilder Foote, *Three Centuries of American Hymnody*, Boston, 1940. See also Percy A. Scholes, *The Puritans and Music*, London, 1934. Charles A. Place has numerous observations and useful data on this subject in his "Forms of Worship in North America", typescript, American Antiquarian Society.

2. Pp. 8-9. The booklet itself measures 3 x 5 inches.

3. *The Grounds and Rules of Music Explained; or an Introduction to the Art of Singing by Note, fitted to the meanest Capacity*, Boston, 1721, p. 5.

4. Reprinted, *Essex Institute Hist. Coll.*, II (1860), 99.

5. Dec. 28, 1705, *Diary*, II, 151; July 5, 1713, *Diary*, II, 391. See also III, 164.
6. In its printed form he called it *An Essay to Silence the Outcry that has been Made in Some Places against Regular Singing*, Boston, 1725.
7. *Utile Dulci, or a Joco-Serious Dialogue Concerning Regular Singing*, Boston, 1723, p. 29.
8. Selected, pp. 11ff. Each of these "theological" points is annotated.
9. *Diary*, III, 285.
10. *Publications, Col. Soc. of Mass.*, XXVIII (1931), 188-189.
11. *Reasonableness*, p. 5.
12. *Ibid.*, p. 6.
13. *Ibid.*, pp. 10-11.
14. *Ibid.*, p. 11.
15. *Ibid.*, p. 14.
16. *Ibid.*, pp. 14-15.
17. *Cases of Conscience, An Essay Preached by Several Ministers of the Gospel Concerning the Singing of Psalms*, Boston, 1723. Question 12 concerned the companion question as to the right of women to sing. "Undoubtedly they may and ought" was the answer.
18. The young people are similarly favored in all surviving *Singing Sermons*. Solomon Stoddard announced his purpose in *Cases of Conscience* as "to stir up young men and maidens to praise the Lord".
19. *Utile Dulci*, p. 20.
20. *Ibid.*, p. 21.
21. *Ibid.*, p. 35.
22. *Ibid.*, pp. 51-52.
23. Quoted by William Cothren, *History of Ancient Woodbury, Connecticut*, Waterbury, 1854, pp. 226-227.
24. Quoted by E. B. Huntington, *History of Stamford, Connecticut*, 1868, p. 152.
25. *A Brief Narration of the Practices of the Churches in New-England*, written in private to one that desired information therein, by an Inhabitant there, a Friend to *Truth* and *Peace*, London, 1645, pp. 15-16.
26. By Richard Rich, *News from Virginia*, London, 1610. 22 stanzas, of which this is the last line of Stz. 13. The "news" was the safe arrival in England of Sir Thomas Gates and his companions after their hazardous voyage to Virginia and the long sojourn in "the Island of Devils (otherwise called Bermuda)".

Chapter XI

1. From the section "Of Censures", Thomas Hooker, *A Survey of the Summe of Church Discipline*, London, 1648.

2. Some detail on this episode is supplied by William I. Budington, *History of the First Church in Charlestown*, Boston, 1845, pp. 56-58.

3. The John Swift *Diary*, formerly owned by the Framingham Historical Society, disappeared some years ago and in spite of diligent search has not yet come to light. This excerpt was quoted by Josiah Adams in his *Centennial Address, delivered at Acton, July 21, 1835*, Boston, 1835, p. 8.

4. From the manuscript records of the First Church, by courtesy of the Massachusetts Historical Society.

5. *Magnalia*, I, 485.

6. The Massachusetts Historical Society owns a sermon of George Weeks preached on this episode, Aug. 6, 1726. His theme was to God be the glory of it all, including the position of the jutting rock which prevented the victim's fall to a lower depth. This was the same George Weeks of the wig arguments. Cf. Note 29, Ch. VI, *supra*.

7. From the manuscript records of the Second Church, by courtesy of the Massachusetts Historical Society.

8. *Ibid.*

9. Roxbury Church Records, as included in *A Report of the Record Commissioners*, 1881, pp. 95, 99.

10. *Ibid.*, p. 99.

11. Action of Plymouth, 1639. In the detail of church consent for a marital choice, this case is not typical.

12. *Essex Institute Hist. Coll.*, XXXV (1899), 189.

13. New Haven Church Records, 1644. This case is summarized in Leonard Bacon, *Thirteen Historical Discourses—of the First Church in New Haven*, New York, 1839, pp. 296-306.

14. Records of the Second Church, cf. Note 7, *supra*.

15. Roxbury Church Records, p. 83. This was a case of 1642.

16. *Ibid.*, p. 85.

17. *Records of the First Church at Dorchester in New England, 1636-1734*, Boston, 1891, p. 164.

18. Dec. 11, 1722.

19. *Records of Brewster Congregational Church*, 1700-1792. Privately printed (25 copies), Merrymount Press, Boston, 1911, pp. 123-124.

20. *Ibid.*, p. 125. Apr. 4, 1764.

21. *Ibid.*, p. 134. Apr. 5, 1767. The original incident belonged to July, 1762.

22. He was first accused Feb. 10, 1733/34; the formal admonition was voted Apr. 28, 1734. There is no further record.

23. Article 4 in a new covenant of the church in Dunstable, Massachusetts, May 12, 1757. Elias Nason, *History of the Town of Dunstable*, Boston, 1877, p. 93.

24. Abijah P. Marvin, *History of the Town of Lancaster, Massachusetts,* Lancaster, 1879, p. 381.

Chapter XII

1. Urian Oakes, Chauncy's successor, was his eulogist. Chauncy died Feb. 19, 1671, aged eighty-two.
2. Ebenezer Gay, at the ordination of Joseph Green of Barnstable, May 12, 1725. *Ministers are Men of Like Passions with Others* was his title.
3. *Diary* of the Rev. Jacob Eliot, 1716-1764, Coll. & Deciphered by Wm. Inglis Morse, Cambridge, 1944.
4. Quoted by Josiah Adams, *Centennial Address,* p. 8.
5. Sept. 12, 1728, and Mar. 1, 1744. *Journals of the Rev. Thomas Smith, and the Rev. Samuel Deane,* Portland, 1849, pp. 69, 113.
6. These items are selected over the years. *Essex Institute Hist. Coll.,* Vols. VIII, X, XXXVI.
7. *Ibid.,* X, 101.
8. *Ibid.,* X, 78-79.
9. Thomas Smith's *Journal,* p. 113. Entry for Mar. 10, 1744.
10. *Ibid.,* p. 89.
11. Samuel Deane's *Journal,* p. 327. Entry for Feb. 8, 1770.
12. Entry of Nov. 1, 1746.
13. "A Journal from Rhoad Island to New York a Josepho Hull, anno 1724", manuscript owned by the American Antiquarian Society. The "best bed" sleepers are identified as "Mr. Eales & his deacon".
14. *Essex Institute Hist. Coll.,* X, 90.
15. Under date of Aug. 15, 1723.
16. *Ibid.,* entry of Apr. 11, 1765.
17. *New Eng. Hist., Geneal. Register,* VII, 239.
18. A Groton item of May 8, 1706. They had also built him a house, 38 x 20, with an 11 ft. lean-to.
19. This question had concerned the salary of John Wilson, first Teacher of the first Boston church. At that date, Aug. 23, 1630, the amount was fixed at £30 annually.
20. Connecticut Election Sermon, *The Firm Union of a People,* 1717, pp. 49, 52.
21. Pp. 11, 18, 19.
22. Pp. 6-7. John Tufts' name was not on the title page.
23. *Ibid.,* p. 27.
24. *Ibid.,* p. 28.
25. A few such items from the Church Book are included in *Records of*

the Church of Christ in Cambridge (ed. Stephen Paschall Sharples), 1906, pp. 183-185.

26. As quoted by Samuel C. Damon, *History of Holden*, 1667-1841, Worcester, 1841, pp. 50-51.

27. *Diary*, entry of May 3, 1724. From the original, by courtesy of the American Antiquarian Society.

28. Judd's *History of Hadley*. In 1742 he had 60 "ordinary" loads; by 1751 he had advanced to 100 "good" loads; *good*, meaning a full cord or more.

29. He was later dismissed.

30. Quoted by Ithomar Sawtelle, *History of the Town of Townsend*, 1676-1878, Fitchburg, 1878, pp. 78-79.

31. *Town Records of Topsfield, Massachusetts*, 1659-1739, I, 303-304.

32. George Willis Cooke, *A History of the Clapboard Trees*, Boston, 1887, pp. 41-43.

33. Entry of Oct. 5, 1724. At that time the Westborough church numbered "12 beside the Pastor Elect w[h]o signd ye Covt & ansd to ye Names in ye Assembly".

34. At the ordination of Joseph Emerson, 1721. *Romans* 11, 13, "I magnify my office", was his text.

35. At the ordination of James Varney, Oct. 24, 1733. Boston, 1733, p. 5. In fairness to Nathaniel Henchman, it must be said that he was attempting to "describe the Pastor after God's Heart".

36. Cf. Note 34, *supra.*, p. 9.

37. *Obedience and Submission to the Pastoral Watch and Rule over the Church of Christ*, Boston, 1737. He was honoring the ordination of James Diman. Pp. 25, 35.

38. *Ministers, Spiritual Fathers in the Church of God*, Boston, 1726, p. 46.

39. This was the title of his sermon, preached Sept. 12, 1739.

40. To a "Convention of ministers of the Province", and as it was hoped, in this time of bitter division among the clergy, "a brotherly Convention"; hence the "Dove of one accord" theme, on authority of *John*, 1, 32.

41. *Diary*, entry of Jan. 6, 1745.

42. *The Temple Measured*, London, 1647. Quoted by Coffin, *Sketch of the History of Newbury*, pp. 72-73.

43. *Ibid.*, p. 74.

44. *The Piety and Duty of Rulers to Encourage the Ministry of Christ*, Boston, 1708, pp. 13-14.

45. This was in reply to the printed announcement of his successor which had appeared in a preceding issue.

46. An entry of June 14, 1739. Quoted by Josiah Adams, *Centennial Address*, pp. 7-8.

Chapter XIII

1. Selections from this manuscript are printed by courtesy of the Congregational Library in Boston.
2. Brewster Church Records, Oct. 17, 1731.
3. *Newbury, 1st and 3rd Churches, 1743-6. Papers relating to separation of members.* In manuscript. By courtesy of the Congregational Library in Boston. The petition quoted is dated June 7, 1746. It is addressed to Jonathan Parsons, minister of the First Church. John Lowell, minister of the Third Church, had refused to grant dismission to these applicants, 83 of whom signed this formal appeal to Jonathan Parsons. One name is scratched out.

Chapter XIV

1. Preached Jan. 30, 1749; published, Boston, 1750. Preface.
2. *Ibid.,* p. 53.
3. *Ibid.,* p. 54.
4. To his Election Sermon, 1754. Preface, pp. II, III.
5. *Ibid.,* pp. 37-38.
6. *Ibid.,* p. 42.
7. *Thanksgiving Sermon for National Blessings,* 1759, p. 149.
8. *Religion and Patriotism the Constituents of a Good Soldier,* preached Aug. 17, 1755, p. 12 footnote.
9. Election Sermon, 1754, p. 46.
10. *Religion and Patriotism,* pp. 1, 2, 11.
11. Artillery Sermon, 1756, pp. 8, 19.
12. *The Expediency and Utility of War,* Artillery Sermon, 1758, p. 28.
13. Artillery Sermon, 1759, pp. 25, 26.
14. Artillery Sermon, 1763, pp. 36-37.
15. *The Curse of Cowardice,* preached May 8, 1758, pp. 3-4.
16. *New England Pleaded with, and pressed to consider the things which concern her Peace,* Cambridge, 1673, p. 53.
17. James Lockwood, Connecticut Election Sermon, *The Worth and Excellence of Civil Freedom and Liberty Illustrated—,* New London, 1759, p. 26.
18. Connecticut Election Sermon, *The Welfare of a Government Considered,* New London, 1747, pp. 15, 17-18.
19. *The Present Principle of Resistance,* London, 1644. Preached before the House of Commons.
20. Jonathan Ingersoll, Connecticut Election Sermon, New London, 1761, pp. 27, 44.

21. *God's Eye on the Contrite*, Massachusetts Election Sermon, Boston, 1685, pp. 14, 17.

22. *The Churches Quarrel Espoused*, 1710. Boston ed., 1715, Principle V, Principle VII, pp. 93-94.

23. *Ibid.*, "The Epistle Dedicatory", pp. 8-9; 102.

24. *A Vindication of the Government of New-England Churches*, Boston, 1717, p. 33. For a recent discussion of John Wise and his ideas of democracy, see Clinton S. Rossiter, "John Wise, Colonial Democrat", *New England Quarterly*, XXII (1949), pp. 3-32.

25. *A Vindication*, p. 61.

26. First published anonymously in 1690, with the avowed intent to prove King William III king of England by consent of the people. Recently reissued, with an Introduction by Thomas I. Cook, New York, 1947.

27. *Political Rulers Authoriz'd and Influenc'd by God*, Boston, 1750. The sermon begins in these words.

28. *The Dignity and Duty of the Civil Magistrate*, Boston, 1751, p. 33.

29. *Wisdom, Knowledge, and the Fear of God*, Boston, 1753, p. 40.

30. Preached at Pembroke, Oct. 10, 1757, p. 22.

31. *The pious Soldiers' Strength & Instruction*, Boston, 1757, p. 24.

32. *The Worth and Excellence of Civil Freedom and Liberty Illustrated* —, New London, 1759, p. 24.

33. *Ibid.*, p. 12.

34. *A Sermon*, Boston, 1763, p. 44.

35. The Stamp Act was passed, Feb. 27, 1765; became law, Mar. 22; came into effect, Nov. 1; was repealed, Mar. 18, 1766. News of repeal reached America, May 6, 1766.

36. Included by Charles Hudson, *History of the Town of Lexington*, Boston, 1913, I, 69-70.

37. *A Sermon*, Boston, 1765, p. 5.

38. *Ibid.*, p. 7.

39. *Ibid.*, p. 18.

40. *Ibid.*, pp. 20-21.

41. *Ibid.*, p. 43.

42. *Ibid.*, p. 48.

43. *Ibid.*, p. 52.

44. *Ibid.*, p. 52.

45. *Ibid.*, pp. 53-54.

46. *Ibid.*, p. 33.

47. Preached July 24, 1766, pp. 13-14.

48. *Ibid.*, 19, 27, 32.

49. *A Thanksgiving Sermon*, Boston, 1766, pp. 13, 22.

50. *Ibid.*, p. 29.

51. *Ibid.*, pp. 31-32.

52. Preached May 23, 1766, and published immediately, pp. 20-21.

53. *Ibid.*, p. 26.

54. *Ibid.*, p. 39.

55. *Ibid.*, p. 42.

56. *Ibid.*, pp. 28, 32.

57. Connecticut Election Sermon, Hartford, 1768, pp. 7, 32.

58. Feb. 2, 1766. Included in *Sketches and Chronicles of Litchfield*, 1859, Sec. VI, p. 85.

59. *A Sermon*, 1768, pp. 6, 68.

60. *Ibid.*, p. 20.

61. *Diary*, III, 195. Entry of Sept. 14, 1718.

62. *The Literary Diary of Ezra Stiles*, (ed. Franklin B. Dexter), New York, 1901, 3 vols., I, 8-9.

63. *Ibid.*, I, 53.

64. *Ibid.*, I, 53.

65. *A Sermon*, Boston, 1769, pp. 48-49.

66. *A Sermon*, Hartford, 1769, p. 41.

Chapter XV

1. *Town Records*, quoted, *Semi-Centennial Celebration of the One-Hundred and Fiftieth Anniversary of the Incorporation of Abington, Massachusetts*, Boston, 1862, Appendix D, p. 104.

2. Town Records, quoted by John G. Metcalf, *Annals of Mendon*, Providence, 1880, pp. 316-318. The moving spirit in the formulation of this protest was said to be Joseph Dorr, an ordained minister, representative to the General Court and delegate to the Continental Congress.

3. His *Diary* is extant in 10 manuscript volumes. For portions quoted, see *Proceedings at the Centennial Celebration of Longmeadow*, Oct. 17, 1883, Longmeadow, 1884, pp 207-211.

4. Other Episcopal clergymen did likewise.

5. *Innocent Blood Crying to God from the Streets af Boston*, Boston, 1771, pp. 5-6.

6. *Ibid.*, p. 7.

7. Pp. 20, 21, 22, 25.

8. *The Dignity and Importance of the Military Character*, p. 21.

9. Artillery Sermon, 1773, p. 21.

10. *Ibid.*, p. 28-29.

11. P. 38.

12. Preached on an occasion of Thanksgiving, pp. 14-15.

13. *Ibid.*, p. 16.

14. *Ibid.*, 38-39.

15. In a sermon of 1799, in which he pleads "to unite Patriotism and Religion in the American character", and urges America once more to put herself "in a posture of defence".

16. John Lathrop's Artillery Sermon, 1774, p. 28.

17. Timothy Hilliard, *The Duty of a People Under the Oppression of Man*, 1774, p. 29.

18. Andrew Eliot, "The Excellency of the Human Soul," included in *Twenty Sermons*, 1774, p. 50.

19. Massachusetts Election Sermon, 1774, pp. 46-47.

20. *Love of Our Country*, Boston, 1774, p. 26.

21. Election Sermon, Boston, 1780, pp. 41-42.

22. This was the Samuel Cooke, who at his ordination had been told that "ministers should carefully avoid giving offence in anything".

23. Massachusetts Election Sermon, 1775, pp. 9, 11, 19.

24. *A Sermon*, 1777, p. 34.

25. *Ibid.*, p. 27.

26. P. 12. This "called of God" motivation is repeated in nearly every sermon.

27. *A Sermon*, Boston, 1776, p. 27.

28. *Ibid.*, p. 56.

29. *Sin Destructive of temporal and eternal Happiness*, Boston, 1776, from the text, "Woe unto them that call evil good, and good evil" (*Isa.* 5, 20). "They call evil good, who say it is good to submit to the will of tyrants, or tamely part with liberty at the summons of any *king or ministery* on earth."

30. *Ibid.*, pp. 26, 27, 28.

31. *Journal of Nicholas Cresswell*, 1774-1777, (ed., Samuel Thornely), New York, 1924. He was twenty-four years old when he came to America. On Jan. 22, 1776, he wrote from Virginia, "Nothing but Independence talked of. The Devil is in the people". From Newark, Sept. 6, "The Army here is numerous, but ragged, sickly, and ill-disciplined. If my Countrymen are beaten by these ragamuffins, I shall be much surprised". Of George Washington, July 13, 1777, "Though my enemy, . . . I should be sorry if he should be brought to an ignominious death".

32. *Copy of the Diary of Deacon [Israel] Litchfield* made by Wilford J. Litchfield, 1906. New England Historic Genealogical Library. Previous to his formal enlistment, he had been under training with sixty other men and boys of Scituate.

33. He reports of the Lexington-Concord news, "When we first heard the

rumor Some Discredited it and Some Believed it." Home from the minister's at 9:00 P.M.", he was ordered "to Larrum the Street".

34. On May 17 (four days earlier) he reported, "In the Evening We Saw a great Light aboute in the Range of Boston which made us Suspect that Boston was on Fire".

35. Entry of Sept. 16, 1776, *Journal*, p. 234.

36. Entry of Oct. 21, 1765.

37. Church Records, Aug. 27, 1770; May 16, 1771.

38. *The Diary of William Pynchon* (ed. Fitch Edward Oliver), Boston, 1890, p. 37.

39. Among many treatments of preaching during the Revolution, that of Alice M. Baldwin, *The New England Clergy and the American Revolution*, Durham, North Carolina, 1928, is particularly useful.

Chapter XVI

1. William Pynchon's *Diary*, pp. 63-64.

2. This was Sturbridge, Massachusetts, according to local tradition.

3. Town Records, quoted by Joseph Merrill, *The History of Amesbury*, Haverhill, 1880, p. 291.

4. Moses Mather, Connecticut Election Sermon, 1781, pp. 11-12.

5. James Dana, Connecticut Election Sermon, Hartford, 1779. He was pleading for a more nearly equal distribution of land, as a safeguard of every man's freedom.

6. *Journal* of Thomas Smith, p. 241. Later entries on almost any page of anyone's private record make these prices sound like bargains.

7. *A Sermon*, Boston, 1782, p. 57.

8. *A Sermon*, Boston, 1783, pp. 33-34.

9. *The United States Elevated to Glory and Honor*, New Haven, 1783, p. 14. The text was *Deut.* 26, 19, "And to make thee high above all the nations which he hath made". . . .

10. *Extracts from the Itineraries and Other Miscellanies of Ezra Stiles*, 1755-1794 (ed. Franklin B. Dexter), New Haven, 1916, pp. 51-52.

11. *The United States Elevated*, pp. 20-21.

12. *Ibid.*, pp. 32-33.

13. P. 38.

14. P. 51.

15. P. 56.

16. P. 36.

17. P. 32.

18. P. 98.

19. *Oration* before the Society of the Cincinnati, 1787, p. 12.

20. Thanksgiving Sermon, 1796, pp. 5, 9, 12.

21. End of the "Credo" prefaced to *The Age of Reason,* 1794.

22. He terminated his connection, Sept. 11, 1786, to become pastor of Federal Street Church, Boston.

23. Quoted by Frankelyn Howland, *A History of the Town of Acushnet,* New Bedford, 1907, p. 206.

24. Dennis Donovan and Jacob Woodward, *The History of the Town of Lyndeborough, New Hampshire,* Boston, 1906, pp. 294, 296.

25. Church Records, quoted by L. H. Thayer, *The Story of a Religious Democracy,* Portsmouth, 1921, p. 48.

26. *Record of the Centennial Celebration,* Manchester, 1866, pp. 19-20. Walter Harris had enlisted as a boy of sixteen and had served three years. After the war he went to Dartmouth College, and in 1788 was "hired for 1 year" at Dunbarton, where he remained.

27. Church Records, quoted by George Willis Cooke, *A History of the Clapboard Trees, or Third Parish,* (Dedham) Boston, 1887, p. 110.

28. Samuel A. Clarke, *Centennial Discourse at the . . . 100th Anniversary,* Boston, 1851, p. 42.

29. Town Records, quoted by Edwin R. Hodgman, *History of the Town of Westford,* Lowell, 1883, pp. 97-98.

AMERICAN HISTORY TITLES IN THE NORTON LIBRARY